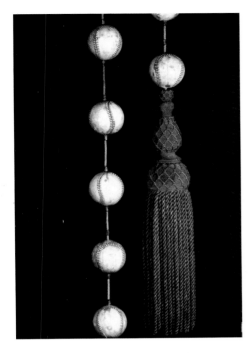

STRAND FROM THE BASEBALL SHOW
CURTAIN FROM *DAMN YANKEES*. (EC)

The Performing Set

The Broadway Designs of William and Jean Eckart

THIS BOOK IS DEDICATED TO: THE MEMORIES OF
MY GOOD FRIENDS JEAN AND BILL,
AND MY NEPHEW MARIO TORRES.

The Performing Set
The Broadway Designs of William and Jean Eckart

Andrew B. Harris

Foreword by Carol Burnett

Preface by Sheldon Harnick

University of North Texas Press

Denton, Texas

Now I want
Spirits to enforce, art to enchant

William Shakespeare, *The Tempest*

FRONT AND BACK OF JACKET: WILLIAM AND JEAN ECKART,
DESIGNS FOR *CINDERELLA* (1957), *MAME* (1966), AND
THE EDUCATION OF H*Y*M*A*N K*A*P*L*A*N (1968)

DESIGNER: SARAH FLOYD

10 9 8 7 6 5 4 3 2

Permissions:
University of North Texas Press
P.O. Box 311336
Denton, TX 76203-1336

The paper used in this book meets the minimum requirements of the American National Standard for Permanence of Paper for Printed Library Materials, z39.48.1984. Binding materials have been chosen for durability.

Library of Congress Cataloging-in-Publication Data

Harris, Andrew B. (Andrew Bennett), 1944-
  The performing set : the broadway designs of William and Jean Eckart / Andrew B. Harris ; foreword by Carol Burnett ;
preface by Sheldon Harnick.
    p. cm.
  Includes bibliographical references and index.
  ISBN-13: 978-1-57441-212-3 (cloth : alk. paper)
  ISBN-10: 1-57441-212-4 (cloth : alk. paper)
1. Eckart, William. 2. Eckart, Jean. 3. Theaters--Stage-setting and scenery--New York (State)--New York. I. Title.
PN2096.E23H37 2005
792.02'5092273--dc22
                    2005029355

MODEL OF APPLE TREE FROM *THE GOLDEN APPLE.* (EC)

Picture Credit Abbreviations

Contents

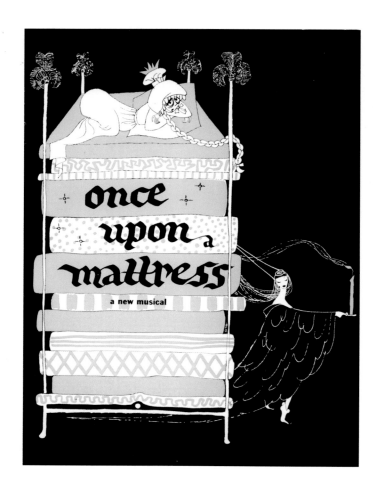

CAROL BURNETT AS PRINCESS WINNIFRED IN THE SIGNATURE IMAGE OF *ONCE UPON A MATTRESS*. THE ECKARTS NOT ONLY DESIGNED SETS AND COSTUMES BUT ALSO SERVED AS PRODUCERS. (EC)

Foreword by Carol Burnett

My sister Chrissy was home from school on spring vacation and found me crying over losing a job. I was that close. She was trying to comfort me:

"Sissy, it's okay… it's okay… Remember what you always say: One door closes; another one opens?"

I wanted to punch her in the nose. Then the phone rang.

"Is this Carol Burnett?"

"Yes."

The voice belonged to Jean Eckart. I knew who she was. William and Jean Eckart were Broadway designers, whose names I had seen in advertisements and on original cast albums. Jean spoke very quietly but ever so clearly, "Are you free to audition for a show this afternoon? We're starting rehearsal in two weeks, and we open in May at The Phoenix Theatre."

"Uh…"

"It's a musical based on 'The Princess and the Pea,' the Hans Christian Andersen fairy tale. Would you be interested in trying out for the lead? George Abbott's directing."

There it was. One door closes, and another one opened. As a student at UCLA, I had visualized myself as a performer in a musical directed by George Abbott. I was certain that circumstances would arrange themselves.

The audition was on stage at The Phoenix Theatre downtown. I had this tremendous feeling of support. Not that there weren't other actresses; there were, and a couple of very well-known ones, too; but the atmosphere—and that started with Jean—was more like that of a family, and it extended to everyone in that show. We were all a part of the Eckart family, and somehow they were presenting me to Mr. Abbott.

There were quaint little footlights that lined the edge of the stage and beyond them an auditorium of seats, covered by white dustcovers. In the center of the third row, sat the legendary Mr. Abbott who had directed a string of Broadway hits that spanned more than three decades. To his right were Jean and Bill Eckart who I learned were not just designing but producing the play. On Abbott's left were Mary Rodgers (the composer) and Marshall Barer (the lyricist). Earlier when I stopped at Marshall's apartment on 28th Street and Third Avenue to go over the songs, they gave me all kinds of advice not only about the songs but also about what to wear. As I stood on the stage, I just relaxed. How could I not succeed?

Jean called me a half hour later to tell me, "You have it."

CAROL BURNETT LEADS THE PICKET LINE, "ON STRIKE, WE NEED A THEATRE." (EC)

CAROL BURNETT RECEIVED THE FIRST ANNUAL
(AND ONLY) "TRUCKIE AWARD" FOR THE "MOST
MOVING MUSICAL ON BROADWAY" FROM
HENRY SCHUMER OF THE SCHUMER THEATRICAL
TRANSFER COMPANY. DURING THE FIRST YEAR
OF ITS RUN, THE PLAY MOVED FIVE TIMES. THE
ECKARTS RECORDED EACH MOVE WITH A PHOTO
OF THE THEATRE MARQUEE. (EC)

As producers, their excitement was absolutely infectious, and as designers, they were at the top of their form achieving miracles on a pea-sized budget. *Mattress* was a period show, yet everything felt totally fresh and contemporary.

We opened Off-Broadway in May 1959 for a six-week run and quickly became the surprise hit of the season. We were all having so much fun that it seemed a shame to close it just so the theatre could bring in its next attraction. So, I started a picket line. Bill and Jean painted signs and we all marched with them in the curtain calls: "On Strike, We Need a Theater," "A house! A house! My kingdom for a house!" "Big Hit, No Errors, Need Run." From atop of my twenty mattresses, I pitched the show. We got not only one theatre; we got five. But none for very long so we just kept moving from the Alvin, to the Wintergarden, the tiny Cort, and then the St. James. There has never been anything like it either before or since. We did that for an entire year, and still audiences found us. At each new location, the Eckarts and Tharon Musser (the lighting designer) would hang the lights and slap in a rough focus. With no rehearsal, we would look to see how far back the back wall was, and then we would open. The show wasn't miked, but nobody had any trouble hearing us.

I believe the theatre is a living institution. Maybe, it is possible for it to be that joyous again. But for me, the show that Jean and Bill offered me, gave me my big break. And so they were not just brilliant designers and producers but also really good friends.

Carol Burnett

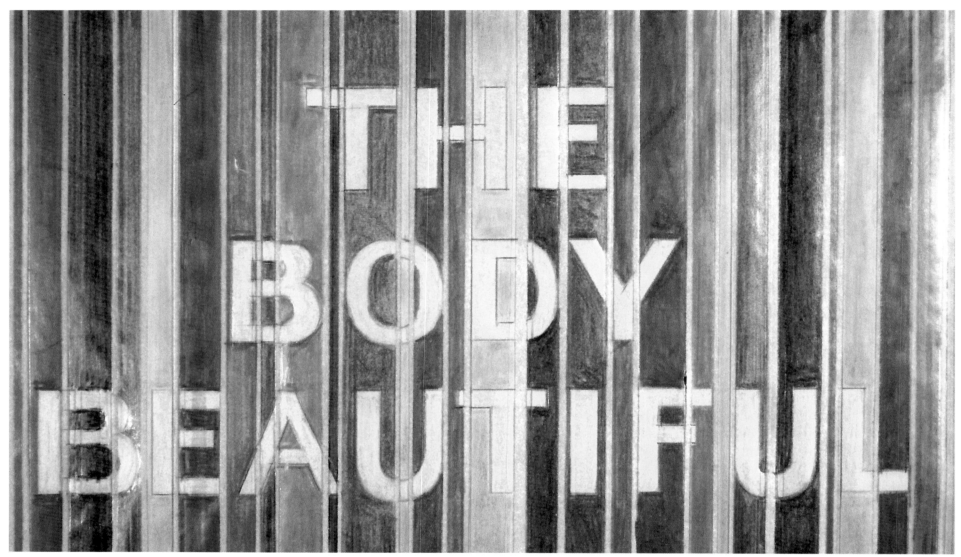

THE SHOW CURTAIN FOR *THE BODY BEAUTIFUL* WAS MADE OUT OF COLORED SATIN STREAMERS, THE SAME MATERIAL AS BOXING TRUNKS. WHEN THE OVERTURE BEGAN, THE AUDIENCE SAW ONLY A BLACK CURTAIN. AT A CERTAIN POINT IN THE MUSIC, THE RIBBONS WERE RELEASED IN QUICK SUCCESSION AND STREAMED DOWN, WHIZZING ACROSS THE STAGE FROM LEFT TO RIGHT AND SPELLING OUT "THE BODY BEAUTIFUL" IN PURPLE, YELLOW, ORANGE, AND RED. "THE FIRST TIME I SAW IT, I WEPT," SAID SHELDON HARNICK. (EC)

Preface by Sheldon Harnick

Nineteen hundred fifty six was a watershed year for me; I met Jerry Bock. We had been teamed by Jerry's music publisher to write the score for a new musical, *The Body Beautiful*. For me, this was a dream come true. Until then, I had scraped along by placing songs in revues when what I really wanted—what every theatrical songwriter wanted—was to do the complete score for a book show. The producers assembled an experienced, professional production staff but, in retrospect, it seems clear to me that no one approached this project with the freshness and invention of our set designers, William and Jean Eckart.

At that point in my career, although I was shown sketches of the sets as a courtesy, I wasn't stage-wise enough to envision how they would look in the theatre. So the actuality of the sets, as they eventually looked and functioned onstage, came as a thrilling surprise.

The Body Beautiful was a tale that unfolded in the milieu of professional boxing. The Eckarts had created a variety of locations, three of which remain particularly vivid in my mind's eye some forty years later. The first was a gym where the boxers worked out and where our opening number took place: "Where Are They," the plaintive cry of a fight manager (Jack Warden) forever in search of his next money-maker.

The set looked real enough to be rented out during the day to professional boxers—you could practically smell the stale sweat—but at the same time it was unmistakably theatrical. As real as this set was, it only prepared the way for the climactic moment in Act II when the stage suddenly blossomed into a boxing arena (if that isn't some sort of oxymoron).

The Eckarts had magically transported the audience to Madison Square Garden, lights, smoke, crowd noises, and all.

Although I didn't know it at the time, I learned later that the Eckarts, in addition to being superb artists, had the reputation of being superb craftsmen, which is to say that their designs worked onstage. They did not have to be forced to work by harried stage crews who cursed the set designer under their breaths when parts that were supposed to mesh didn't quite.

My third memory is of a set that needed that kind of meticulous craftsmanship: it was a Turkish bath. Its creators not only needed to be architects, engineers, plumbers, and safety experts, but they also had to be gifted with the eye, hand, and wit of a Daumier. In the scene that had been written by our bookwriters, Joe Stein and Will Glickman, the fight manager had come to plead with a promoter to set up a match using one of his boxers. Clouds of steam hovered over the stage, with more steam constantly hissing onto the set. The promoter was sensibly attired in a Turkish towel while Jack wore a suit and tie which grew progressively limp and waterlogged during the scene. Alas, this pre-dated the days of the Lincoln Center Archives, so the scene is not available for viewing. You will have to take my word that the scene itself, what with the pleading, soggy Jack Warden plus the perfectly realized steam room set combined to create one of the most hilarious scenes I have ever witnessed.

SKETCH OF GYMNASIUM—THE ECKARTS' SET HAD AN ELEMENTAL MASCULINITY. THIS WAS EXPRESSED IN THEIR USE OF VERTICAL LINES TO INDICATE THE HEFT OF THE BAGS, THEIR USE OF COLOR, AND THE INDICATIONS OF GRAPHIC RELIEF. (EC)

THE ECKARTS RECONSTRUCTED A THREE-DIMENSIONAL *LIVING* WORK OF ART ON STAGE USING THE FAMOUS GEORGE BELLOWS PAINTING, "STAG AT SHARKEY'S." THE SET STARTED WITH A VIEW OF THE BACK OF THE BLEACHERS. THEN THE BLEACHERS SPLIT DOWN THE MIDDLE AND PARTED, REVEALING THE BOXING ARENA AND THE GRANDSTANDS. THE SET GAVE THE ENTIRE EXPERIENCE OF THE PLAY A SENSE OF AUTHENTICITY. (EC)

LEFT TO RIGHT, MARK ALLEN (CAMPBELL) AND JACK WARDEN (DAVE) IN THE STEAM BATH SCENE FROM *THE BODY BEAUTIFUL*. IN ADDITION TO LOOKING LIKE A STEAM BATH, THE STEAM POURED OUT FROM UNDER THE BENCHES. (BILLY ROSE THEATRE COLLECTION, NYPL-PA)

The Eckarts had also provided an "Overture Curtain" constructed so that during the Overture spools of lustrous fabric (made from the same material as boxing trunks), unrolled one by one from the top of the proscenium arch to the stage floor. The effect was so theatrically imaginative and exciting that the first time I saw it, I wept. Would that the entire show had been as exciting and imaginative.

On opening night, there was a traditional celebration at Sardi's restaurant. Jerry and Patti Bock and I sat at a long, long table crowded with festive guests. When the first disappointing review came out, half the guests silently snuck out. When the second review appeared, the rest of them left. Jerry, Patti, and I were depressingly alone at that endless table. The Eckarts came to our rescue, introducing us to the eminently successful producers Harold Prince and his then partner Robert Griffith. Although Griffith and Prince admitted to having reservations about the show as a whole, they told us how much they liked our score. So, thanks to the Eckarts, we salvaged something from the evening.

Hal and Bobby obviously meant what they said because within a year Jerry and I were hard at work on their new musical, *Fiorello!*, as were Bill and Jean. By now, I was beginning to know the Eckarts. Jean made the stronger immediate impression: slender, handsome, quick, bright, thoughtful, and articulate. Bill, good looking, quiet, and reserved, spoke less frequently but his comments were shrewd and intelligent and delivered with a charming, residual southern drawl.

The *Fiorello!* experience was exhilarating. (Our orchestra conductor, Hal Hastings, commented that he had never experienced such a happy, relatively trouble free pre-Broadway tryout.) I had never worked with George Abbott before. Someone on the production staff remarked that Mr. Abbott, unlike most directors, chose not to work closely with the set designers. According to my informant, Abbott engaged people he trusted, and when shown renderings of the sets, asked only the simplest technical questions, such as "Do the doors open in or out?" I have no idea whether this is truth or myth but with or without Abbott's guidance, the Eckarts came up with wonderfully atmospheric sets (and, in this case, costumes and lighting) that evoked an old New York constructed of

homely, warm-toned brick and family friendly neighborhoods. And for the finale of Act I, they provided a set that was every bit as impressive, in its way, as the boxing arena had been in *The Body Beautiful*. The entire upstage area became a World War I troop transport ship and down its gangplank marched squadrons of soldiers—indeed, a memorably stirring theatrical moment.

I had the pleasure of working with Bill and Jean once more when Hal Prince invited them to design and light *She Loves Me*. It's difficult to conceive of three shows more dissimilar in look and tone, scenically, than the three we did together. It's a tribute to the Eckarts' wide ranging versatility that they could move so successfully from the gritty realism of *The Body Beautiful*, to the nostalgic little-old-New York atmosphere of *Fiorello!* to the delicious Old World, Art Nouveau charm of *She Loves Me*. For this last show, what the Eckarts created was so in tune with our score and Joe Masteroff's book that it left an indelible, glowing memory in the minds and hearts of those aficionados of the musical theatre who saw it.

After *She Loves Me* closed, my wife Margie and I stayed in touch with Bill and Jean. We saw various shows they designed and continued to admire their versatility, freshness of vision, and invention. But there seems to be a curious phenomenon regarding set designers. When a designer is associated with a string of hits, he or she becomes endowed with an aura of success and, for a while, becomes the designer of choice. This continues until that designer, through no fault of his or her own, is associated with several flops. Then the mantle passes to someone else. Meanwhile, other designers are offered the less "sure-fire" shows.

There was a period when the Eckarts found themselves in that position. They lavished their consummate artistry on every show they chose to do. But, as they told us, if they wanted to continue to make a living in the New York theatre, they were obliged to accept shows about which they had serious reservations. So it wasn't too surprising that when the opportunity arose to join the faculty of Southern Methodist University, they seized it.

New York theatre's loss was the SMU students' gain. I can't help but envy those students who got to work with Bill and Jean, absorbing lessons in craft and theatrical legerdemain, which the Eckarts were uniquely qualified to impart. And, as someone vitally interested in the health of the legitimate theatre, it is deeply gratifying to me to think of artists like the Eckarts passing on their expertise to future generations of theatre professionals.

Acknowledgments

BILL CREATED THIS PAINTING FOR THE COMEDY THRILLER *BETTER HALF DEAD*. THROUGHOUT THE PLAY, THE PAINTING WAS IDENTIFIED AS "PORTRAIT OF RENA." RENA WAS A CHARACTER IN THE PLAY HAVING AN AFFAIR WITH A SUCCESSFUL MODERN ARTIST. IN THE DISCOVERY SCENE AFTER THE ARTIST'S DEATH, THE PAINTING WAS TURNED UPSIDE-DOWN TO REVEAL THAT THE PAINTING THE AUDIENCE HAD BEEN LOOKING AT ALL EVENING WAS A RE-WORKING OF GIOTTO'S "KISS OF JUDAS," WHICH IDENTIFIED RENA AS THE MURDERER. (COLLECTION OF THE AUTHOR)

The task of one who writes on visual subjects is a difficult one, and it is only made more difficult by the temporal aspect of theatrical production. Capturing the feel and texture of a play in performance and making it compelling for readers many of whom have never seen the original production is like catching butterflies in a windstorm. Like Shakespeare's Prologue to *Henry V*, we must urge the reader to work on his or her "imaginary forces." Yet it does no good to counsel the reader if one can't take the advice oneself. I have indeed been fortunate by having as expert guides, William and Jean Eckart. Although Jean Eckart died in 1993, a full two years before work began on this volume, I was able to rekindle my memory of her through Ronald L. Davis' Oral History for the Southern Methodist University Oral History Program. Davis' interviews were made in 1986, during the period I chaired the Theatre Department at Southern Methodist University. As a new arrival from New York City—a place the Eckarts thought of as their hometown—Jean and Bill went out of their way to welcome my wife Ann and me to Dallas, and we became instant friends. I often found Jean's opinions about our new surroundings refreshing, and when I could I would sneak down to the costume shop either to sit in on a class or corner her in the hall for advice. During those years, Bill and I met frequently on departmental business and became close friends. Off campus, we worked on several productions together, most notably *Better Half Dead* for which he designed sets and costumes. His contributions to that production (and many others) went far beyond the role of designer. Bill understood the collaborative nature of theatrical production, and he became actively involved in all aspects of production including, but not limited to, rewrites. Since the play was about the murder of a modern artist and its subsequent cover up, Bill's design and execution of an incredible painting that unlocked the central mystery of the play was a key to the play's success. Therefore, it was not a surprise when Bill solicited my involvement in this volume. Although I had seen and admired many Eckart productions over the years dating back to my youth in New York, I told him that I would not undertake a book of this kind without his active involvement. He told me quite candidly that he would not have it any other way, and true to his word, he was at my side through the first draft of this volume, and through subsequent revisions. We were at work on a total revamping of the manuscript when his health made it impossible for us to continue as we had. Obviously, I am indebted to him not only for his painstaking help with the text, but also for much more—not the least of which was the furthering of my theatrical and visual education. Truly, this volume would have been impossible without Bill's active participation in almost every phase of the project. My only regret is that he is not here to enjoy the completed work.

I wish to acknowledge the generosity of both Carol Burnett and Sheldon Harnick. Each has made a unique contribution to this volume giving us another perspective and point of view about our subjects. Bill and I felt particularly fortunate that they were able to take the time from their busy professional lives to meet with us and then to write about their first hand experience. I was also fortunate to have the enormously helpful support of the Eckart family but most importantly, the Eckart children Peter and Julie, Jean's stepmother, Herta Hess Kahn, and Bill's sister Rosemary Bernard. Over a period of several years, I interviewed a number of other individuals who knew and/or worked closely with the Eckarts. I wish to thank them for their assistance. They are: Richard Adler, Julie Andrews, Marty Aronstein, Bea Arthur, Lyn Austin, Kaye Ballard, Ken Billington, John Bos, John Bowab, Marc Breaux, Joe Brown, Patton Campbell, Bob Chambers, Ted Chapin, Jack Clay, Alvin Colt, Bea and Danny Daniels, Rondi Hillstrom Davis, Andre De Shields, Sharon (Shore) Denoff, Jules Fisher, Aaron Frankel, Burry Frederik, Robert Fryer, Peter Gennaro, Richard Grayson, T. Edward Hambleton, Jim Hancock, Sheila Hargett, Terry Hayden, Marjorie Hayes, Allen Heaton, Jerry Herman, Burnett Hobgood, Earle Hyman, David Jacques, Mesrop Kesdekian, Angela Lansbury, Arthur Laurents, Jerry Lawrence, Ming Cho and Elizabeth Lee, Ed Levy, Terry Little, Charles Marowitz, Elliot Martin, Dorothy Monohan, Tharon Musser, Cecil O'Neal, Stuart Ostrow, Hal Prince, Charlotte Rae, Charles Nelson Rielly, Mary Rodgers Guettel, Herbert Ross, Hazel Roy, Tim Saternow, Haila Stoddard, Tao Strong, Michael Sullivan, Susanna Moross Tarjan, Giva Taylor, Robert Taylor, Jay Thompson, Jac Venza, Gwen Verdon, Ellen Violett, Robin Wagner, Tony Walton, Onna White, and Deedee Wood.

Before I became involved in this project, I talked with Jerome Weeks, columnist for *Dallas Morning News.* Since he had interviewed the Eckarts several times, I asked him for his advice. Weeks encouraged me to take it on and he said he would help in whatever way he could. True to his word over the years, he has been there providing editorial advice, insight, criticism, and words of encouragement.

I owe a special debt of gratitude to Joan Torres for her help in structuring this volume. She provided invaluable assistance for which I cannot even begin to express my appreciation. Sherri Small Truitt, Dena Davis, and Geneva Snider lent valuable assistance at different times during the extended process of revisions and rewrites. Sarah M. Floyd also had a profound impact on this project as graphic designer and consultant. Without the assistance of these individuals, this volume would not be what it is today. I also wish to thank Michele Baker who assisted me on my earlier volume *Broadway Theatre* (Routledge, 1994) and who made an important contribution to this volume as well. Shari Watson and later Rayna Runge helped to organize research and provided valuable computer assistance. In New York, Steffi Wallis researched photographs.

There were also a number of helpful people at libraries and photo archives. Although Bill had an extensive archive of drawings and models as well as photographs, the visual record would not have been what it is in this volume were it not for Ron Mandelbaum at Photofest, and special thanks to Alan Gomberg for his post-production editorial assistance. We are thankful that Mrs. Fred Fehl and the Estate of Al Capp took a personal interest in this project. We also wish to thank the McNay Art Museum of San Antonio for their permission to use several sketches from the Robert L. B. Tobin Collection.

In all likelihood this book would have remained a dream if it were not for key grants from the Robert L. B. Tobin Foundation and the Faculty Research Grant Program of the University of North Texas.

Ultimately, a book needs an editor and a publisher, and I could not have found better than Karen DeVinney and the University of North Texas Press.

And finally, I would not have been able to devote the time to this effort were it not for the continued support of my wife without whose love, patience, and enthusiasm a work of this kind would not have been possible.

ABH   July 2005

BILL ECKART CHECKING PAINTER'S ELEVATION CONSTRUCTION OF *DAMN YANKEES*, 1955 ·
(PETER STACKPOLE, EC)

JEAN ECKART AT THE COSTUME PARADE WITH A DANCER FROM *DAMN YANKEES*, 1955 (PETER STACKPOLE, EC)

Getting Together

"Jean and I always believed that the nature of theatre is collaborative." William Eckart

BILL AND JEAN AT WORK IN THEIR STUDIO, NOVEMBER 1957 (EC)

"Can I represent the two of you on *Mame*?" Abe Newborn asked when Jean Eckart answered the phone at the Eckarts' apartment. It was December 1965. She told him she'd get back to him. Once she'd hung up she turned to Bill, her husband and collaborator. "That was Abe Newborn, Onna White's agent."

Onna White was to be the choreographer for *Mame* and Bill and Jean had worked with her on a previous musical, *Let It Ride*. That show had turned out to be a turkey. The Eckarts knew they were in trouble with it when George Abbott, who'd written the original play *Three Men on a Horse*, refused to get involved with the musical version. They had joked with Onna White that it was tough to build a musical around the deadpan TV comic, George Gobel, a man who couldn't sing, dance, or act. There was one memorable song that summed up the whole experience: "An Honest Mistake." In spite of the outcome, they'd loved working with Onna White and knew she must have been behind their being asked to work on *Mame*.

The phone was frequently ringing with offers. The Eckarts were at the top of their profession as theatrical designers and American musical theatre itself was still thriving. Yet neither Bill nor Jean were thrilled by the idea of designing *Mame*. *Auntie Mame* had been done too often and too well by their friend, Rosalind Russell. Making a musical of the same material seemed superfluous. "Why are they doing a musical of *Auntie Mame*?" Bill asked. "It's practically a musical already." The Eckarts were being offered what would become the biggest hit of their Broadway careers yet they hesitated. They were no longer sure of their choices.

BILL, JEAN, AND GEORGE ABBOTT (LEFT TO RIGHT) IN 1959 DISCUSSING *ONCE UPON A MATTRESS* IN WHICH BILL AND JEAN SERVED IN DUAL CAPACITY OF DESIGNERS AND PRODUCERS (FRIEDMAN-ABELES)

THE ECKARTS PREFERRED DESIGNING MUSICALS AND WORKED WITH SOME OF THE GIANTS OF THE GOLDEN AGE, HERE SHOWN WITH OSCAR HAMMERSTEIN, II AND RICHARD RODGERS AT A PLANNING SESSION FOR TELEVISION'S FIRST MUSICAL *CINDERELLA* (1957) (EC)

For the better part of the 1950s and 60s, the Eckarts had at least one show running on Broadway. They were the preeminent husband and wife design team to share joint credit in the history of the American theatre. Bill and Jean Eckart were fortunate that their talent came to fruition during the Golden Age of American Musicals. It was the musical that provided them with the opportunity to break away from the literal realism that had typified the American theatre. If the audience could accept the improbability of characters expressing their emotions through song and dance, then they could also accept sets changing in front of their eyes. Keenly aware of designing as much for dancers as for actors, the Eckarts wanted the same sense of movement to flow throughout the entire production. They saw scenery as integral, not decorative, and they saw themselves as storytellers.

This technique also made what happened *between* the scenes important. With storytelling in mind, they experimented with, developed, and perfected a variety of innovative scene change systems: a winch driven device that guided set pieces silently across the stage on hidden tracks;

mini-drops (or flying set pieces) that occupied only a small section of the visible stage area; a series of turntable systems that sometimes moved concentrically, sometimes in opposition; and the adaptation of a minimalist style which utilized a sophisticated modern art shorthand for communicating ideas. The Eckarts became known not just for designing but for choreographing set changes and making the changing of scenery part of the performance. Their innovations were to lead to a revolution in scene changing techniques that continues today with computer mechanized sets. They made changing sets an integral part of the art of set design.

As anyone knows who works in or follows the theatre, not every show can be a hit, and the Eckarts had their share of flops. But they also had a few setbacks due to other circumstances. Producer Elliott Martin remembers, "My very first play on Broadway, *Never Too Late*, was directed by George Abbott, the great comedy and farce director, who at that time was 76 years old and who eventually lived to the age of 107. Abbott asked for Bill and Jean to design his set. I made a minimum union offer to them

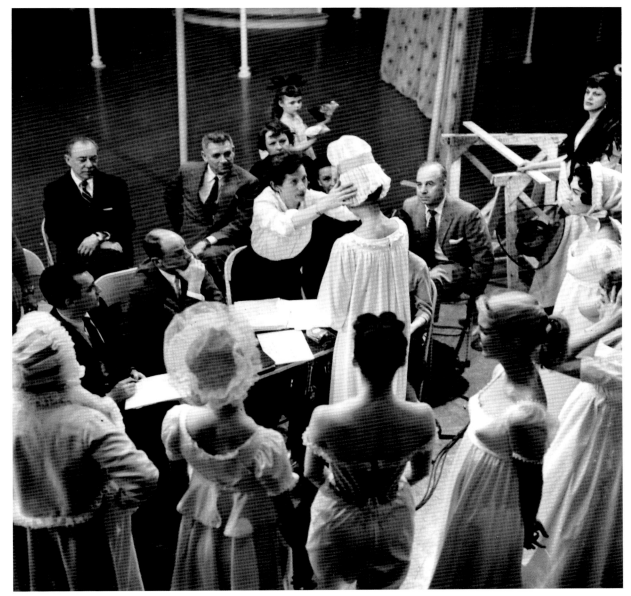

COSTUME PARADE FOR *CINDERELLA*—TOP ROW, LEFT TO RIGHT: RICHARD RODGERS, OSCAR HAMMERSTEIN, II, JEAN ECKART (STANDING), AND KAYE BALLARD (UPPER RIGHT CORNER). CENTER ROW, LEFT TO RIGHT SEATED: JOSEPH PAPP (STAGE MANAGER), RICHARD LEWINE (PRODUCER), AND RALPH NELSON (DIRECTOR, SEATED ON JEAN'S LEFT) (EC)

which they did not wish to take. They wanted a much higher fee because they thought it wouldn't run. So, I suggested we give them the higher fee, but then we would not pay them a weekly royalty during the run. They couldn't wait to sign. Fortunately for me, and unfortunately for the Eckarts, the play ran over three years on Broadway, and five years on the road." When Abbott found out, he chided them, "Never doubt the old man." They were still smarting over losing *Gypsy*, a blockbuster hit they were initially promised. Bill and Jean learned they were off that show from *Gypsy*'s author, Arthur Laurents, when he informed them Hal Prince was withdrawing, and David Merrick, the show's new producer and his production team would be taking *Gypsy* to Broadway. But the most painful of all was when their friend Jerome Robbins dropped them from another big hit, *Fiddler on the Roof*. They were at work on researching Chagall paintings when Nora Kaye, a dancer and future film producer, persuaded Robbins that Boris Aronson was the only designer who was right for the show. "He's lived through it," she said. "He's from Russia, and he's Jewish." By 1965, the Eckarts were no longer sure if it was bad luck or infelicitous circumstance, but it seemed as if "the big ones" were always getting away. Then they were offered *Mame*.

Within the next five years, the Broadway theatre that had given rise to the Eckarts would fade away and change forever. The Golden Age of American Musicals was over. The music that America was listening to wasn't coming from Broadway shows anymore but from the Beatles, Bob Dylan, Nashville, and Motown. The new music was inhospitable to the lyrical subtlety that was needed to tell a story on stage. It also tended to alienate the slightly older

DESIGNERS FOR *LIFE*

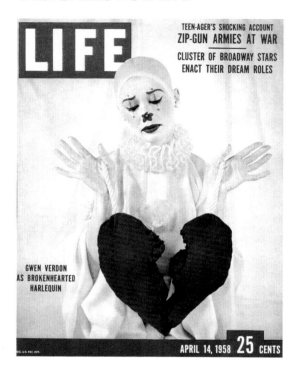

GWEN VERDON AS BROKENHEARTED HARLEQUIN

APRIL 14, 1958 25 CENTS

BILL AND JEAN ALSO DESIGNED FOR *LIFE* MAGAZINE (APRIL 14, 1958, COVER STORY), A PICTURE STORY OF BROADWAY STAR DREAM ROLES. GWEN VERDON PLAYED A BROKEN HEARTED HARLEQUIN AS HER DREAM ROLE. YEARS LATER, THE ECKARTS USED THEIR IMAGE, ENLARGING THE BROKEN HEART TO CREATE THE NUMBER "ALL MY LAUGHTER" FOR DOROTHY LOUDON, IN THE SHOW *THE FIG LEAVES ARE FALLING*. (GETTY IMAGES)

JEAN AND BILL AT THE *LIFE* STUDIOS DRESSING A SET FOR ONE OF A SERIES OF "DREAM ROLES," THIS ONE FOR JUDY HOLIDAY (AMANDA) IN *THE GLASS MENAGERIE*. OTHER ACTORS INCLUDED IN THIS STORY WERE: SHIRLEY BOOTH, SUSAN STRASBERG, ANTHONY PERKINS, TYRONE POWER, JASON ROBARDS, JR., JULIE HARRIS, BERT LAHR, RODDY MCDOWELL, AND PETER USTINOV. (ELIOT ELISOFON, EC)

Broadway audiences. By the end of the 1960s, Jean noticed that the money behind Broadway was changing as well. It no longer seemed to matter what was "best for the show or the people working on it." Instead of creative producers, corporate executives wearing white-on-white shirts were calling the shots. On *Maggie Flynn*, a show that the Eckarts designed for the husband and wife team of Jack Cassidy and Shirley Jones, there was a legion of these producers whose connection to the theatre seemed to be limited to having offices that looked out on Broadway from the upper floors of the Brill Building. They hadn't a clue about what to do to improve a show that was in trouble except to keep throwing money at it. If nothing else, the cash infusions kept the show running long after audiences had forsaken it. For Bill and Jean, the idea of working for faceless bosses bankrolling overdone productions wasn't worth the sacrifices it required. Their clarion call had always been "less is more." They believed in the minimalism they had developed over the years. Suddenly, they were faced with an era that sought to counteract

vanishing audiences by conspicuous spending, as if spectacle alone could somehow make up for everything else that was lacking.

As the kind of theatre they believed in vanished from Broadway, so too did the Eckarts' ability to tolerate the instability of working in the New York theatre. They were facing increasing demands as the parents of two young children. Their old way of life spent in rehearsal halls and on the road had permanently altered. If they wanted to survive, they realized they'd have to move on. They left New York City and in the fall of 1971 set about building a new program in theatrical design at Southern Methodist University in Dallas, Texas.

The Eckarts believed that collaboration was at the heart of the theatrical process. It was also the cornerstone of their marriage. In conversation, each used the first person plural, as in "we look at it this way." They developed a kind of designer shorthand to express their ideas to each other: a doodle on a lined phone pad became an iconic tree (*The Golden Apple*) and a sketch of tenements drawn with kids' crayons became the key to the main character in *Fiorello!* Sometimes one drew while the other added color or vice versa. A visual record of their work makes ascribing individual authorship to their drawings impossible.

"We never really established which one of us was going to do what," Bill said. "We just let it evolve." But according to Jean, it wasn't always quite so easy. "I was always more competitive than Bill, and I can remember how painful it was to be in class at Yale, doing the same assignments, facing one another so we couldn't see what the other one was doing. All the while I was thinking, 'Oh, my God, he's doing something brilliant and I haven't got an idea in my head.' It was so important for me to feel that I was always pulling my weight that I felt obligated to grind out drafting plates, which I detested." Only later did Jean discover how good she was at brainstorming and synthesizing ideas. They came to accept Bill doing the drafting while Jean, whose drawings were better, sketched the costumes. "If one of us had a good idea," Bill said, "we literally couldn't remember *which one of us it was*." What remained constant was their ability to analyze each other's work and benefit from each other's critical acuity. According to designer Ming Cho Lee, the Eckarts had a perfect creative union. "They truly complemented one another." Their collaboration in life as well as theatre was all the more remarkable considering the differences in their backgrounds.

The Early Years

Bill was brought up in New Iberia, Louisiana, a small agricultural Southern town famous for sugar cane and Tabasco sauce. Jean was raised in Glencoe, along Chicago's exclusive north shore. Bill's Bayou Teche and Jean's big-city suburb were about as far apart culturally as one could get and still be in the continental United States.

The Eckart family was of Swiss extraction, arriving in New Orleans in 1839. They were watchmakers and jewelers, but Bill's father, William Joseph, Sr., left the family business to become a traveling salesman. Bill's mother, Annette Cecile Brown, was a plantation belle educated in a Carmelite convent. Bill Eckart was born October 21, 1920, and was William and Annette's youngest child.

Jean's family, the Levys, were German Jews who had emigrated to Chicago in the mid-nineteenth century after the collapse of the great lib-eral revolution in Europe in 1848. Jean's mother was distantly related to Albert Einstein. Jean's father, Herbert Levy, started as a mailroom clerk in the Chicago branch of the New York brokerage firm Paine Webber. Eventually he rose to the rank of partner. Jean was the oldest of three children and was born August 18, 1921.

Bill's interest in stage design emerged in early childhood. Rosemary Bernard, Bill's older sister, remembers how Bill "liked to play under the family's oak desk, cutting up pieces of paper to make columns, platforms and step units for his imaginary stage." Bill saw his first stage show at the age of six. It was *The Gorilla* by Ralph Spence, and it featured a gorilla that came out of the audience and chased the actors around the stage. What Bill never forgot were the two grown men who escaped by climbing into a small valise brought out and placed on the stage. Bill couldn't understand how they fit into that little valise. Afterwards, he insisted on going backstage. There he discovered the traps in the stage floor. Bill would always enjoy this kind of theatrical wizardry, and used similar tricks in many of the shows he designed.

BILL SITTING ATOP THE DUGOUT FOR *DAMN YANKEES* (1955) AT MACDONALD'S SCENIC STUDIO (PETER STACKPOLE, EC)

BILL WITH HIS MOTHER AND SISTER ROSEMARY IN 1929. ACCORDING TO ROSEMARY, "FATHER HAD NO TASTE BUT WAS VERY SMART. MOTHER HAD GREAT TASTE AND NO BRAINS. BILLY GOT THE BEST FROM BOTH." (EC)

JEAN'S FAMILY IN 1929: EDITH, HERBERT, BABY EDWIN, CATHARYN, AND JEAN (EC)

AT AGE FIFTEEN, JEAN BEGAN PAINTING PORTRAITS OF THE FAMILY MAIDS. HER MOTHER WAS SO IMPRESSED SHE HUNG THEM IN THE FAMILY LIVINGROOM. (EC)

But the touring Chautauqua tent show was the theatre Bill remembered seeing most often as a child. By age nine, Bill had made up his mind. He decided to stage his own backyard production using an old awning as a curtain and a tumbledown shack at the rear of the property as a stage house. He was producer, designer, director, playwright, and star. He organized the entire event down to making up the tickets and collecting them. He seated family, friends, and neighbors on the lawn. Then Bill climbed onto the stage where he discovered he couldn't remember his lines. "That's when I knew that I was not going to be an actor."

When Bill was eleven, his mother cut a deal with the local movie theatre manager. She traded the family piano for free passes to all the picture shows. "Between age eleven and thirteen, I saw every single movie at that theatre, as many as four films a week." The Hollywood musicals of the 1930s whetted Bill's taste and influenced many of his later designs.

By age fifteen, Jean had begun painting. More cosmopolitan than Bill, Jean had seen touring Broadway shows in downtown Chicago while she was growing up. She'd always remembered the thrill she felt when she heard an overture, "That's when you know that you are going to see a show!" There was never any question that she would attend college or that she would major in art.

Bill graduated from high school at fifteen. He began college at nearby Southwestern Louisiana Institute in Lafayette but during his second year he found out a local man named Guggenheim had endowed a scholarship. Bill applied, stating his wish to become an architect. He received not only his full tuition and an allowance for books but a stipend of $35 per month, enough in those days to pay for room and board as well. At seventeen, Bill, soft spoken, introspective, and shy, was off to Tulane University.

Jean did not want to go east to one of the Seven Sister schools (Smith, Radcliff, Wellesley, etc) like most of her suburban friends. She was a rebel and couldn't wait to get away from Chicago's north shore. She decided to pick a school which "would be near a reputable art school, would accept all my credits and would not be too far away from a boys' school." Jean was attractive, outspoken, and competitive. She chose Sophie Newcomb, the Women's College of Tulane University.

Bill and Jean became involved with Tulane University Theatre for entirely different reasons. Jean initially wanted to act and to meet people. Bill joined the backstage crew in order to enhance his status as a fraternity pledge.

Because he was training to become an architect, Bill was already thinking in terms of space rather than of flat planes and using a kind of notation that required him to think in more than one dimension. The theatre's director, Dr. Monroe Lippman, recognized his ability immediately and in his freshman year promoted him to the rank of resident set designer. While at college, Bill designed more than a dozen shows. Norris Houghton, the author of *Moscow Rehearsals* and *Theatre U.S.A.* was visiting Tulane when he saw Bill's set for *Liliom*. Of the several productions he had seen, none had solved the change-over the way Bill had. Houghton asked Lippman to take him backstage to meet the young designer. (Years later, the Eckarts would work for Houghton and T. Edward Hambleton Off-Broadway at The Phoenix Theatre in New York.)

Since Tulane's University Theatre was a small organization, Bill and Jean were bound to get to know one another. But it was not until they met a newcomer to the art faculty, a young instructor named Heinz Thannhauser (1918–1944) that their relationship with each other began to develop in earnest. Thannhauser, although only two years older than Bill, had had an extraordinary visual education. A German Jew by birth but educated at Cambridge and Harvard, Heinz was a trained art historian. He was also the eldest son of Justin Thannhauser, one of the great modern European art collectors. (The Thannhauser Collection at the Guggenheim Museum in New York gives an idea of the range of the family's holdings.) Before the Nazi regime forced his family to flee, Heinz was greatly influenced by his family's personal connections to such figures as Pablo Picasso and Henri Matisse.

AT TULANE, BILL SOUGHT OUT THEATRE AS AN EXTRACURRICULAR ACTIVITY AND HIS MENTOR BECAME DR. MONROE LIPPMAN. WHEN "DOC" FOUND OUT BILL WAS STUDYING ARCHITECTURE, HE PROMOTED HIM TO A SET DESIGNER, A POSITION HE HELD FROM HIS FRESHMAN THROUGH HIS SENIOR YEARS. SET DESIGNER STATUS WAS USUALLY RESERVED FOR SENIORS. "I TRIED IT, I LIKED IT, AND I'VE BEEN DOING IT EVER SINCE," BILL SAID. (EC)

TWELFTH NIGHT CAST AND CREW PHOTO, TULANE UNIVERSITY (MAY 1942). LEFT TO RIGHT: FIRST ROW ON LEFT IS HEINZ THANNHUSER (FESTE), SECOND ROW—FIFTH FROM THE LEFT IS JEAN (LIGHTING, PUBLICITY), THIRD ROW—THIRD FROM LEFT IS BILL (VALENTINE, HEAD OF PAINTING, SET DESIGNER). (EC)

YOU CAN'T TAKE IT WITH YOU, TULANE UNIVERSITY. ACT II. BILL ECKART'S SET DESIGN SHOWS HIS INDEBTEDNESS TO DONALD OENSLAGER (ORIGINAL BROADWAY PRODUCTION DESIGNER) WHO WOULD LATER BECAME HIS PROFESSOR AT YALE. (EC)

He was intrigued by the idea of having modern artists design theatrical pieces and became a magnetic force for Bill and Jean. It was Jean who persuaded Heinz to offer a course in theatrical design, something that had never been done before at Tulane. Bill would later say "Heinz knew about as much as we did about stage design, but he offered us a totally different design aesthetic." The course was a turning point for the Eckarts. On an academic level, Bill and Jean were exposed to significant trends in modern art: Expressionism, Cubism, Constructivism, and Abstraction. Under Heinz's tutelage Bill had his first success with a non-realistic set. He designed a University Theatre production of William Saroyan's *Jim Dandy*, which clearly drew on the work of European sur-realist Salvador Dali. It was the first time Bill had used the work of a modern artist to open up the world of a play. Bill and Jean would con-tinue to employ this kind of an approach to design again and again in their mature work.

It was in the ferment of this kind of intellectual stimulation that the couple opened up to one another and formed a bond. When asked when he knew he had fallen in love with Jean, Bill later said "It evolved."

Jean was putting the finishing touches on the Newcomb Alumnae's production of *The Gondoliers*, in December 1941, when the Japanese bombed Pearl Harbor. Once war was declared, Bill was fast-tracked through college and graduated with a BS degree in architecture. He enlisted and was later accepted into the Army's Officers' Candidate School. During a battery of tests, one consisting of translating a made-up language, Bill scored so well he was transferred to an intelligence unit. There he received specialized training in Japanese.

Jean had to continue at Sophie Newcomb for another year to get her degree. She became the first BFA theatre major at Tulane. This would be the first of many firsts for Jean during her career.

With Bill in basic training, their courtship had to be carried on by phone and through the mail. Then just before starting the Army's lan-guage program at Georgetown University in Washington, D.C., Bill

JIM DANDY BY WILLIAM SAROYAN, TULANE UNIVERSITY THEATRE, JANUARY 1942, WILLIAM ECKART'S FIRST USE OF MODERN ART AS A WAY OF OPENING UP THE WORLD OF THE PLAY. INSPIRED BY SALVADOR DALI, THE SET STRUCK A LOCAL CRITIC AS "VIVIFIED AND INTENSIFIED TO A POINT OF STUNNING INCREDULITY." BILL STARTED WITH THE IDEA EXPRESSED IN SAROYAN'S DIRECTION, "THE FICTION ROOM OF THE PUBLIC LIBRARY IN SAN FRANCISCO" AND WENT ON FROM THERE. (EC)

was given a three-day leave. "It was a Thursday. I called Jean in Chicago and asked her to marry me over the phone. She said she'd be there on Saturday." Bill and Jean Eckart were married Saturday afternoon in Baltimore. It was 1943.

Jean went to work for the Army creating pictographs while Bill completed his courses. When the Navy seized a top-secret Japanese codebook, Bill was able to get Jean hired to work on the code with him. "It was all very hush-hush," Jean said later. "I don't know that we won the war, but the work was very interesting, and we were surrounded by a remarkable group of people. Then once the fighting stopped we spent our mornings making up double-acrostic puzzles and swapping them in the afternoon." The Eckarts' passion for puzzles and problem-solving continued for the rest of their lives, and they seldom missed a day doing *The New York Times* crossword puzzle.

After the war was over and Bill was discharged from the army, he and Jean wanted to follow in the footsteps of Tulane profs Monroe and Ruth Lippman and become the nurturing couple the Lippmans had been for them. Lippman had been like a father to Bill. He'd taught both Bill and Jean how to read plays, analyze text, make floor plans, and many of the other practical aspects of theatre production. Ruth Lippman was equally involved. She did the costumes, worked the box office, and helped to promote the plays. Together they had created an extended family of the promising students, and Bill and Jean were favorites. To pass on to others what the Lippmanns had done for them, Bill and Jean knew they had to go to graduate school, get degrees, and then find teaching positions at a university.

The Yale School of Drama had the best theatre program in the nation, but neither Bill nor Jean thought they were advanced enough to be accepted. Nonetheless, they applied together and then visited the campus where Bill met with Donald Oenslager who was in charge of the design program. Oenslager was a working professional designer, and Bill was in awe of him. He knew that Oenslager had designed the original production of *You Can't Take It With You* by Moss Hart and George S. Kaufman, a play that he had designed at Tulane. Neither Jean nor Bill could believe how readily Oenslager accepted them into Yale. They were so overwhelmed, they scurried back to Chicago and promptly signed up for summer courses at Northwestern University. They wanted to be prepared for the advanced technical work they assumed

JEAN ON THE EVE OF HER MARRIAGE IN 1943 (EC)

COMPANIONS OF THE LEFT HAND, YALE. JEAN'S SKETCH SELECTED FOR THE SCHOOL PRODUCTION IN 1948. THE ECKARTS SEEM TO HAVE UNCONSCIOUSLY ADOPTED A SIMILAR DRAWING STYLE. (EC)

would be required at Yale. Bill later joked about what hayseeds they'd been. Technical craft was not what Yale was all about.

The student body at Yale after World War II was mature and determined; the average age of the students was twenty-five. It was the combination of serious students, the exposure to the out-of-town Broadway tryouts that passed through New Haven each season, and a faculty that included working Broadway professionals, which would alter the course of the Eckarts' creative lives. At Yale, students were not isolated into specific disciplines, so design students were constantly interacting with actors, directors, and playwrights. The emphasis was on working together if not actually on collaboration. "We not only designed plays," Bill said "but we produced, wrote, directed, and acted in plays." When they entered Yale, Bill and Jean thought they wanted to be academics. By the time they left, they knew they were going to be professionals.

Donald Oenslager combined teaching with a successful professional designing career and commuted back and forth to New Haven. He worked not only with Kaufman and Hart but with such figures as Robert Edmond Jones, Eugene O'Neill, and Kenneth MacGowan. None of these seminal figures thought of set design as a decorative art. Instead they believed set designers needed to be "thinkers with imagination." But it was Robert Edmond Jones, an occasional lecturer at Yale, who would provide the Eckarts with their working aesthetic. A charismatic personality, he enthralled students, including Bill and Jean, with portions of what was to become *The Dramatic Imagination.* Stage design to Jones was poetic, giving expression to *the essential quality of a play,* and that meant boiling a show down to its essence. A designer, he maintained, needed to find the dramatic root of a play and then work with the core. This approach became Bill and Jean's professional credo.

COMPANIONS OF THE LEFT HAND, YALE. BILL'S COMPETING SKETCH—EVEN THOUGH JEAN WON THE COMPETITION, BILL HELPED HER PAINT THE SET. (EC)

BILL IN HIS SERVICE UNIFORM IN 1942 (EC)

It matched their individual talents precisely. Finding the essence required an analytical frame of mind, a natural talent of Jean's. During the war, Bill's ability to see patterns had given him a key position in military intelligence. When the Navy was getting incomplete signals from Japanese ships, Bill was given a series of three transcriptions to decipher. If a pattern existed, Bill could see what was needed to complete it.

Donald Oenslager watched the two work at Yale and saw Bill and Jean as very individual spirits. "Jean worked practically while Bill had the quality of the visionary. They'd work separately on projects and they always did the same things well, but given the same design problem they'd come up with very different answers." In a designing competition for a Yale production of *Companions of the Left Hand,* each of them entered sketches. Jean's simplified approach was selected and produced, but once the show was in production, Bill and Jean painted the sets together. "Often our solutions were similar because we talked, but we were treated as individuals," Bill said. The combination of their talents would mature over their shared careers and would eventually lead to their best work in the theatre.

Another powerful influence at Yale was Professor Frank Poole Bevan. Bevan was also a theatre professional, although during the years the Eckarts were at Yale, he dedicated himself exclusively to teaching. He had elevated the teaching of costume design from a study of craft to a rigorous academic discipline, developing the first program for systematically training costume designers. But Bevan's greatest contribution to the Eckarts at Yale was accompanying him to the Broadway "tryouts" that played the Shubert Theatre in New Haven. Bevan demanded of them that they learn to get beyond the level of accepting the show as audience members. He contended that if they remained at that level, they

THE ALCHEMIST, BY BEN JONSON, DECEMBER 1947, YALE EXPERIMENTAL THEATRE. PHOTOGRAPH OF JEAN'S DESIGN SHOWS THE INFLUENCE OF RUSSIAN CONSTRUCTIVISM. BOLD COSTUMES AND A GEOMETRICALLY PAINTED CEILING HELPED TO COMPLETE THE STAGE PICTURE. (EC)

HENRIK IBSEN'S PEER GYNT, (1949). JEAN'S THESIS PROJECT WAS A MODERNISTIC PRODUCTION WITH JAPANESE OVERTONES ALTHOUGH THIS COSTUME SKETCH, "WOMAN IN GREEN," OWES SOMETHING TO PABLO PICASSO. (EC)

were bound to remain consumers. They would never ask the right questions to become creative in the theatre. Bevan insisted they discuss the plays afterwards, concentrating on the failures as much as the successes. To the Eckarts these professional tryouts became a kind of laboratory. This exposure to shows on the road in tryout gave Bill and Jean a chance to measure themselves against others working in the business. The idea of designing professionally, which at one time seemed so remote, now seemed to be just a short distance off.

Although musicals at mid-century were a Broadway staple, Yale students seldom had any direct experience with the form. But Bill and Jean more than made up for what was lacking in the curriculum by taking in the shows at the Shubert and occasionally in New York. During the time they were attending Yale, the Eckarts saw such musicals as: Bambi Linn in *Great To Be Alive*, Carol Channing in *Gentlemen Prefer Blondes*, Kurt Weill and Maxwell Anderson's *Lost in the Stars*, Irving Berlin and Robert Sherwood's *Miss Liberty*, Alan Jay Lerner and Kurt Weill's *Love Life* and Lerner and Frederick Loewe's *Brigadoon*, Frank Loesser's *Where's Charley?*, Cole Porter's *Kiss Me Kate*, Rodgers and Hammerstein's *South Pacific* and *Allegro*, Jule Styne's *High Button Shoes*, John Latouche and Jerome Moross's *Ballet Ballads*, Latouche and Duke Ellington's *Beggar's Holiday*, and E. Y. Harburg and Burton Lane's *Finian's Rainbow*.

When Michael Rubin, a fellow student, first brought his musical spoof of Hollywood entitled *Gwendolyn* to Jean, she was so enthusiastic about it, she agreed to direct it. Then she worked out an arrangement with the faculty so

POSSUM TROT, YALE, (1949). BILL'S THESIS WAS THE SET FOR A PLAY BASED ON THE WORKS OF BLACK POET PAUL LAWRENCE DUNBAR AND RELIED HEAVILY ON DROPS AND CURTAINS. THE BACKDROP WAS A MAP OF THE PLACE THAT DIDN'T "MAKE NO PRETENSIONS TO BEIN' GREAT AND FINE." BILL DREW INSPIRATION FROM HIS LOUISIANA ROOTS WHERE HE HAD SEEN AFRICAN AMERICAN QUILTS. (EC)

GREEN PASTURES, BY PAUL GREENE, YALE (1948)—BILL CREATED A DESIGN FOR OENSLAGER'S CLASS USING BOLD LINES FOR THE TREE TRUNKS, CREATING PORTALS WITH A STRONG SENSE OF MOVEMENT. HE DREW HEAVILY ON IMPRESSIONISTS AND MODERN ART. IN THIS SET HE IS INDEBTED TO HENRI ROUSSEAU. (EC)

she and Bill could produce the show together as an extracurricular activity with Bill doing the set design. This was to be their first joint production, and it was a hit. When *Gwendolyn* sold out, the faculty finally embraced the project and underwrote additional performances. *Gwendolyn* was to be the first of many successes for Rubin. He went on to write the books for *Hello, Dolly! Carnival*, and *Bye Bye Birdie* under his new name, Michael Stewart. At Yale the Eckarts would meet many future collaborators and life-long friends, such as Tharon Musser (lighting designer), Anne Shropshire (actress), Patton Campbell (costume designer), and Bill Goodheart (playwright).

During the summers, the Eckarts took jobs working together in summer stock. In 1947, they brainstormed by designing six shows, one a week, for the Barnstormers in New Hampshire. The following summer, they did half a dozen shows in Ridgefield, Connecticut. Among the shows was *All the Way Home* written by Lynn Riggs (not to be confused

with the Tad Mosel drama of the same name). Riggs had previously written the play on which the musical *Oklahoma!* was based. One of Broadway's most prominent designers, Ralph Alswang, was hired to design the set. But, as Richard Grayson, the company manager, recalled "Ralph had only done a preliminary floor plan and a water color sketch for the elevation. The program should have read 'sets by William and Jean Eckart based on an *idea* of Ralph Alswang.' They also did the lighting and a really smashing job." Grayson was so impressed with the quality and imagination of the Eckarts' work, he decided they'd be valuable people to know in the future. That fall, he would make a special trip to visit them in New Haven. Afterwards, he invited them to join him in New York for Thanksgiving. It would be during Thanksgiving dinner they would meet Eli Wallach, Anne Jackson, and Terry Hayden.

The summer stock season in Connecticut brought another unexpected break their way. Bill and Jean were not only designing but building all

DESIGNERS FOR TELEVISION

their own sets. The bookkeeper at the theatre accused them of buying too many nails and suggested instead that they straighten out the old ones and re-use them. The Eckarts were understandably frustrated and exhausted. One evening towards the end of the summer they were out front watching *The Late George Apley* when the stage manager missed the curtain call cue. "The curtain went up just as all the actors turned to leave and came down just before they could take their bows. It was like something out of a Marx Brothers movie." Bill and Jean couldn't stop laughing. "The director—who was unfortunately also the star of the show—told us, 'If you can't control yourselves, you shouldn't be in the theatre.' So we quit." In the time between the abrupt end of their summer stock season and the beginning of fall classes, the Eckarts went to New York. Although they were determined to complete their studies and obtain Yale graduate degrees, their ready acceptance by seasoned theatre professionals such as Richard Grayson convinced them their future lay in professional New York theatre.

Towards the end of the following semester the opportunity they needed came to them through the chaotic early days of live television. "The idea of television at the time we all started was unknown," said Jac Venza, an early colleague of the Eckarts and currently a producer for PBS. "In those days television hired only two kinds of people: those who had failed in radio and those who never had any career at all. Television then was not part of anyone's career plan." A Yale schoolmate who had to leave a position at NBC television in New York asked Bill to fill in for him, and he seized the opportunity. He moved to New York to take the job while Jean packed up their few possessions and followed. Yale was to help out by allowing them to finish their masters work off campus. There was a big problem in New York, though. They would have to become members of the United Scenic Artists Union or permanent work as designers would not be possible. During the Great Depression, employment possibilities had been so grim that the Union's leadership had stopped giving entrance exams and accepting new members. Then in the summer of 1948, the Union, due to the scenic demands of live television, suddenly decided to reverse its stance. "They wanted $500 just to take the exam," Bill said. "We didn't have enough for both of us, so we flipped a coin and I got elected to try first." Jean had to wait to take her exam the following year.

Television threw challenges at designers very quickly. "Often," Bill said, "we would get a script in the morning and later that same day, we'd have a production meeting with the director, by which time you were expected to have a basic design for the show. We had to work so fast there was no time to worry." Like summer stock, early TV had a one-week turn around and the actors first got to work on the set at noon on the day of the live telecast. After six months of working at NBC, Bill walked over to CBS and asked them if they'd like to hire him. The new medium was that wide open. CBS told Bill to report for work the following week. Jean, after getting her union card, became the first woman to be hired as a designer in television. She also got a job at CBS and started by designing quiz shows, such as *What's My Line?* Then she graduated to *Big Town,* a dramatic show. Unlike *Suspense*, one of Bill's shows, *Big Town* had what Jean thought of as a "huge budget." "And so I was always designing something, adding in a fireplace that I didn't need, so that we'd have it in stock and it was available for other people to use."

Live television taught the Eckarts to work efficiently and quickly. But from another perspective, it was all about limitations. The size of the early television image and its low quality of resolution encouraged design simplification. On the positive side this dovetailed perfectly with Robert Edmund Jones' *finding the essence* and using symbols to relay meaning to the viewer. There was no color so television painted pictures with light. Bill and Jean learned a great deal more about lighting, such as how to create an area of sharp focus by using just a few lights and how to backlight a specific object so it would dominate the on-screen picture. They were also told that they couldn't use objects that were black or white, but they refused to accept this and found black and white could be used, just not up against one another. Other limitations they refused to accept had to do with their democratic ideals. In spite of the courageous stand being made by CBS News' Edward R. Murrow against McCarthyism, CBS was still insisting that everyone at the network sign a loyalty oath swearing allegiance to the United States and disavowing any affiliation with Communism. The Eckarts refused to sign. The network backed down, but Bill and Jean were left with an uneasy feeling about the medium.

On top of the other problems with television, it was not artistically satisfying. "It was lucrative," said Jean, "but really we were just grinding it out. Maybe one week in seven we'd turn out something we were proud of." Jac Venza looked at it differently. "The Eckarts acquired from television what they really wanted to do, which was to design for the theatre."

The big break came in 1951. The Westport Country Playhouse near New York had a resident designer accustomed to doing one-set shows. He balked at doing *The Little Screwball* by Walt Anderson because it required ten sets. Since Westport was near New York and the Theatre Guild was the producer, the Eckarts jumped at the chance to design it. They took time off from CBS hoping the show would move to Broadway. "But when it came to signing the contract," Bill said, "the Union told us, 'You can't take a one week job in stock. Two weeks is the minimum.' We told the Theatre Guild and they offered us a second show."

"LAMP UNTO MY FEET" (1951). JEAN AND BILL'S DESIGN FOR THE INSPIRATIONAL PROGRAM THAT AIRED ON CBS SUNDAY MORNINGS. (EC)

THE BIG BREAK

A TRAINED ARCHITECT, BILL DESIGNED A SUMMER HOME FOR BEN ROSSIN IN MONTANA. THE DESIGNS WERE A WAY OF THANKING ROSSIN'S WIFE HELEN CLAYTON, JEAN'S ROOMMATE AT TULANE. HELEN WAS RESPONSIBLE FOR THE ECKARTS' FIRST BREAK IN PROFESSIONAL THEATRE WHEN AS A CHORUS MEMBER IN *SOUTH PACIFIC* SHE OVERHEARD A CONVERSATION THAT WALTER ABEL NEEDED A DESIGNER FOR THE SHOW HE WAS GOING TO DIRECT AT THE WESTPORT PLAYHOUSE, AND SHE RECOMMENDED THE ECKARTS. ROSSIN, A SCION OF THE LEWISOHN FAMILY, BUILT THE HOUSE INTO A HILLSIDE. BILL CONSIDERED THE DESIGN TO BE AN HOMAGE TO FRANK LLOYD WRIGHT SINCE IT FOLLOWED WRIGHT'S IDEA OF SUITING THE ARCHITECTURE TO THE SITE. (EC)

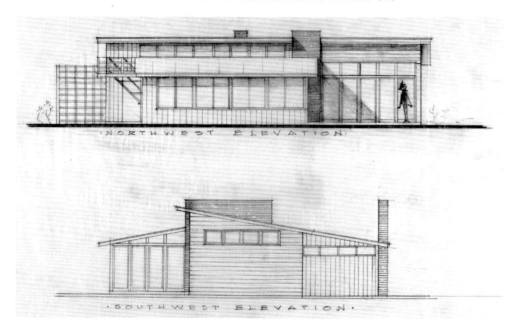

·NORTHWEST ELEVATION·

·SOUTHWEST ELEVATION·

THE LITTLE SCREWBALL, WESTPORT COUNTRY PLAYHOUSE (JULY 1951)—ACTORS (LEFT TO RIGHT) SARINA MINEO, MURIEL BERKSON, SANTY FRANK JOSOL, JR., SALVATORE MINEO, JR. SAL MINEO WAS JAMES DEAN'S FRIEND "PLATO" IN *REBEL WITHOUT A CAUSE* (1955) AND BECAME A STAR. (PHOTO: BOB GOLBY, EC)

In spite of the Eckarts' innovative designs for the ten scene changes, *The Little Screwball* did not make it to Broadway. The play was set in Spanish Harlem and dealt with a plucky eleven-year-old played by Sal Mineo. The story took place in a series of flashbacks before a judge. The Eckarts' design solution was to use tight focus lighting to create the multiple locales. Stage right became the courtroom and stage left the chaos of the streets. Center stage remained undefined. The action moved fluidly from one location to another without ever halting to change the scenery. For a scene in Central Park, a piece of scrim floated down from above. Bill and Jean projected light patterns onto the scrim to make the fabric function like a large umbrella. The effect turned the entire stage into a diaphanous canopy of leaves. According to one reviewer "Special applause was given time and again as the change of scenes appeared." *Variety* panned the play but singled out the Eckarts for their "atmospheric and flexible sets."

Broadway's Harald Bromley produced *Glad Tidings*, the second show on the Eckarts' contract. Bromley had received a bid of $17,000 from a commercial shop to design and build the show. To get him to open the show in Westport first, Lawrence Langner, Westport's executive producer, bragged to Bromley that his shop could design and build it for less. Bill and Jean were given the assignment. They rummaged through warehouses of old Theatre Guild sets, took pieces from several other shows

and then crafted everything into their new design. They came in under $3,000. Elliott Martin, who ran the scenic studio at Westport, believes few designers would have had the craft to pull this off. "The set was so lovely," said Halia Stoddard (producing with Harald Bromley), "it was practically ready to take into New York and that's quite a tribute." The Eckarts found these reactions flattering but amusing. They'd been whipping out scenery for CBS every week with even lower budgets.

Glad Tidings starring Melvyn Douglas and Signe Hasso turned out to be the Eckarts' ticket to Broadway. It opened October 11, 1951, at Broadway's most venerable theatre, the Lyceum. Critic Brooks Atkinson (*The New York Times*) wrote "[The] actors… have the advantage of playing inside a beautifully designed set of a manor house." John Chapman (*Daily News*) found it "handsome and imposing." *Glad Tidings* ran for more than one hundred performances. The Eckarts were on their way.

They got their next Broadway show when producer/director Herman Shumlin discovered the designer he had hired for *To Dorothy, A Son*, had-

n't even read the script. The volatile Shumlin fired the man only weeks before the play was to open. Then desperate, he called Charles Bowden, the Production Manager at Westport. Bowden recommended the Eckarts. "We had to get our entire design drawn up in a week," Bill said. "Then we were told to use a cheap scene shop. When we set up out-of-town, we found the color on one part of the set didn't match the color on the other part. The shop simply hadn't finished the work." The Eckarts hand-painted the scenery themselves rather than see a botched job open in New York. Their perfectionism and economy were appreciated by Shumlin, who was so financially strapped at the time he had the Eckarts use his own living room furniture on stage. Although once considered a Broadway heavyweight, with a string of hits that included *Grand Hotel*, *The Children's Hour, The Little Foxes, The Corn is Green*, and *Watch on the Rhine*, Shumlin was going through a dry spell. The truth was he hadn't had a hit in seven years, and *To Dorothy, A Son* wasn't an exception. In spite of everyone's best efforts, it flopped and closed after only eight

THE FIRST VERSION OF BAGNOLD'S GEORGIAN COUNTRY HOUSE IN *GERTIE* (1952) (EC)

FINAL VERSION OF *GERTIE* ELIMINATING PANELING AND ADDING THE COLOR, WHICH BAGNOLD DESCRIBED AS "OCHRE AND SPIRITS" (EC)

performances. Shumlin would have to wait another three years before *Inherit the Wind* brightened his prospects.

"We weren't accustomed to working with anyone as explosive as Shumlin," Jean said. "When we were out-of-town with him I remember eating a lot of pre-digested food, like oatmeal and egg salad sandwiches."

CBS in the meantime was becoming impatient. The Eckarts had been able to cover themselves until then but now were informed they were taking too much time off to design theatre. CBS gave them an ultimatum: a good paying job in television or the theatre. They chose the theatre. Their three years in television would be the final leg of Bill and Jean's design apprenticeship.

Amazingly, Shumlin was able to find the money to mount another production that season. Once more, he hired the Eckarts. The play was *Gertie* by English novelist Enid Bagnold, and it was to be British film star Glynis Johns's Broadway début. Bill noticed the normally manic Shumlin getting so tense when Enid Bagnold was at a rehearsal "that his head would go off to the side and lock." Bagnold, the wife of Sir Roderick Jones, insisted she be addressed as Lady Jones. The Eckarts dubbed her "Lady Bag."

"Lady Bag" took exception to the Eckarts' set. They'd designed an English country house in faded color, Georgian, and very genteel. Bagnold wanted the color to be heavier and talked about mixing "ochre and spirits." "It's all off, all off," she kept shouting. "We never could figure out what she meant," Jean said, "but we changed the colors, eliminated the paneling, and showed her the new sketch. She finally approved." Yet when the show went into rehearsal, Bagnold exploded again. This time about some blue and white ginger pots. "They're Tottenham Court Road. "THIS is an ENGLISH house. You've made it into a lodging house near Euston (London) AND one that takes in Indians!"

Lodging house or Georgian mansion, according to George Jean Nathan, *Gertie* was "stage mush." It opened on Wednesday and closed on Saturday. Shumlin cancelled the two other productions he had planned for the season.

The Eckarts were able to find employment doing industrials. They designed for a wide variety of clients such as Oldsmobile, DuPont, and Borden. But like so many of their contemporaries who had come to New York after the Depression and the war, they were idealists. They were anxious to be contributors to a living theatre and to raise the level of its art.

During the early months of 1953, the Eckarts learned that Teresa Hayden, whom they had met while still at Yale, was planning to produce a month-long season of plays in the new venue of Off-Broadway. Bill and Jean were delighted with the eclectic choices she had made. Hayden had persuaded Cheryl Crawford, one of the founders of the then new Actors Studio, to let her use the School's space for rehearsals. The Theatre de Lys (now the Lucille Lortel Theatre) was a small, converted movie house on Christopher Street, located within easy walking distance of the Eckarts' Greenwich Village apartment. The Eckarts agreed to paint and build their sets in the alley adjacent to the theatre. Because of Crawford's involvement, there were lots of young actors and directors who were impatient with the compromises of commercialism and willing to work at the Theatre De Lys for practically nothing. Because of the proximity, Bill and Jean's Washington Mews

home became a natural gathering place for the entire company and all the opening night parties were held there. Bill and Jean had rented the eighteenth-century carriage house the second year they were in New York. They'd read an ad for a one-room house "thirty squared feet." Curiosity about a place that measured "3 feet by 10 feet" drove them to see it. NYU, the landlord for The Mews, had made a slight mistake in the ad. The room was actually 30 feet square or nine-hundred square feet. It was also twenty-one feet high with a skylight. Bill and Jean redesigned the space into a home and studio. People who visited The Mews never forgot it. In an era that spawned tract houses and conformity as national pastimes, the Eckarts' conversion of an old stable into a dramatic open area and work place was extraordinary.

BACKDROP RENDERING. WHEN THE ECKARTS SEVERED THEIR TIES WITH CBS, THEY DID A VARIETY OF INDUSTRIAL SHOWS. THE OLDSMOBILE SHOW, WHICH WAS STAGED IN THE ZIEGFELD THEATRE, WAS ONE OF THE MOST PRESTIGIOUS AND FROM A DESIGN STANDPOINT EVERY BIT AS DEMANDING AS A BROADWAY SHOW. THEIR USE OF COLOR AND FORM SHOWS THE INFLUENCE OF NEW YORK ABSTRACT ARTIST ROBERT RAUSCHENBERG. (EC)

THE ECKARTS BEGAN THEIR EXPERIMENTATION WITH STAIRCASES IN THEIR WASHINGTON MEWS APARTMENT IN GREENWICH VILLAGE. IN THE MEWS, THEY WERE DEALING WITH A TWO-STORY SPACE THAT WAS NARROW, BUT THE STAIRCASE TRANSFORMED IT INTO A STYLISH THEATRICAL SETTING. PEOPLE WHO VISITED THEIR HOME NEVER FORGOT IT. THE STAIRCASE WASN'T JUST AN ATTENTION GETTER; IT OPENED THE ENTIRE APARTMENT, PROVIDING ACCESS TO LOFT WORK AND SLEEP AREAS FROM THEIR LIVING ROOM WITHOUT REQUIRING AN UPSTAIRS HALLWAY. NOVEMBER 1957. (PHYLLIS TWACHTMAN, EC)

BILL AND JEAN IN THEIR WASHINGTON MEWS APARTMENT, NOVEMBER 1957 (PHYLLIS TWACHTMAN, EC)

The repertory for Hayden's Off-Broadway season was as exciting as it was diverse: *The School for Scandal, The Scarecrow, Maya,* and *The Little Clay Cart.* Each play was written in a different period. Each demanded a different style of presentation. The format appealed to actors eager to be noticed by agents and critics. The host of young acting talent available from The Actors Studio was staggering: James Dean, Anne Jackson, Eli Wallach, Kay Medford, Salem Ludwig, Leo Penn, Mark Rydell, Martin Ritt, Sono Osato, Patricia Neal, Bradford Dillman, David J. Stewart, John Randolph, Rebecca Darke, Vivian Matalon, and Albert Salmi. "It was the caliber of the acting that attracted all of the first string critics," Hayden said. "It certainly wasn't the salaries. Everyone received a token $25 per week for each week worked. The union situation was different then. They cooperated."

For Bill and Jean, the month-long Off-Broadway season was a major turning point. Until then they'd been known as "the designers of last resort." Bringing in shows at the last moment, in record time on low budgets. Although the Eckarts were able to accomplish marvelous things under difficult conditions, they hadn't really had a chance to show what they could do. The Theatre de Lys gave them their opportunity. Each production, they decided, would have an entirely different look. Because of the limited budget, Bill and Jean undertook to oversee the costumes and made them as well in more than a few instances.

The season opened with *Maya* by Simon Gantillon, a new translation of a French play previously banned in New York because of its direct treatment of prostitution. Naturally, it caught the attention of the press. "I originally had selected the piece for Jo Van Fleet," Hayden said. "It was her idea to get Susan Strasberg for the role of a girl who makes the journey from innocent to woman of the world. She was such a pretty little girl. We asked Lee Strasberg if he would let us use his daughter in the play. The condition was we take her to school and then home after rehearsals and performances." The play was to be Susan Strasberg's stage début. Her performance resulted in her next getting the lead in *The Diary of Anne Frank*.

Maya opened to generally favorable notices, but the set made of discarded shutters received rave reviews. Brooks Atkinson (*The New York Times*) found the set completely charming. "It combines the cheapness and mysticism of M. Gantillon's theme better than the playwriting does," he wrote.

The second play, *The Scarecrow* (in which James Dean had one of his early stage roles) critics from *Variety*, *Cue*, the *Herald Tribune*, and the *Journal-American* echoed Atkinson's praise. Walter Kerr (*Herald Tribune*) wrote, "William and Jean Eckart have created a glowing forge, with sunlight filtering down through suspended wagon-wheels, which is far more atmospheric than the performance it graces." The Eckarts were less

THE ECKARTS' SET SKETCH FOR *MAYA*, THEATRE DE LYS 1953 (EC)

FOR THE MARSEILLES PROSTITUTES IN *MAYA*, THEY DESIGNED CLOTHES THAT WERE ALL FLUFF AND PLUNGE, HELD TOGETHER BY A LITTLE NET. FOR SUSAN STRASBERG'S CHARACTER, WHO MADE THE WORLDLY JOURNEY FROM CHILDHOOD INNOCENCE TO WOMAN OF THE WORLD IN A SINGLE DRESS, THEY CREATED A VOCABULARY OF ADD-ONS USING A RAKISHLY DRAPED RED SASH, STILETTO HEELS, DARK STOCKINGS, AND A STYLISH HAIR-DO. (EC)

THE ECKARTS POSE ALONGSIDE A MONDRIAN INSPIRED SERIES OF FRAMES THE PANELS OF WHICH HELD BRIGHTLY COLORED CHINA SILK. DESIGNED FOR *THE LITTLE CLAY CART* AT THE THEATRE DELYS, THE ENTIRE SET WAS MOVED TO CONDE NAST'S "VOGUE" STUDIO IN JUNE 1953 WHERE THIS PHOTOGRAPH WAS TAKEN. (EC)

successful with *The School for Scandal* (the third play). They attempted to hide stage hands in scene shifts the way the actors tried to hide their American roots behind periwigs, snuff boxes, and fake British accents. But they triumphed once again with the final and most difficult show, the East Indian drama, *The Little Clay Cart*.

In their research, Bill and Jean had discovered some interesting similarities between Indian art and the paintings of the abstract artist Piet Mondrian. Each broke space into planes. They loved the way Mondrian dealt with flat design and made it dimensional. Bill said, "We never set out to imitate or copy Mondrian or any of the other post impressionists but we wanted to get away from painted drops." The Eckarts felt if they could use panels, they could compose objects in space. Part of a new generation of academically trained designers, the Eckarts were beginning to differentiate themselves from other designers who were not as visually sophisticated. "We developed the scenery along the lines of East Indian prints," Jean said. "We used their primitive architecture. The strange perspective we got as a result was created out of China silk which had been dye-painted. It had a glow." It not only had a glow, but the set created a small sensation. Someone from *Vogue* magazine saw it, and thought it would be appropriate as a fashion background. When the show closed, the Eckarts' vermilion and shocking pink set was moved to the Condé Nast Studios where it was photographed with fashion models in front of the scenery. People who were knowledgeable and who set trends were taking notice of Bill and Jean's work.

John Keating of *Cue* magazine noted the Eckarts had come off better than almost any other members of the company. "The sets of William and Jean Eckart demonstrate that there will soon be a new addition to the all-but-closed ranks of Mielziner-Oenslager-Bay-Ayers-Alswang." Bill and Jean were beginning to be mentioned alongside the top ranked theatrical designers of the time.

Cheryl Crawford was not only director of The Actors Studio but an established Broadway producer, and she was so impressed with the Eckarts. she hired them to design her next Broadway production, *Oh, Men! Oh, Women!* by Edward Chodorov. *Oh, Men! Oh, Women!* was a stylish comedy about a New York psychoanalyst

ONE SET PER ACT, PLEASE!

IN *OH, MEN! OH, WOMEN!* THE ECKARTS USED THE CHANGEOVER TIME DURING INTERMISSION WELL AND PRESENTED THE AUDIENCE WITH THREE TASTEFUL INTERIORS. ACT I IS A PSYCHOANALYSTS OFFICE. 1953 (EC)

OH, MEN! OH, WOMEN! ACT II, BETSY VON FURSTENBERG'S APARTMENT. JEAN HAD TO ADMIT AFTERWARDS THAT USING PINK AS THE PREDOMINANT COLOR IN THE SET'S APARTMENT CAUSED MORE TROUBLE SETTING THE LIGHTS THAN IT WAS WORTH. 1953 (EC)

IN *OH, MEN! OH, WOMEN!* ACT III, A SET DESIGNED AFTER A STATEROOM ON THE *S. S. UNITED STATES* OCEAN LINER. 1953 (EC)

(Franchot Tone) and his young fiancee (Betsy Von Furstenberg), a woman with a past. Larry Blyden and Gig Young (Broadway début) each had cameo appearances. The audience's clear favorite, however, was to be newcomer Anne Jackson who played a wacky patient and stopped the show each night.

Oh, Men! Oh, Women! called for three complete set changes, one for each act, an approach popular in realistic plays of the fifties. Opera continues this tradition today. Playwrights wrote to this formula because they dreaded the disorder and loss of pace that came with changing sets during the middle of an act. The designers' art was supposed to impress the audience with realistic detail and sumptuous decor. Bill and Jean actually received fan letters from members of the audience asking where they might purchase items they'd seen on the stage set.

Oh, Men! Oh, Women! opened on Broadway to favorable reviews. For the first time in their professional careers, the Eckarts were involved with a long running Broadway hit. *Oh, Men! Oh, Women!* ran for 382 performances and spawned a successful road company with Ralph Bellamy replacing Franchot Tones, Peggy Cass for Anne Jackson, and Patrick O'Neal for Gig Young. Tony Randall eventually came into the New York production. When the play was turned into a Hollywood motion picture Randall was retained making *Oh, Men! Oh, Women!* his feature film début. For Bill and Jean, the success of the show meant a source of regular income as they received a percentage of the gross box office receipts.

The next play they designed was unpromisingly called *Dead Pigeon*, starring Lloyd Bridges in his Broadway début. It was one of the last "box" sets the Eckarts did. They did not like placing an actor in a realistic room with the fourth-wall removed, a style which had become popular in the nineteenth century. *Dead Pidgeon* didn't last long, closing after only twenty-one performances.

Everything about how the Eckarts got their next show and their first musical was unusual. It began with a call from their summer stock friend, Richard Grayson. He invited Bill and Jean to a backers' audition of the new Jerome Moross and John LaTouche musical *The Golden Apple*. Five years earlier Bill and Jean had seen Moross and Latouche's *Ballet Ballads* and had admired how the experimental one-acts combined dance and song. They were eager to hear the new show. *The Golden Apple* was even more ambitious. "The show was fresh and innovative and we felt it broke new ground. Jean and I wanted to see if we could do the same with the scenery. We were thrilled by the challenge and decided to approach designing the show as if it were a class project at Yale."

Several weeks of working on the project passed when they heard Moross and Latouche were suspending their search for backers and leaving town. Moross, with a family to support, had to accept a composing job in Hollywood doing the ballet music for the film *Hans Christian Anderson*. John LaTouche was headed for Vermont "to brood and eschew the doldrums of the theatre forever." The Eckarts decided to invite the composer and lyricist to the Mews. They had built a small marionette-like model. Their design concept differed completely from the realistic descriptions found in LaTouche's stage directions. LaTouche later wrote, "Working independently of us, they had found

bold and ingenious ways to bring out the shifting moods and unbroken pace that our show demanded." Then something unexpected happened; LaTouche met with a Vermont neighbor, Norris Houghton, and discovered he and T. Edward Hambleton were planning to start a new theatrical venture to be known as The Phoenix. The new theatre group sought to provide a large audience with the best professional theatre for the least money. It would become the first permanent company to be established Off-Broadway. When LaTouche found the planned theatre's first season didn't include a musical, he got Houghton and Hambleton to listen to *The Golden Apple*. "They listened to it, they liked it, and suddenly three long years ended in a whirl of activity," LaTouche wrote. The composer and lyricist were so impressed with the Eckarts, they insisted the theatre hire them. Were it not for their enthusiasm, it is likely The Phoenix would have hired an established musical designer, such as Jo Mielziner (*Death of a Salesman, Streetcar Named Desire, Guys and Dolls*), Lemuel Ayers (*Oklahoma! Kiss Me Kate, The Pajama Game*), Oliver Smith (*On the Town, Brigadoon, My Fair Lady*), or Raoul Pene du Bois (*Panama Hattie, Call Me Madam, Wonderful Town*). But instead, the new theatre took a chance with new talent, and the Eckarts were in place to design their first musical.

For the most part, designers do not to get to select the shows they work on. Bill and Jean not only had the luxury of discovering the project they wanted, but they had the time to consider many new ideas and approaches to the material without the pressure for quick results. They also reaped one of the early benefits of the Off-Broadway experience: direct contact with the originators and the creators of *The Golden Apple*.

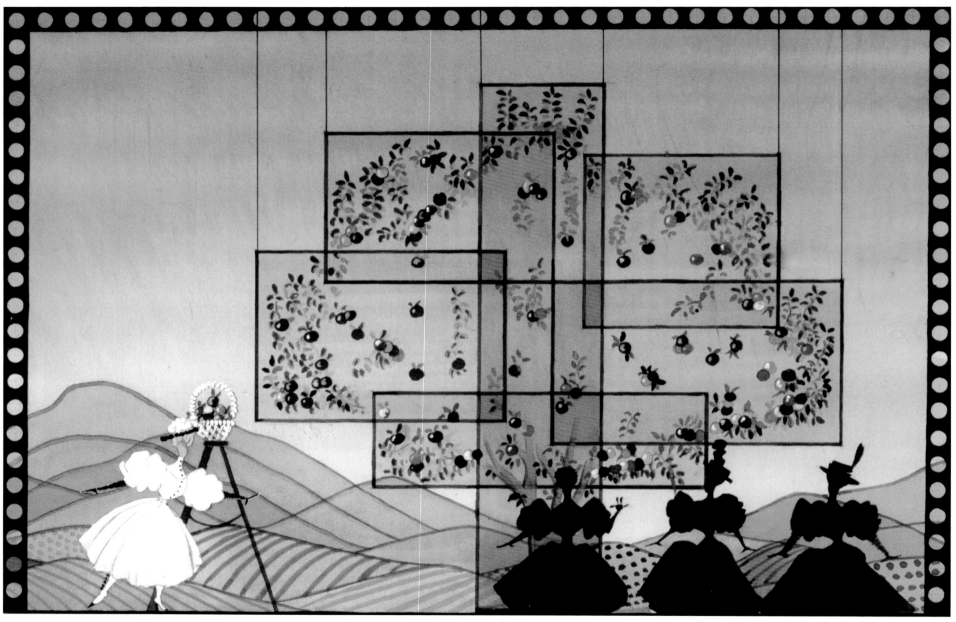

THE FINAL DESIGN SKETCH, ACT I, SCENE I. THE ECKARTS' STYLIZED BACKGROUND, AN APPLE TREE COMPOSED OF SIX RECTANGLES OF TRANSLUCENT MATERIAL APPLIQUÉD WITH APPLES AND LEAVES. THIS LIGHT AND AIRY COMPOSITION WAS THE ECKARTS' CUBISTIC EVOCATION OF AN APPLE ORCHARD IN THE FICTIONAL TOWN OF ANGEL'S ROOST. (COLLECTION OF THE MCNAY ART MUSEUM, GIFT OF ROBERT L.B. TOBIN)

Enchantment: The Golden Apple

1954 Marionette Scenery: Mini-drops

A MODERN RETELLING OF *THE ILIAD* AND *THE ODYSSEY* SET IN WASHINGTON STATE AT THE TURN OF THE CENTURY. THE HERO RETURNS FROM WAR DISILLUSIONED, IS LURED TO THE BIG CITY WHERE HE WINS EASY SUCCESS, ONLY TO BE UNDONE BY DECEIT AND CORRUPTION AND FINDS HIMSELF HAVING TO RETURN HOME.

"Our interpretation was really very sassy, and what I call presentational as opposed to representational. It is in a sense, a background rather than an environment. It freed us to just let our imaginations ride."

Jean Eckart

PENELOPE (PRISCILLA GILLETTE) AND ULYSSES (STEPHEN DOUGLASS) "IT'S GOING HOME TOGETHER" (PHOTOFEST)

"Our idea for the apple tree was that it was frankly scenery, so that when we wanted to do a scene we built what we called "mini-drops," and they were simply small screens, with the ropes that supported them quite visible. Everything flew in and out and moved in sight of the audience and traveled and galloped around so that it was really like staging scenery to the music, as you would stage actors or choreograph dancers," Jean said. *The Golden Apple* was not only the Eckarts' first musical and the first musical to move from Off-Broadway to Broadway, but it was also the Eckarts' first performing set. *The Golden Apple* was that rare commodity: a sung-through musical. It built on John LaTouche (lyricist) and Jerome Moross's (composer) experimental *Ballet Ballads* (1948), which was, as its title suggests, a three-part folk ballet made of ballads.

Dispensing with spoken dialogue was a major departure from the Rodgers and Hammerstein formula of book scenes interspersed with songs. So fluid was *The Apple's* structure that it bore a closer resemblance to the earlier *Ballet Ballads* than it did to traditional opera and operetta.

As is the case with all innovations, LaTouche and Moross found it was hell to get *The Golden Apple* produced. Their auditions of the show for Broadway producers were met with rejection upon rejection and soon hope evaporated into despair. It was at one of these many auditions that the Eckarts heard the show, and according to Bill, "It was love at first hearing." In the first flush of their enthusiasm, Bill and Jean decided to design this show for free.

THE ESSENCE: FROM ABSTRACT SCRIBBLES, THROUGH REALISM . . .

BEGINNING THOUGHTS. A ROUGH IDEA SCRIBBLED ON INEXPENSIVE, LINED COFFEE-STAINED TABLET (EC)

THE NEXT STEP: THE EMERGENCE OF APPLE TREES BROKEN INTO OVERLAPPING PANELS (EC)

DEVELOPMENT OF THE IDEA. THE ORIGINAL SCRIPT SPECIFIED AN APPLE ORCHARD IN THE TOWN OF ANGEL'S ROOST ON THE EDGE OF MT. OLYMPUS IN WASHINGTON STATE JUST AT THE END OF THE SPANISH-AMERICAN WAR. "INEXPLICABLY, WE GOT THE IDEA OF EXPLODING THE SCENES INTO OVERLAPPING SEE-THROUGH PANELS," BILL SAID. "WE SEEM TO HAVE STARTED WITH TREES AND A BLAZING SUN WHICH GRADUALLY DEVELOPED INTO AN ORCHARD REPRESENTED BY A SINGLE APPLE TREE."

THE ORCHARD HAS BECOME A SINGLE "REALISTIC" APPLE TREE BROKEN INTO GEOMETRICALLY FRAMED LAYERS OF SCRIM PANELS. THE PATCHWORK QUILT MOUNTAINS IN THE BACKGROUND ARE SIMILAR OVERLAPPING PANELS, BUT WITH ORGANIC SHAPES. AS THE PANELS RECEDE THEY CHANGE FROM OPAQUE TO TRANSPARENT. A PIERCED, LATE NINETEENTH CENTURY GINGERBREAD PORTAL FRAMES THE STAGE PICTURE. ALL THE ELEMENTS ARE FLAT, BUT ARRANGED IN DEPTH. (EC)

AND BACK TO ABSTRACTION

"BUSY LITTLE SEWING BEE," ACT II, SCENE VI. LEFT TO RIGHT: PENELOPE (PRISCILLA GILLETTE) AND THE OTHER LADIES OF ANGEL'S ROOST, LOVEY MARS (BIBI OSTERWALD), MISS MINERVA (PORTIA NELSON), AND MRS. JUNIPER (GERALDINE VITI) ACCOMPANIED BY MEMBERS OF THE CHORUS WAITING FOR ULYSSES TO RETURN. (FRED FEHL, EC)

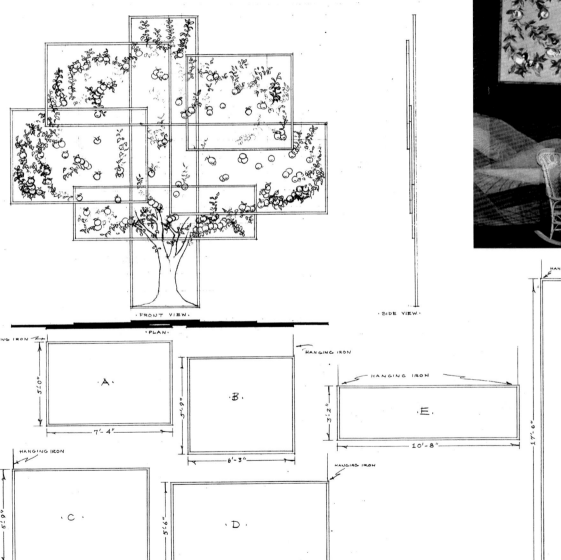

WORKING DRAWINGS SHOWING
THE CONFIGURATION OF PANELS TO
CONSTRUCT THE APPLE TREE (EC)

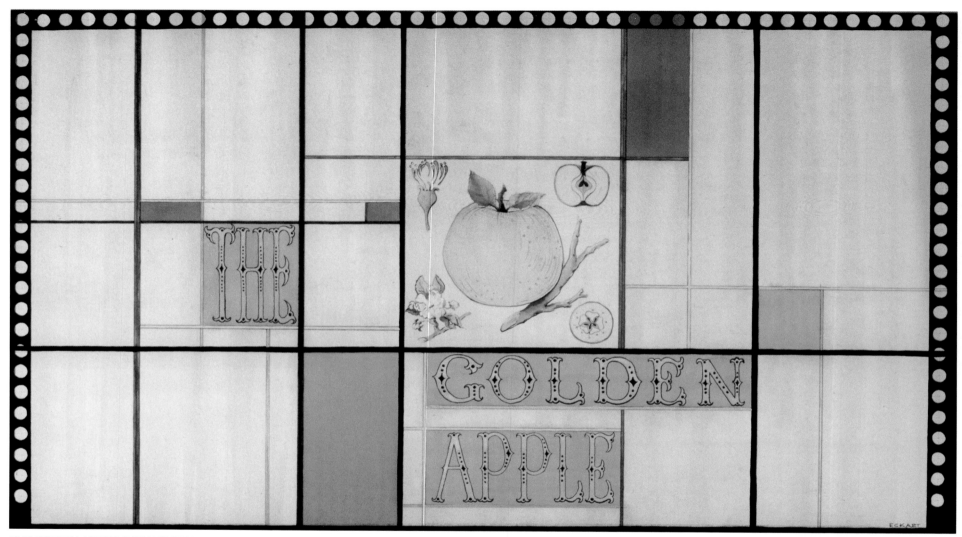

THE GOLDEN APPLE'S SHOW CURTAIN—AN EXPRESSION OF THE SPIRIT OF THE PIECE—A COMBINATION OF THE OLD (AS REPRESENTED BY THE 19TH CENTURY LETTERING STYLE AND BOTANICAL PRINT) AND THE NEW (A MONDRIAN INSPIRED COMPOSITION). THE PANELS WERE TRANSLUCENT CHINA SILK SET IN TUBULAR METAL FRAMES. (COLLECTION OF THE MCNAY ART MUSEUM, GIFT OF ROBERT L.B. TOBIN)

DURING INTERMISSION, THE BOTANICAL PRINT WAS REPLACED BY A LITHOGRAPHIC PORTRAIT OF HELEN (KAYE BALLARD) AS IF SEEN FROM THE FRONT PAGE OF THE CITY OF *RHODODENDRON BUGLE* FOR THE OPENING NUMBER OF ACT II, "OH, IT'S GRAND TO SEE MY PICTURE IN THE PAPERS." (CORNELL CAPA, GETTY IMAGES)

They told Richard Grayson (Stage Manager) that they were going to design the show as if it were a class project at Yale, and he gave them a copy of the libretto. At the time, the Eckarts had no idea that they were violating union rules by working without pay, an infraction that would later result in a stiff fine. And although they hoped that *The Golden Apple* would eventually find a producer, they had no idea that the producer would be T. Edward Hambleton's new Off-Broadway producing unit, The Phoenix Theatre.

What appealed to the Eckarts? Obviously, it was the challenge, but it was also the injustice of it all. Here was a literate (based on the Homeric epics), historical (set in Spanish-American War era), and contemporary (in musical sound and point of view) musical that was being ignored, perhaps because of its virtues. "The music felt something like Aaron Copland (*Billy the Kid, Appalachian Spring, Rodeo*)," Bill said. "It's an impression of American music. The themes are there, but it is witty and evocative rather than a direct recreation of a specific period." According to LaTouche, the new musical would be based on dances such as waltzes, ragtimes, blues, rumbas, and vaudeville turns to comically reflect "the classical influences, on the way we think nowadays." Something about this pastiche with its emphasis on dance clicked. What *The Golden Apple* was trying to do was to translate classical heroism into an urban, contemporary American framework. Against the post-war generation's sense of lost youth, dashed dreams, and disillusionment, Moross and LaTouche were erecting a multi-layered perspective. Their Ulysses would wrestle with a series of new challenges: Scylla and Charybdis as crooked stockbrokers, Calypso as a socially prominent hostess, and Circe aptly described by LaTouche's lyrics as "a woman without mercy."

To get down his first thoughts, Bill began scribbling his impressions on a lined pad. He was seeking to find the play's essence. Instantaneously, the idea emerged of breaking an apple tree into hard-edged separate planes. Bill and Jean realized that their approach brought them squarely into the abstract world of Piet Mondrian. Unconsciously, Bill had retraced the steps of that great modern artist as he came to champion New York's urban environment, the idea of living in a grid. The Dutch painter had begun with the abolition of figure-ground relationships, replacing them with

"A WELCOME HOME BANNER OF SUCH BRAZEN GAYETY THAT YOU IMAGINE NO ONE HAS EVER USED A WELCOME HOME BANNER IN A MUSICAL BEFORE."

WALTER KERR, *HERALD TRIBUNE*

THE TOWN SQUARE. A CELEBRATION FOR ULYSSES AND HIS MEN AS THEY RETURN FROM THE SPANISH-AMERICAN WAR. A FLAGPOLE (APPLIQUÉD ON A SCRIM PANEL), A BANNER, BLEACHERS PAINTED RED, WHITE, AND BLUE (EC)

"THE HEROES COME HOME." CENTER, MRS. JUNIPER (GERALDINE VITI) SINGS TO THE RETURNING HEROES (RODERICK MACARTHUR, COURTESY SUSANNA MOROSS TARJAN)

simplified, overlapping planes. This kind of abstract composition expressed in line and color the essence of an aesthetic which because of its linear rhythm had been called by critics a form of visual jazz. Mondrian, building on this comparison, entitled the triumph of his final period, "Broadway Boogie Woogie" (1942–43). Ironically, the Eckarts' experimentation with his approach had the unlikely outcome of bringing Mondrian to Broadway.

To achieve this objective, Bill and Jean constructed Cubist-style panels of translucent fabric. On the surface of the panels, they silk-screened apples. When the panels were lit, the audience could see through the surface of the scenery to other panels hung in different planes. This conception of layering visually paralleled LaTouche and Moross's point of view of playing one time period off against another. Because the Eckarts' dimensional use of stage space was hard to visualize on paper, they constructed a three dimensional model made of translucent paper, wooden battens, and string. When the model was complete, it resembled a marionette figure.

The design process was marked by several efforts toward and in retreat from abstraction. Eventually, Bill and Jean decided to abandon realism and free themselves from the clumsy conventions it required. They would unapologetically show the hemp lines from which their panels were suspended and let the audience know that the sets were part of the show. To emphasize this point, they were determined to change the sets in full view of the audience, a style which had not been popular since the Italian Renaissance when it was described as *à vista*.

With The Phoenix as *The Golden Apple's* producer came director Norman Lloyd, a member of the theatre's acting company and later TV's *St. Elsewhere's* Dr. Auschlander.

"LAZY AFTERNOON." HELEN (KAYE BALLARD) SEDUCES THE NON-SPEAKING PARIS (JONATHAN LUCAS), A TRAVELING SALESMAN. "LAZY AFTERNOON" BECAME A HIT AFTER MARLENE DIETRICH RECORDED IT. MORE RECENTLY, BARBRA STREISAND MADE THE SONG THE TITLE TRACK FOR AN ALBUM. (PHOTOFEST)

HELEN'S HOUSE, A BIT OF RURAL NOSTALGIA—THE HOUSE, PORCH, AND FENCE WERE FLAT CUT-OUT PIECES. THE CHAIR IS DIMENSIONAL. THE BACKGROUND OF MOUNTAINS REMAINED CONSTANT IN EVERY SCENE THAT TOOK PLACE IN ANGEL'S ROOST. (COLLECTION OF THE MCNAY ART MUSEUM, GIFT OF ROBERT L.B. TOBIN)

Lloyd had never directed a musical before, but he was John LaTouche's friend. "He came down to see the models and sketches," Bill said. "We hadn't completely designed the whole show yet, but we had the basic scheme, one which LaTouche and Moross had found 'bold and ingenious for the shifting moods and unbroken pace' of their show. Lloyd looked at it, and he didn't understand it or like its 'preciosity.' Jean and I had no idea what he meant. It was a word unfamiliar to us. In our youth and strong belief in what we were designing, we arrogantly announced to all concerned that this was the way we were going to do the show, and we weren't changing anything. And they (the management) backed us up. We never had much to say to Norman after that. We worked with choreographer Hanya Holm and 'Deli'" (Alfred de Liagre, Jr. co-producer).

As the work on their design concept continued, the Eckarts decided to make the show curtain (a visual presentation of the major themes of the show displayed during the overture) an homage to Mondrian. They kept the convention of inscribing the show's title and complemented it with nineteenth century graphics, but the Eckarts' curtain was dimensional. It was created in two planes: a front section made out of wood and fabric and an upstage section of solid fabric. Actors could enter between the two, a novel idea used at the top of Act II when Helen (Kaye Ballard) pierced the front section of the curtain by popping through her image as if to obliterate the gossipy reports of her fall from virtue.

If Mondrian was the inspiration for the show curtain, the work of American regionalist painter Grant Wood

PAINTER'S ELEVATION OF PARIS' HOT AIR BALLOON—THE ONLY DIMENSIONAL ELEMENT WAS THE BASKET (EC)

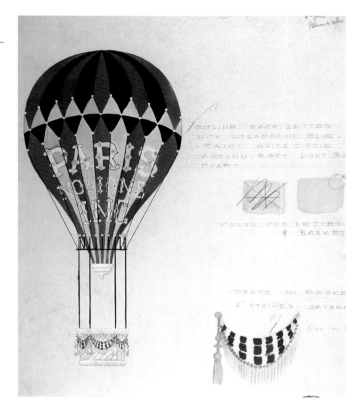

THE OPEN SET CHANGE. HELEN IS PURSUED BY A DOZEN MEN TRANSPORTED IN A SINGLE BOAT-SHAPED COSTUME. (CORNELL CAPA, GETTY IMAGES)

"THE DEPARTURE FOR RHODODENDRON"—PARIS AND HELEN LEAVE IN HIS BALLOON. (PHOTOFEST)

was the inspiration for Helen's house. The Eckarts established consistency of style between Mondrian and Wood by retaining the use of two-dimensional, cut-out panels suspended by visible hemp lines. They embellished the cutout with appliquéd scrim panels. The contoured hills echoed Wood's more representational style as seen in *Stone City, Iowa*. This use of translucent scenery established an airy lightness that complemented the pastel yellows, greens, and whites in the color palate.

The lightness of the scenery made it economical to build and permitted it to be changed easily in full view of the audience throughout the play. At $60,000, it was one-fifth the cost of a conventional Broadway musical of that era. Once the play was in rehearsal, however, problems developed with director Norman Lloyd. "[I] was coming from pictures," Lloyd explained, "where if one scene doesn't work, you substitute another." Lloyd was fired (although his name remained on the program) when he cut a musical bridge without consulting the composer. It was clear that Lloyd didn't understand the unique quality of this show. "The entire fabric was music and lyrics; if any part was disturbed, it all unraveled," Lloyd later commented. Since Bill and Jean had already been working closely with choreographer Hanya Holm, who took over directing duties, they plotted all the set changes and transitions with her so that the musical flowed as the sets seemed to dance on and off. "It was a joy and an invaluable learning experience for us," Bill said, "one which we were to draw upon often during our careers."

Fate of the Show

Opening night was a tremendous success, even though musical director Hugh Ross dropped the score right before Kaye Ballard was set to sing "Lazy Afternoon," leaving Ballard fending for herself while he gathered up the pages. "She improvised brilliantly," Bill said, "pretending her fan was a mirror and preening into it."

As a modern "folk opera," *The Golden Apple* reaped universal praise. Robert Coleman (*Mirror*) was the most enthusiastic while Brooks Atkinson, in *The New York Times*, was more restrained. The sets caught everyone's eye. Atkinson wrote, "*The Golden Apple* is not a heavy production, it has been designed in impeccable taste by people who love form and color . . . This is a light, gay, charming production." Harold Clurman in *The Nation* wrote, "Great credit is due to the airy, delicate, and precise coloration of William and Jean

Eckarts' settings—which employ some of the decorative discoveries of the non-objective painters with handsome theatrical effect." Walter Kerr in the Sunday *Herald Tribune* devoted two paragraphs to what he called "an extraordinarily simple but extraordinarily captivating series of stylized backgrounds." He was bowled over by the Eckarts' careful attention to detail: "At one point a scenic cutout is being lowered to the stage floor, and the designers have had the imaginative insight to attach a few crepe-paper streamers to it. The streamers disappear, of course, the minute the piece hits the floor, but the momentary effect has been out of all proportion to the scanty materials used. Instead of a flat, square line being lowered with a thump, something light and fanciful has floated in from above."

THE BIG SPREE—ULYSSES WINS
HELEN BACK FROM PARIS IN A
PRIZEFIGHT. BUT HE IS WAYLAID
BY A SERIES OF DECEPTIVE CELE-
BRATIONS. HIS TRIP BACK HOME
BECOMES "THE BIG SPREE," A
NIGHT ON THE TOWN, A DRUNK-
EN BENDER. THESE SHORT SCENES
WERE CREATED AS A SERIES OF
VAUDEVILLE TURNS. ULYSSES FALLS
VICTIM TO THE EVILS OF THE CITY.
EACH OF ULYSSES'S ENCOUNTERS
WAS DESIGNED IN ONE VIVID
COLOR WITH BLACK AS THE UNIFY-
ING THEMATIC ELEMENT.

MADAME CALYPSO'S PARLOR—
ULYSSES AND THE BOYS ARE
LIONIZED BY THE BE-FEATH-
ERED, SELF-APPOINTED SOCIAL
ARBITER OF RHODODENDRON
(GERALDINE VITI) AT A VICTORY
BALL. EVERYTHING WAS SHIM-
MERING GOLD, YELLOW, AND
PEARL WITH GLEAMING CHAN-
DELIERS AND SCONCES. (FRED
FEHL, EC)

THE ALL BLACK AND WHITE BROKERAGE OFFICE
OF SCYLLA AND CHARYBDIS—THIS SCENE WAS
PERFORMED AS A GALLAGHER AND SHEEN
VAUDEVILLE NUMBER "IN-ONE." THE CURTAIN
AT THE REAR WAS BLACK VELOUR. BLACK SATIN
STRIPES WERE ADDED TO GIVE IT GREATER
VIBRANCY. AT THE END OF THE NUMBER, AJAX,
HAVING BEEN DUPED INTO BUYING WORTH-
LESS STOCK, JUMPS THROUGH THE PAPER WIN-
DOW IN DESPAIR. (EC)

"GOONA GOONA"

SKETCH OF "GOONA GOONA"—A GARISH, TAWDRY WATERFRONT DIVE INSPIRED BY A CONEY ISLAND SOUVENIR PILLOW BILL HAD WON FOR JEAN ON THE BOARDWALK. IT WAS A NETTED MINI-DROP WITH NO ATTEMPT TO HIDE THE NETTING. THE COLORS WERE HOT PINK, ORANGE, AND MAGENTA. (EC)

ULYSSES (STEPHEN DOUGLASS) IS LURED BY THE HEAD SIREN (BIBI OSTERWALD) SINGING "BY A GOONA GOONA GOONA, BY A GOONA GOONA GOONA LAGOON" WHILE THE SIRENETTES STRUM THEIR LEIS—A PRIME EXAMPLE OF HANYA HOLM'S WITTY CHOREOGRAPHY. (PHOTOFEST)

In their mail the next day was a letter from Jo Mielziner, the dean of American set design, which read, "I tried to locate you after the opening last night, to tell you what a delightful, fresh, and completely right design job you both did."

Since The Phoenix Theatre had one more play left to its season, *The Golden Apple* transferred uptown for a commercial run. The Eckarts' featherweight scenery made the journey with ease. Yet, in spite of the show's critical success downtown, there was nothing certain about Broadway. It was the end of the season when *The Golden Apple* opened just as New York was entering its long summer doldrums. A decade earlier, a run of 173 performances would have been considered profitable, but by the mid-1950s, it was not. In the days and weeks to follow, a series of articles appeared about the Eckarts. They were instant celebrities. The New York Drama Critics named *The Golden Apple* the "Best Musical of the Year" and the industry recognized the Eckarts with a Donaldson Award for the Best Scenic Design for a Musical.

Following the New York run, an outdoor engagement was booked in Washington, D.C. at the Carter Barron Theatre, Rock Creek Park. The Eckarts arranged to have Paris' balloon float to the stage suspended from a crane resting in a nearby gorge. The effect was spectacular. *The Golden Apple* has been revived several times. In 1995, the Light Opera Works in Evanston, Illinois, utilized the Eckarts' designs but mistakenly executed them on opaque muslin rather than on translucent China silk.

"DOOMED, DOOMED, DOOMED," AT THE HALL OF SCIENCE—SCIENTIST (PORTIA NELSON) IS PREPARING TO LAUNCH A JULES VERNE TURQUOISE ROCKET INTO SPACE. ULYSSES (DOUGLASS) WATCHES HER AS SHE INSTRUCTS HER ASSISTANTS. (CORNELL CAPA, GETTY IMAGES)

"CIRCE"—CIRCE (ANN NEEDHAM) IS LURING THE LAST OF ULYSSES' BAND. PARTIALLY FOR ECONOMIC REASONS, THE SAME RHODODENDRON PANELS WERE USED, BUT HERE AGAINST A SOLID BLACK BACKGROUND AND WITHOUT THE "MINI-DROP." WHEN ULYSSES THINKS OF HOME THE LIGHTS COME UP BEHIND RHODODENDRON AND THE STAGE RAPIDLY CHANGES OVER TO REVEAL PENELOPE'S HOUSE IN ACT I. (FRED FEHL, EC)

RENDERING FOR *WEDDING BREAKFAST* (EC)

A Split Screen and a "Style" Show

1954

"Film had changed theater. Playwrights began writing cinematically and that meant in Wedding Breakfast *seeing both sides of the telephone conversation."*

William Eckart

L TO R: LEE GRANT IN HER EASTSIDE APARTMENT AND UPTOWN: HARVEY LEMBECK, VIRGINIA VINCENT, AND TONY FRANCIOSA. THE UNLOCALIZED ACTING AREA WAS LOCATED IN FRONT OF THE APARTMENTS. (FRED FEHL, EC)

*T*he *Golden Apple* garnered the Eckarts tremendous praise. Suddenly, they were the "Lunts of stage design," after the famous acting couple, and in time, a wag rhymed their names with other celebrities in a "Hate Song" at Greenwich Village's The Upstairs at the Downstairs:

I hate Eileen Heckart
Jean and William Eckart
I hate Gregory Peck-art, too.

Hollywood agent Irving "Swifty" Lazar heard that Sam Goldwyn wanted the Eckarts for the Frank Sinatra/Marlon Brando film of *Guys and Dolls* and asked to represent them. "We knew nothing about film," Bill said, "but this was what we were suddenly being thrust into. We were relieved not to get that job."

Much more to their liking was an offer from the set designer of *Oklahoma!* and producer of *Kiss Me Kate,* Lemuel Ayers, who had optioned a new musical entitled *Saturday Night* written by the Epstein twins (Julius J. and Philip G.), Academy Award winners for *Casablanca.* According to Miles White, the costume designer for *Oklahoma!* it was a great tribute that Ayers, a noted designer, had chosen the Eckarts. *Saturday Night* was to be Stephen Sondheim's debut as composer/lyricist. Unfortunately, Ayers took ill while designing George Abbott's *The Pajama Game* and the Sondheim project had to be abandoned. With Ayers no longer available, Abbott, who had seen and admired *The Golden Apple,* sought the Eckarts' services for two of his upcoming projects, the film of *The Pajama Game* and his next Broadway musical, *Damn Yankees.* Bill and Jean would not get a chance to work with Sondheim until nearly a decade later on *Anyone Can Whistle.*

But before the Eckarts could take on Abbott's projects, there were two new Broadway shows and neither of them was a musical. The first, via Herman Shumlin, was *Wedding Breakfast,* a class melodrama by Theodore Reeves, which Shumlin had changed into a contemporary comedy. The central character, played by Lee Grant, was a snobbish Helen Gurley Brown-type who rejects a perfectly likable young man, played by Tony Franciosa, because he hails from Buffalo and sells hardware. The Eckarts strengthened Shumlin's attack by making Grant's upscale eastside apartment tiny and claustrophobic. For all her pretensions, Grant's apartment was so cramped that maneuvering around it induced knowing laughter from audiences familiar with the problems of city living. "It was modeled after our first New York apartment," Bill said, "so we didn't have to really make up anything." By contrast, Franciosa lived in a rather spacious, uptown tenement, with high ceilings and tall double-hung windows. The Eckarts backed the set with a soft focus scrim of the city skyline. But the most striking feature of their design was showing simultaneously the two apartments, one upper-middle-class and the other working class. As in *The Little Screwball*, the Eckarts added to the realistic apartments an unlocalized acting area downstage. This acting area functioned something like the medieval stage's *platea* and was used to present public places, such as the Staten Island Ferry and Central Park. These locales were established minimally with a railing or a bench. *Wedding Breakfast* was a modest success due to outstanding performances from Grant and Franciosa.

The second play was an adaptation by William Archibald of Henry James' novel *Portrait of a Lady*, directed by José Quintero and starring Jennifer Jones, Academy Award winner for *The Song of Bernadette* (1943) and star of *Madame Bovary* (1949) and

Carrie (1952). Backed by her husband, Hollywood producer David O. Selznick (*Gone with the Wind*), *Portrait* would have a sumptuous production budget as evidenced by the presence of the noted English costume designer and fashion photographer Cecil Beaton, best known for his designs for *My Fair Lady* (1956), *Quadrille* (1952), and *Lady Windermere's Fan* (1946). The Eckarts were looking forward to this collaboration, but as it turned out, "We met Beaton exactly once during tryouts at the Colonial Theatre in Boston," Bill said. "Jennifer was a pretty woman, beautiful skin, she lighted very well; but she was not a very good actress for this period piece. A lot of the cast was English, and they were so much better than she was. We knew we were in trouble when out-of-town Selznick began coming to rehearsals with his secretary and writing memos. The next day, everyone would get five or six single-spaced typed pages of notes. It was decided that José's direction was static so he was asked to redirect. What he did was to swap everything; what had been staged on stage right he restaged on stage left, etc. He spent weeks doing that." In Washington, Jay Carmody (*Evening Star*) opined that the Eckart and Beaton physical production was so magnificent that it might be sufficient to keep *Portrait* running as a "style" show. But a week after opening on Broadway, the show closed.

PHOTOGRAPH OF THE MODEL FOR *PORTRAIT OF A LADY*—BILL AND JEAN CONSTRUCTED A MODEL FOR THIS PSYCHOLOGICAL STUDY SO THEY COULD CONCENTRATE ON MOOD LIGHTING. (EC)

RENDERING FOR *PORTRAIT OF A LADY*, ACT I, AN ENGLISH MANOR HOUSE (EC)

ARGUABLY, THE MOST FAMOUS COSTUME OF ANY 1950s MUSICAL

LOLA'S COSTUME WAS BUILT TO SHOW OFF DANCER GWEN VERDON'S LEGS. JEAN ECKART CUT THE TOP OF THE LEGS UP TO THE HIP. THE NEW FAUX BIKINI CUT CREATED AN ORIGINAL FASHION. SOON AFTER THE SHOW OPENED IN NEW YORK, WOMEN'S MAGAZINES BEGAN SHOWING UNDER-GARMENTS WITH JEAN'S BIKINI CUT. THE LOOK IS STILL WITH US TODAY. VERDON LATER SAID, "WHEN WE DID THE MOVIE, THE STUDIO WOULD NOT ALLOW ME TO WEAR A CUT LIKE THAT. BILL AND JEAN HAD TO ADD A PIECE OF FLESH COLORED FABRIC. THEN THEY MADE A SORT OF A LACE THING AROUND THE TOP OF THE LEG." (PHOTO: FRED FEHL, EC)

DAMN YANKEES WASN'T A GREAT BOX OFFICE HIT WHEN IT OPENED IN NEW YORK. INITIALLY CONCEIVED AS A BASEBALL SHOW, THE FIRST DISPLAY ADVERTISING FEATURED STAR GWEN VERDON DRESSED IN A BASEBALL JERSEY. THE QUALITY OF SEDUCTION WAS ADOLESCENT, AND THE POWER OF EVIL WAS ABSENT. TO BOOST SALES, THE PRODUCERS DECIDED TO USE A CANDID SHOT (LEFT) OF VERDON TAKEN IN NEW HAVEN. TICKET SALES ROSE IMMEDIATELY. (FACING PAGE: ORIGINAL BASEBALL JERSEY ADVERTISEMENT) (EC)

Damn Yankees

1955 Collaborating with Mister Broadway

IN A REWORKING OF THE FAUST LEGEND, A MIDDLE-AGED MAN, JOE, SELLS HIS SOUL TO THE DEVIL SO HE CAN HELP HIS FAVORITE BASEBALL TEAM, THE WASHINGTON SENATORS, BEAT THE YANKEES. THE DEVIL TURNS JOE INTO A YOUNG INVINCIBLE BALLPLAYER, BUT THEN SENDS HIS CHIEF SEDUCTRESS, LOLA, TO ENSNARE HIM. LOLA'S LOVE HELPS YOUNG JOE WIN THE PENNANT. SHE OUTWITS THE DEVIL SO JOE CAN RETURN TO HIS FORMER SELF AND BELOVED WIFE.

"In solving any problem for any show the solutions are step by step. You start somewhere and then you keep going. Sometimes the result bears little relation to the starting point."

William Eckart

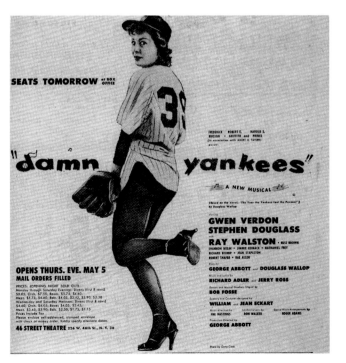

Months before *Damn Yankees* opened, Gwen Verdon met with Bill and Jean Eckart at their Mews House for an important costume meeting. "Jean's idea was to start my first number 'Whatever Lola Wants' in a rumba skirt which zipped down the back. It was a striptease," Gwen Verdon said. "I'd just come off coaching Marilyn Monroe on *Gentlemen Prefer Blondes*. She'd worn these terrific Capri pants and I wanted Jean to make them part of my costume. She was willing to work with me. In the number I had to sit on the floor and wriggle backwards while stripping off the Capris over high heels. It was very difficult. I kept practicing on their floor trying to take off the toreador pants while Jean kept making the slits up the sides higher and higher."

It was a three-part continuously revealing costume with the undergarment delivering the final blow to the young Joe Hardy when Lola vamps him in the locker room. The Eckarts' sexy first act costume would bring out one of the defining themes of the show—and the image of Gwen Verdon at the end of the dance eventually became the show's selling point.

George Abbott wanted whomever he brought on board to be his collaborators. Gwen Verdon's story points out how open that collaboration process was on an Abbott production, for the amazing aspect of Verdon's costume meeting at the Eckarts' is that George Abbott was not present. Why wasn't the director known as Mister Broadway there? The answer is trust. Although ultimately Abbott would take responsibility for all creative decisions on a show, he was so confident in his own judgments that he let the show evolve through the creative people he hired. "I know from my own experience that it is no fun to have someone peering over your shoulder critically when you are in the formative stages of your work," Abbott said in his autobiography, *Mister Abbott* (1963). His team was free to develop their ideas on their own because

"WHATEVER LOLA WANTS" WAS INTENDED AS A STRIP TEASE. GWEN VERDON HAD TO BE ABLE TO GET OUT OF THE THREE PART COSTUME SMOOTHLY WHILE DANCING. BY THE TIME THE COSTUME WAS FINISHED, BOB FOSSE HAD ALL THE TOOLS HE NEEDED TO DESIGN A SHOW-STOPPING NUMBER. HE AND GWEN VERDON MADE THE MOST OF IT. (EC)

(TALBOT, EC)   (FRED FEHL, EC)   (FRED FEHL, EC)

as far as Abbott was concerned, there wasn't anything his collaborators could do that he couldn't rework. The safety net lay in Abbott's ability to read an audience and to reshape a show on the road. In the 1950s, that's what the out-of-town try-outs were all about. For Abbott no show was complete until it played in front of an audience. In the days and weeks that followed during the try-outs, the show received "the Abbott touch." Sometimes, as in the case of *Damn Yankees*, it continued to evolve and be revised even after the last New York reviews were written.

The Eckarts admired Abbott tremendously and were thrilled for the opportunity to work with him. They knew changes were the order of the day on an Abbott production but changes were also what created the excitement of working with him.

Abbott liked to develop a show by having several of the numbers and book scenes written but the balance of the material in various stages of development. The bestselling novel by Douglass Wallop, *The Year the Yankees Lost the Pennant*, would be simply a road map for Abbott and his team of collaborators. *Damn Yankees* actually encompassed three stories: Joe Hardy selling his soul to the Devil to help his favorite team, the story of Joe's love for his wife whom he must leave behind in his deal with the Devil, and buried in the soup was the third story, that of Lola, the Devil's procuress, who attempts to seduce Joe but instead falls in love with him.

Three stories in one play are a theatrical liability. They tend to cancel each other out. What an audience looks for at the top of a show is a "grabber." With three choices to make, Abbott and his team initially picked the wrong one. Their original misread of what the show was about is reflected in the newspaper advertising that ran weeks before it was scheduled to open in New York. The creative team thought they were developing a musical about baseball, even though baseball was considered to be a jinxed subject in the theatre. There hadn't been a show about the sport in more than fifty-one years. The curse was just another challenge for George Abbott. He thought of it

TWENTY CENTS   JUNE 13, 1955

TIME
THE WEEKLY NEWSMAGAZINE

GWEN VERDON
of
"DAMN YANKEES"

$6.00 A YEAR   VOL. LXV NO. 24

GWEN VERDON AND THE ECKARTS' COSTUME MADE THE COVER OF *TIME* MAGAZINE. A LARGE SPREAD ON THE SHOW APPEARED IN *LIFE* AS WELL. (GENE COOK, GETTY IMAGES)

in much the same way he thought of the unexpected success the year before. Then, he'd taken a book about labor unrest and turned it into the hit musical *The Pajama Game*. With *Damn Yankees*, even with the same composer and lyricist, Ross and Adler, the task wasn't going to be as easy. What they all discovered on opening night in New Haven was that *Damn Yankees* was not a show about baseball, and it was partially the Eckarts' input that would reveal the show's true appeal.

The designer's role is different from those of the rest of the creative team. Major scenic elements and costumes have to be built and in place before the out-of-town tryouts. This means the designer has to cast a wide net when trying to conceptualize a show. The elements must be able to change and move if needed. Abbott realized several things on opening night in New Haven. At the top of the play, the mechanics of how old Joe was transformed into a young ballplayer, something Abbott had insisted Bill Eckart spend weeks trying to figure out, was something the audience simply wasn't interested in. They also weren't interested in whether Joe got his wife back or not. What they wanted to see was more of the Devil, Applegate (played by Ray Walston), and Lola, the temptress (Gwen Verdon).

The Eckarts struggled with the show curtain that would appear during the overture and would set up the major themes of the play. They experimented with many approaches trying to discover the essence of the show. They started with ballparks, then went to fences, then scoreboards, and eventually baseballs. Designers are not conventionally logical in how they arrive at a concept. As Bill would often say, "You don't necessarily know where you are going when you start."

This seems the case with not only the show curtain, but the whole way in which *Damn Yankees* evolved. By the time Bill and Jean arrived at the show curtain made of strings of multicolored baseballs, they had been through two dozen other schemes. Ironically, they were now satisfied with a design in which baseballs had nothing to do with the sport, but instead were used as large beads in a curtain which was eye-catching, clever, and above all sexy. What they didn't realize was that they had accidentally stumbled onto the core idea of the play: seduction. Though it seemed obvious to this author that a swaying, hot, beaded curtain was a sign for a bordello or a siren's bedroom, no one in the company at the time was aware of the connection between the curtain and Lola. Fifty years later, when I pointed the connection out

SEX AND BASEBALL—HOW THE CURTAIN DEFINED THE SHOW

PRELIMINARY #1—BILL AND JEAN WERE SEARCHING FOR THE SHOW'S ESSENCE WHEN THEY MADE THEIR EARLIEST DRAWINGS OF A WHITE PLANK CHAIN-LINK FENCE WITH A BALLFIELD BEHIND IT, *DAMN YANKEES* SCRAWLED IN GRAFFITI ACROSS IT, BATTING WIRE, AND TECHNI-COLOR PIGEONS. "WE KNEW IT WASN'T RIGHT. IT WAS TOO PRETTY AND TOO WHIMSICAL," SAID BILL ECKART. (EC)

PRELIMINARY #2—THEIR SECOND SKETCH SUPERIMPOSED A SCOREBOARD WITH ADDED PANELS OF CHAIN-LINK FENCE, HYDRANTS, HANGING VINES, AND ONLY ONE PIGEON. "IT WASN'T AS PRETTY BUT IT WAS STILL TOO WHIM-SICAL," SAID BILL ECKART. ONE MAJOR CURTAIN CONCEPT (NOT SHOWN) WAS TO SUSPEND A GIANT BASEBALL CENTER STAGE FLANKED BY THE CAPITOL DOME ON ONE SIDE AND THE NEW YORK SKYLINE ON THE OTHER. IT WAS AN IMPORTANT TRANSITION BECAUSE IT MADE THE ECKARTS THINK ABOUT USING BASEBALLS IN THE CURTAIN. (EC)

PRELIMINARY #3—THEIR NEXT ATTEMPT WAS THE BREAK-THROUGH. BASEBALLS MAKE THEIR FIRST APPEARANCE AS POR-TAL DECORATIONS. "WE WERE GETTING CLOSER, BUT IT WAS STILL TOO REMI-NISCENT OF AN EARLIER PERIOD—THAT OF 'TAKE ME OUT TO THE BALLGAME,'" SAID BILL ECKART. (EC)

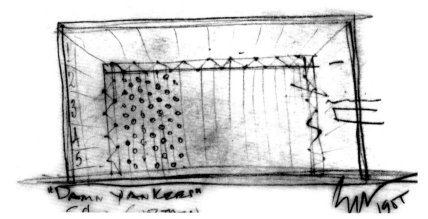

PRELIMINARY #4—BASEBALLS IN THIS VERSION APPEAR TO BE EMBEDDED IN THE CHAIN-LINK FENCE AS IF SLAMMED INTO IT BY A GORILLA-LIKE YANKEE SLUGGER. THE NOTION OF THE BEADED BASEBALL CURTAIN BEGINS TO EMERGE. (EC)

STRINGING BASEBALLS FOR THE FINAL VERSION OF THE SHOW CURTAIN—JEAN TOOK THE MOCK UP OF THE BASEBALL CURTAIN TO SPALDING, THE SPORTING GOODS MANUFACTURER. THE COMPANY LIKED THE IDEA SO MUCH THEY NOT ONLY DONATED THE BASEBALLS BUT ALL THE BATS, GLOVES, AND OTHER SPORTS EQUIPMENT USED IN THE SHOW. (PETER STACKPOLE, GETTY IMAGES)

first to Bill Eckart and later to Gwen Verdon, both admitted they'd never thought of it that way. Yet when the show opened in New Haven and Gwen Verdon, entering late in Act I, came on stage with her glowing white skin, black outfit, and bright orange hair, mirroring the look and feel of the show curtain, the audience made the connection immediately.

Another instinct Bill and Jean had concerned Ray Walston. The Eckarts gave Walston, who was playing the Devil, a pair of red socks to wear on his first entrance. They thought it would be fun if at some point during the first scene, he hitched his trousers just long enough to reveal the socks and to let the audience make the association. At the dress rehearsal in New Haven, Abbott objected. He disliked sight gags and business. It was just "too much," and he instructed Bill and Jean to "cut the socks." It was one of several notes the Eckarts received requiring costume changes in the first act, and it got lost. The next performance was the New Haven opening, and Walston appeared wearing the "cut" socks. When he hitched up his trousers and the first night audience in New Haven saw the red socks, they howled. It was the first big laugh of the evening. Abbott, who was sitting in the eighth row center orchestra taking notes, was extremely thankful. "Everyone," Abbott wrote in his autobiography, "is there for the same reason: to try to get the show in as perfect condition as possible. And the endeavor

LOOKING THROUGH THE SHOW CURTAIN ON STAGE—AT THE BOTTOM OF EACH STRAND OF BALLS HUNG A HUGE TASSEL SO EACH STRAND HAD MOVEMENT. "LESS IS MORE," BILL SAID. "BASEBALLS, BEADS, AND TASSELS, A COMBINATION OF THE TWO GREAT AMERICAN PASTIMES—SPORTS AND SEX." (PETER STACKPOLE, GETTY IMAGES)

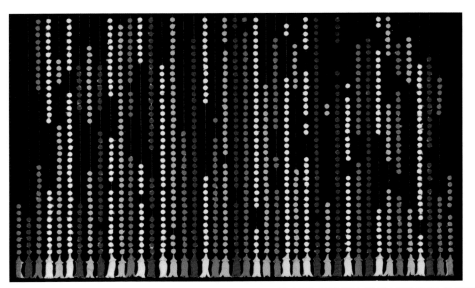

THE ECKARTS DECIDED: WHY NOT REMOVE THE FENCE ALTOGETHER? THEY STOPPED SKETCHING AND BEGAN PUNCHING OUT TINY HOLES OF COLORED PAPER. EACH HOLE BECAME A MINIATURE BASEBALL IN WHITE, ORANGE, AND RED AGAINST A JET BLACK BACKGROUND. EVERYONE LOVED IT. (COLLECTION OF THE MCNAY ART MUSEUM, GIFT OF ROBERT L. B. TOBIN COLLECTION)

UPSCALING THE DEVIL: A SPOOF OF ELEGANCE

A SKETCH OF APPLEGATE'S LAVISH HOTEL ROOM—BILL AND JEAN PLAYED WITH WHAT OTHER KIND OF ACCOMMODATIONS THE DEVIL MIGHT HAVE. THEY PROGRESSED BY STAGES TO SWAGS OF LAVENDER AND TURQUOISE CURTAINS HUNG IN BAROQUE GRANDEUR. (EC)

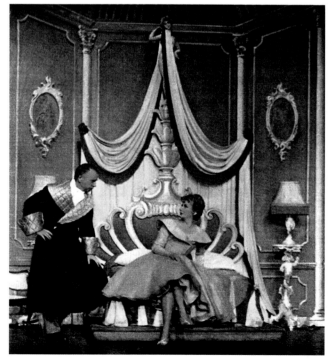

RAY WALSTON (APPLEGATE) AND GWEN VERDON (LOLA)—APPLEGATE HAD RISEN FROM CHEAP CROOK TO A POSITION AKIN TO A POWERFUL WASHINGTON LOBBYIST, ALBEIT ONE WITH QUESTIONABLE TASTE. "WE WANTED AN ORNATE, ARTIFICIAL LOOK," BILL SAID. (EC)

shouldn't involve emotions or personalities or pettiness." True to his philosophy, Abbott's first words after the New Haven opening to Bill and Jean were: "The socks stay!" They have remained part of the show ever since.

Some of the other ideas the Eckarts developed about the Devil helped push his character forward. They created a plush purple satin dressing gown and placed him in a gaudy hotel suite. Much of their work came in great measure out of the prissy way Walston was portraying the Devil. (Later, Marc Blitzstein and others would chide *Damn Yankees* for making the Devil appear to be a homosexual, something neither Bill, Jean, or Abbott had ever intended.) But the lavishly dressed Devil in his baroque apartments was not where the Eckarts had started. The notion they had of the Devil from Wallop's book was totally different.

Initially, they saw Applegate as a penny-pinching tightwad living in a fleabag hotel. But after working and collaborating with Walston, this did not hold up. Could the Devil be marginalized and still be a force to be reckoned with in the story? The Eckarts took Walston out of the residence they'd originally designed for him and punched up his costumes. At the time, Dorothy Draper, a well-known interior decorator in Washington, D.C., had received a great deal of publicity for her redo of the Mayflower Hotel. Bill said, "She was using a white plaster baroque, full of curlicues and moldings. Very ostentatious. Jean and I found the style amusing." With this new point of view, Applegate went from being a Devil who lived in a dive to one who moved in the powerful world of Washington politics. Perhaps he was a highly paid lobbyist, a suggestion that was taken up in one of the show's more recent revivals. In any event, the changes that came about in rehearsal became an essential part of the show's Broadway production.

As a result of the audiences' reactions in New Haven to both Gwen Verdon's first number, "Whatever Lola Wants," and Applegate's presence as the "heavy," Abbott told

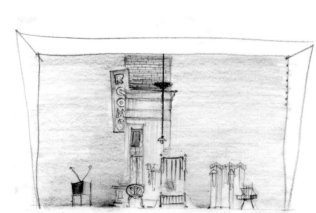

AN EARLY SKETCH OF APPLEGATE'S QUARTERS— BILL AND JEAN BEGAN TO CONSIDER WHETHER THE SEEDY HOTEL ROOM THEY HAD ENVISIONED WITH THE BLINKING LIGHT OUTSIDE THE WINDOW MADE SENSE. THEY KNEW A SET CHANGE WOULD RADICALLY ALTER THE WAY THE AUDIENCE WOULD PERCEIVE THE APPLEGATE CHARACTER.(EC)

ODE TO THE FIFTIES

A SKETCH OF JOE HARDY'S "COLONIAL" TRACT HOUSE IN SUBURBIA, JUST LIKE THE HOUSE NEXT DOOR. THE ECKARTS CHOSE A TRIBUTE TO NORMAN ROCKWELL—RUFFLED CURTAINS, WICKER CHAIRS, VINE COVERED LATTICE, AND POTTED GERANIUMS ON THE FRONT PORCH. IN THE LIVING ROOM—FLORAL WALLPAPER, CHINTZ SLIPCOVERS, AND HIS AND HERS CHAIRS, HIS FACING THE TV SET. THE PORCH AND LIVING ROOM WERE BUILT ON A WAGON WHEELED ON BY STAGEHANDS; THE ROOFTOPS WERE APPLIQUÉD SHARK TOOTH SCRIM. (EC)

"SIX MONTHS OUT OF EVERY YEAR" THE OPENING CHORUS, SHOWING THE ECKART COSTUMES PURCHASED AND PREPARED IN ONE DAY. THE ECKARTS MADE AN UNINTENTIONAL STATEMENT ABOUT CONFORMITY IN THE 1950s. (FRIEDMAN-ABELES, EC)

his collaborators he wanted major rewrites. He wanted additional numbers for Gwen Verdon and Ray Walston throughout the show and he wanted their first appearance to come closer to the beginning of Act I. Richard Adler and Jerry Ross responded with a new song for Verdon before the Lola number called, "A Little Brains, a Little Talent."

To make room for the new numbers, others had to go. A huge fan club ballet, on which choreographer Bob Fosse and the Eckarts had lavished much attention, was one of the most spectacular casualties. Abbott sensed that a big chorus number just before the end of Act I slowed down the pace of the show. Although Abbott wasn't certain what was needed to replace the big number, he knew it had to be small. He suggested giving Verdon another Latin dance to end the first act. Adler and Ross loved the idea of a mambo, back then the current dance craze. As songwriters, they knew that if they could get a popular singer to record a single, the additional work on the road would be more than worth it.

Bill and Jean Eckart, having used up their costume budget on the baseball team mascot costumes, which were clever and expensive, had less to gain and nothing left to spend on new costumes. They had to come up with something fast. They designed a costume to look homemade for the new number, "Who's Got The Pain?" Fosse and Verdon, who were working closely together, went out into the alley behind the theater and retrieved two battered hats from the trash to finish off the costumes. "It might have been then that they decided to get married," Adler said. "There's nothing like a little panic collaboration to get people together." The tightly focused mambo changed the balance of the first act. By the time *Damn Yankees* reached Boston, the entire structure of the musical had changed. Abbott had given Ray Walston and Gwen Verdon almost half of the numbers at the top of the show.

Inadvertently, the Eckarts made another major contribution to the show in New Haven without realizing it. Abbott felt they needed a big sound to open the play and that meant a chorus. The chorus was so important to the look and feel of a fifties musical that no one ever questioned why they were there, or in this instance, who they were. The Eckarts, being new to Broadway, weren't content to leave it that way. They felt that since the first big chorus number, "Six Months Out of Every Year," opened the show that it was crucial to establish that the chorus was made up of individuals. Bill and Jean had seen a photography series by Irving Penn about working people in America, and they decided to individualize the chorus along those lines.

SPECTACULAR CASUALTY TO LATIN DUET

THE ELABORATE MASCOT-GORILLA DANCE NUMBER CHOREO-GRAPHED BY BOB FOSSE COST $5000 IN COSTUMES, REHEARSED FOR FIVE WEEKS, AND WAS CUT AFTER NEW HAVEN. THE COS-TUMES WERE KEPT IN THE SHOW EVEN THOUGH THE NUMBER WAS DROPPED SO THE INVESTORS COULD SEE HOW THEIR MONEY WAS SPENT. SEVERAL OF THE GIRLS' COSTUMES WERE RECY-CLED INTO THE NEXT ECKART SHOW, *REUBEN REUBEN*.

YANKEE SLUGGER AS A GORILLA (EC)

CLEVELAND INDIAN (EC)

DETROIT TIGER LADY (EC)

THE GORILLA NUMBER—FOSSE BASED THE GORILLA NUMBER ON MUSICAL CHAIRS. HE NEVER FORGAVE HAL PRINCE FOR RIDICULING HIS BALLET. IRONICALLY, PRINCE USED THE SAME MUSICAL CHAIRS IDEA IN HIS STAGING OF *EVITA*. (PHOTO: GETTY IMAGES)

"WHO'S GOT THE PAIN?" THE FIRST ACT FINALE, ADDED IN BOSTON WHEN THE GORILLA DANCE WAS DISCARDED. THE ECKARTS IMPROVISED TWO SIMPLE COSTUMES MADE UP OF TOREADOR PANTS AND YELLOW BOLEROS WITH BALL FRINGES. THE COSTUMES WERE DESIGNED TO LOOK HOMEMADE. (EC)

Abbott, according to Gwen Verdon, had already said he wanted "the women to look like housewives who had gotten away from the stove just long enough to sing the song, which is why they were all in 1940s housedresses." After World War II, few women were encouraged or represented on stage as working outside of the home. The distinguishing costumes would be for the men. "Bill and I thought," Jean said, "that we'd show all the people who might legitimately be in the neighborhood: the milkman, the telephone lineman, the delivery boy." The idea seemed logical. At the same time they began focusing in on the middle class Washington suburb where the action took place. Focusing on the physical surrounding they thought would help them further define the characters in the chorus. However, they soon found themselves thinking about New York's sprawling suburb Levittown and its tract homes. Levittown, because of its success, was very much in the news by the mid-1950s. The idea of mass producing housing sprung

from the mind of wartime veteran William Levitt. He used the experience he had in the Navy to build an incredible thirty-six houses a day, turning a potato farm in Hempstead into a village inhabited by 82,000 people. These mass-produced houses were all similar Cape Cod boxes, which critic Lewis Mumford felt created homogenized suburbs inhabited by homogenized people. Levitt, sensitive to Mumford's criticism, tried to address the problem by making a greater variety of houses available the year following the opening of *Damn Yankees*. However, to city dwellers like the Eckarts, the typical suburban house was an anathema. They weren't necessarily looking down their noses at hero and heroine Joe and Meg when they set them in a homey little box as much as trying to fulfill one of the demands of the script by making them typical. But the decision to add an identical gable, representing an identical neighbor's roof next door with an identical television antenna was truly inspired. There was nothing in the script to justify this decision. It was quite simply their choice, but it was one that had vast implications.

When Abbott saw the individualized male chorus number unfold during the New Haven dress, he remarked: "They look like a bunch of bums." Then, knowing the Eckarts would come up with something else and trusting their skills, he added kindly, "But you'll fix it." As Jean remembered the incident, she turned to Bill and said: "How are we going to get sixteen costumes together by tomorrow's performance? Then like a bolt out of the blue we thought, these people are all echoes of Meg and Joe. So, we went to Mallack's (a department store in New Haven) and we bought sixteen loud noisy neckties, all the same, and sixteen red-checked rayon aprons with rhinestones on them."

Without stopping to think about what they were doing, Bill and Jean embarked on a path that would not only give visual continuity to the stage picture but would radically shift the perspective of the play. By pushing Meg and Joe back into the chorus, they heightened the audience's awareness of the play's two truly eccentric characters, Lola and Applegate. (In the film version of *Damn Yankees*, Stanley Donen conveyed the idea that everyone was a reflection of Meg and Joe by having couples appear on a multiple split screen).

LOCKER ROOMS, CORRIDORS, AND BALLFIELDS

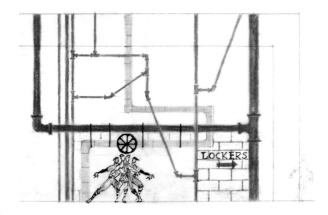

PRELIMINARY SKETCH OF THE IN-ONE LOCKER ROOM CORRIDOR SHOWING ITS "CARTOON" STYLE (EC)

THE FINAL SKETCH OF THE LOCKER ROOM CORRIDOR WAS A CLEANER, SIMPLER STATEMENT. USING "I" BEAMS, PIPES, AND CINDER BLOCKS CREATED A HARD EDGED, INDUSTRIAL TEXTURE. THE DROP WAS CUT TO AVOID COMPLETE FLATNESS. (EC)

THE PLAYERS SINGING "HEART," FROM THE BROADWAY PRODUCTION. THE UNIFORMS WERE REAL, OBTAINED FROM AN OFFICIAL SUPPLIER. LEFT TO RIGHT: RUSS BROWN, JIMMY KOMACK, NATHANIEL FREY, AL LINVILLE (EC)

As a result of the chorus costumes, the number became a tongue-in-cheek social comment. Critics would later say *Damn Yankees* was the first musical to dramatize the conformist nature of 1950s suburbia. But Bill and Jean had come to the idea incrementally: first by doubling the gable, then by multiplying the TV antenna, and then—in a last minute panic—by duplicating all of the costumes. By the mid-nineties, when the show was revived on Broadway, the Eckarts' tract homes and identical costumes had expanded to become a theme and the central joke of the production.

The idea of supplying an ironic commentary on hallowed institutions was inimical to the Eckarts' vision of *Damn Yankees*. Early on in their work on this show, they had looked for a unifying element that would give the entire musical visual continuity. For them, *Damn Yankees* was a slightly off-color comment on baseball. "We decided," Bill

SO THAT GWEN VERDON COULD STRUT HER STUFF IN THE LOCKER ROOM, THE ECKARTS DESIGNED A FULL DEEP STAGE SET. "WE WERE STUMPED ABOUT TRYING TO DO THE LOCKER ROOM," JEAN SAID. "SO WE JUST KEPT TALKING TO EACH OTHER AND FINALLY IT BOILED DOWN TO 'WELL, WHAT IS A LOCKER ROOM ANYWAY?' 'WELL, IT'S LOCKERS.' 'OKAY. SO WHY DON'T WE JUST DO LOCKERS?' WE DID A KIND OF MONDRIAN ARRANGEMENT OF LOCKERS AND BENCHES. WE USED DROP LIGHTS TO COMPLETE THE COMPOSITION. BY USING DIFFERENT SHADES OF RED AND BLUE WE MADE IT FRESH." (EC)

BILLBOARDS ADVANCED THE STORY OF HARDY'S RISE TO SPORTS FAME BY SHOWING HIM ENDORSING A NATIONAL PRODUCT. PEPSODENT REPLACED "WHIFFLE" WHEN THE TOOTHPASTE COMPANY AGREED TO PAY FOR THE DROP. (IN THE FILM MADE OF *DAMN YANKEES* [WARNER, 1958] ON WHICH THE ECKARTS SERVED AS DESIGNERS, A MONTAGE OF GAMES, SUPERIMPOSED OVER NEWSPAPERS TELLING OF JOE'S TRIUMPHS SHOWED THE PASSAGE OF TIME.) (EC)

said, "to go off into variations of red, white, and blue since baseball was the national pastime. We used pinks and oranges instead of red; purples and turquoise instead of blue." The slightly "off" colors Bill and Jean applied to the production were consistent with the musical's irreverent treatment of professional baseball. Producer Hal Prince felt, "[With] their choice of colors the Eckarts made *Damn Yankees* chic and a little cynical. By altering their palette, Bill and Jean created a sense of distance between what the audience expected to see and what was actually presented."

The use of posters and poster art also helped the Eckarts add a missing story element to the show. In the first act, an important transitional scene dramatizing Joe Hardy's miraculous rise to fame was never written. Taking on the role of dramatic collaborators, the Eckarts came up with a large endorsement advertisement on a billboard, the purpose of which was to inform the audience of the change in Joe's status. The billboard also fit in with the show's satirical attack on pop culture.

Working with George Abbott made the Eckarts step away from the kind of innovative scene changing they had introduced in *The Golden Apple*. Instead,

SKETCH OF THE STADIUM AND DUGOUT OF THE WASHINGTON SENATORS. ALL OF THE BASEBALL SETS WERE DESIGNED WITH A GEOMETRIC, POSTER-LIKE QUALITY WITH BROAD AREAS OF RELATIVELY FLAT COLOR—IN THIS SET, RED, WHITE, AND BLUE—IN OTHERS, A VARIATION OF THE SAME SCHEME. AT LEFT IS THE DUGOUT AND THE FIRST SECTION BEHIND THE WALL AND VERTICAL BEAM WITH APPLIQUED SHARK TOOTH SCRIM AND LIT FROM THE REAR TO GIVE THE ILLUSION OF GREATER DEPTH. (EC)

BOB FOSSE'S BASEBALL BALLET SET IN FRONT OF THE DUGOUT (PETER STACKPOLE, GETTY IMAGES)

NO ROCK AND ROLL!

"TWO LOST SOULS"—"WE WANTED THE FEEL OF A BASEMENT," BILL SAID. "THE CANOPY WAS MEANT TO SUGGEST A CAVE." THIS WAS ONE OF MANY ECKART DESIGNS USING SWAGS AND TASSELS, AN ELEGANTLY SIMPLE WAY TO SET THE STAGE. (EC)

they kept the form of the 1950s musical which Abbott had adapted from the nineteenth-century melodrama. What Abbott had wanted was to alternate scenes according to stage depth, the conventional way of permitting large set changeovers. The Eckarts had no recourse but to go along with his dramaturgy. Since Abbott's adaptation indicated that it was not necessary to have full sets for each scene, the show unfolded along more traditional lines. The bigger and more detailed sets were changed behind traveler curtains while briefer scenes were staged "in-one," that is in front of a stylized backdrop. "You Gotta Have Heart," one of the evening's show-stoppers, took place in a stadium corridor between the locker room and the dugout. The Eckarts depicted the wall using a half-drop instead of the more conventional full traveler curtain. The half-drop was unapologetically flown in, and the ballplayers sang in front of it.

The strong basic elements in their design replaced their fanciful earlier conceptions. The progression of sketches records the way in which Bill and Jean were becoming masters at simplification, arriving in time at a geometric minimalism.

When it came to showing the all-important game, Bill and Jean's innovative tendencies found expression in their decision to use the audience itself to complete the staging. The Eckarts knew the game itself couldn't be convincingly shown on stage so they decided to make the dugout and a section of the grandstands face the audience. Choosing this orientation meant the game would be taking place in an imaginary space located somewhere between the audience, the orchestra, and the stage. "On stage we just had the bleachers behind us," Gwen Verdon said. "All the flood lights shone out at the audience. For the first time, we could see them and they (the audience) looked like they were actually attending the game." In a sense, the Eckarts were "breaking the fourth wall" convention of stage realism and forcing the audience into a collaborative role to create the illusion of the ballpark.

But innovation didn't always appeal to George Abbott. When Ross and Adler attempted to introduce "Two Lost Souls" as the first Rock and Roll song to reach Broadway, Abbott wouldn't hear of it. Rock and Roll at the time was being banned by many of the older generation.

Traditional radio stations made much of refusing to play the new music, and church groups, civic leaders, and educators were attempting to suppress recordings because they considered Rock and Roll tasteless, lewd, and corrupting to white American youth. Bob Fosse and Gwen Verdon loved the number and loved the idea of breaking new ground with it on Broadway. Abbott, though, was a staunch advocate of family entertainment. Ross and Adler were forced to change the number. They took the hard edge off the music and retorqued it to resemble a bluesy swing. The Eckarts carried out Ross and Adler's original idea of rebellion by locating the set in an underground dive instead of in an uptown club.

Verdon's tomboy sexiness in just a baseball jersey was the kind of tweaking of the Puritan tradition Abbott felt comfortable with but in retrospect, it seems curious that as a champion of family values, he allowed *Damn Yankees* to be advertised as a girly show. Perhaps raising a few eyebrows was enough. He didn't want to scare away the customers. Yet it speaks volumes about the man that he let the show be represented by the now well-known image of Gwen Verdon in her bikini cut costume. Abbott listened to his audience, and when he found them wanting him to go further than he imagined he could, he took the big plunge. Yes, Abbott was authoritarian, but it was said of him that he'd listen to anybody. He knew how to take ideas from an elderly matron overheard in the lobby or a chorus boy backstage, cull them, find their true worth, and use them to improve his shows. What made him Mister Broadway was his instinct about what to keep and what to discard.

Unquestionably, he also knew how to get the best out of the people around him. With Bill and Jean Eckart, he also knew he'd hired a team who worked well together. By delegating to them the visual elements of the show and allowing them to develop these elements for him, Abbott was able to focus on the big picture. For the Eckarts, *Damn Yankees* was a career high point. This was true in spite of the loss of an elaborate production number, numerous sleepless nights on the road and last-minute costume changes. George Abbott defined for them what creating a musical was all about. During the creation of *Damn Yankees*, he became for them the ultimate collaborator.

The Eckarts would go on to do another eight shows with Abbott.

Fate of the Show

Damn Yankees might have been a play with baseballs in it, but it was clear by the time it had opened that it was not a play about baseball. Gwen Verdon and the Devil had taken over. As opening night critic Walter Kerr (*Herald Tribune*) wrote, "Miss Verdon is, I believe, some sort of a mobile designed by a man without a conscience. As she prances mockingly through a seductive scene, flipping a black glove over her shoulder, as her hips go into mysterious but extremely interesting action, beating the floor idiotically with whatever clothing she has removed, coiling all over a locker room bench while batting absurd eye lashes at her terrified victim, she is simply and insanely inspired." John McClain (*Journal American*) wrote, "Gwen Verdon has never

been given more magnificent material or complimentary costumes and she takes full advantage of both . . . the scenery and costumes are exceptional and original." The play and later the film of *Damn Yankees* had a strong impact on Frank Rich, future drama critic and OpEd Page writer of *The New York Times*. As he recounted in his best-selling memoir *Ghost Light*, "I couldn't take my eyes off Lola herself. She kept taking off her clothing … As the song ended ("Whatever Lola Wants"), Lola was lying arched on her back across Joe's lap, her arms extended as far as they could reach, her breasts practically poking into the ballplayer's face, her nipples almost visible through the black lace. If he reached down and touched her—which he did not—what would happen then?" The question was on everyone's mind. And although the moment occurred only midway through the first act, it was the most dramatic encounter in the show. Such open sexuality was virtually unknown at the time. The quality of danger was palpable. Fosse's choreography and the Eckarts' costume helped to generate Verdon's explosive performance. The groundwork was laid in *Damn Yankees* for a new kind of sexuality on Broadway. Together Fosse and Verdon would push the envelope even further in shows such as *New Girl in Town* (1957) (the "sordid dream" sequence in that show caused a permanent split between Fosse/Verdon and Abbott/Prince), *Sweet Charity* (1966), and *Chicago* (1975).

After *Damn Yankees* opened on Broadway, the marketing department sought to capitalize on Verdon's sexuality and changed the logo, having received the message the Eckarts had telegraphed with their beaded baseball curtain; the kittenish tomboy in the baseball shirt was out. Gwen Verdon as the steamy seductress in the French-cut one-piece bikini was in. From a show that was struggling to survive in New Haven, *Damn Yankees* went on to become one of Broadway's most robust and enduring hits, at 1,019 performances. *Life* magazine did an extraordinary feature story on the show in which the Eckarts figured prominently. A successful film followed, also designed by the Eckarts, and starring most of the original Broadway cast. The show itself has been revived many times. *Damn Yankees* was not only the Eckarts' first pairing with George Abbott but also their first with his young protégé, Hal Prince. *Damn Yankees* would remain one of the Eckarts' biggest hits.

FACING PAGE: OPENING SCENE—THE ECKARTS' DESIGN OF A CITY SUBWAY ENTRANCE SURROUNDED BY TENEMENTS DRAWS ON THE BROODING LONELINESS AND ALIENATION THEY FOUND IN THE PAINTINGS OF EDWARD HOPPER. BILL AND JEAN CHOSE A SUBWAY ENTRANCE BECAUSE IT SYMBOLIZED THE UNDERGROUND ASPECTS OF THE HERO'S PLIGHT. THE FINAL NUMBER WAS A BRIDGE. (EC)

Sets That Move, Shows That Don't

1955–1956 *Reuben Reuben* and *Mister Johnson*

"Against a background of shifting and ingenius sets by William and Jean Eckart the show sometimes flares into brilliance..."

Elliot Norton, Boston Post *(October 11, 1955)*

THE ECKARTS DESIGNED THE COSTUME AND MAKEUP OF "FEZ" AS A BLITZSTEIN LOOK-A-LIKE. (EC)

"When we first met Marc (Blitzstein)," Bill said, "he attacked us. It was guilt by association. He hated *Damn Yankees* because he felt it demonized gays. 'I felt the fires roaring in hell,' Marc said, 'when Abbott made Ray Walston play the Devil (Applegate in *Damn Yankees*) as an old queen.' Jean and I looked at each other. The idea that the Devil was a queen had never occurred to us, and we doubted it had to Abbott, but Marc was personally offended."

It was not an auspicious beginning to a collaborative working relationship on *Reuben Reuben,* Cheryl Crawford's production of Blitzstein's latest musical composition for which the Eckarts had been hired to do everything: sets, costumes, and lights. Since Bill and Jean had worked with Crawford before on *Oh Men! Oh Women!* they knew that leftists from the 1930s had a tendency in the midst of the McCarthy witch-hunts to be hypersensitive. Crawford handled it with reserve. "She was dour, not hysterical, made of New England granite," Bill said, "which reminded us more of Abbott. The difference was that Abbott also had a will of iron while Crawford could become quite sentimental." Perhaps, sentimentality explained the reason she had stayed so close to her old 1930s Group Theatre friend, Robert Lewis, who was set to direct *Reuben Reuben* as well as another play that season which the Eckarts had been hired to design, *Mister Johnson,* an adaptation of the Joyce Cary novel. Crawford had championed Lewis on several occasions, most successfully on *Brigadoon.* In that instance, she backed him and the show when every other producer had rejected it, and she was vindicated when it turned out to be a big hit.

Since Bill and Jean had risen from the alternative theatre movement Off-Broadway, they understood Blitzstein's rage at the commercial establishment with whom Abbott was indelibly connected. For Marc, success was practically a badge of complicity with political oppression. After all, the 1950s marked the height of McCarthyism. Many in the entertainment industry were being attacked for their political as well as sexual affiliations, and Blitzstein was definitely a target.

He had an illustrious history and a fat FBI file. Although he had not been a card carrying member of the Communist Party, his late wife had been. Back in the thirties, he approached Brecht and Weill after the failed New York production of *The Threepenny Opera* and volunteered to translate and adapt the show. It then took him two decades to get the translation produced, and even though it was to become an Off-Broadway institution (running 2,611 performances), his own efforts had been frustrated. The Federal Theatre censored and closed down his *The Cradle Will Rock* (recently the subject of a Tim Robbins film). And then there was *Regina*, his musical retelling of Lillian Hellman's *Little Foxes*, a *succès d'estime* which failed miserably on Broadway. What's worse, his protégé, Leonard Bernstein (who was too young to achieve such colorful notoriety), was racking up a string of commercial hits.

At CBS, the Eckarts had encountered the other side of the coin. They were told to sign a loyalty oath or lose their jobs. They'd refused. They knew that actors and writers were being blacklisted in Hollywood, and they were afraid that if they acquiesced they would hasten the day for censorship throughout the entertainment industry. Confronted by the raging Blitzstein, they couldn't help but be sympathetic, for the play they were hired to design was semi-autobiographical. It was all about how a soldier returning from war loses his voice in the face of strangers and enemies (a condition known as *aphonia*). And this was exactly what Blitzstein believed was happening to him and other leftists. Rather than attack the contemporary political situation head on, *Reuben Reuben* sought to be a play about communication, which Bill would say, "Failed to communicate."

Overcoming Blitzstein's ire wasn't as difficult as it seemed. Even though he was a loner, the Eckarts found he loved an audience. "At his tiny apartment on East 12th Street," Bill said, "he would sit and regale us with songs and stories. If you appreciated his performance, you were friends for life. Jean and I were a great audience."

Reuben Reuben was a dark musical set in the vicinity of the Bowery and the Two Bridges area of the lower east side of Manhattan. Visually, the Eckarts took their cue from the American painter Edward Hopper. Since the action took place in the course of one night, they felt it crucial to maintain the continuity of the action though full set changeovers. The idea of traveler curtains seemed artificial and distracting so there would be no "in-one scenes" during changeovers set downstage. Instead, Bill used full stage sets that could be changed à vista, in front of the audience. And there would be no show curtain. Everything, the entire set, would be visible, nothing would be hidden. Working again with Hanya Holm, choreographer for *The Golden Apple*, they would maintain the somber mood of the piece and make the transitions smooth.

"SAN GENNARO" STREET FESTIVAL—FEELINGS OF ALIENATION FROM EARLIER SCENES WERE CONTRASTED TO THE ITALIAN FOLK CELEBRATION TAKING PLACE IN THE STREETS OF "LITTLE ITALY." THE ECKARTS CREATED AN AMAZING OPEN SCENE CHANGE. THREE RECEDING LIT STREET ARCHES FLEW IN TO CAP THE STAGE PICTURE. (EC)

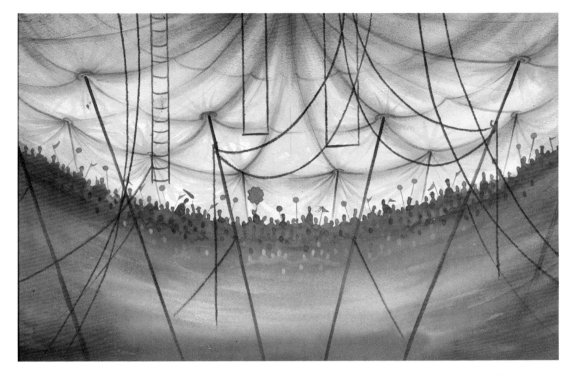

"THE CIRCUS" SKETCH—A LIGHTING CHANGE PERMITTED A BACKSTAGE DROP OF THE CIRCUS TO BLEED THROUGH THE UPSTAGE WALL OF THE NIGHTCLUB, WHICH UNTIL THEN HAD APPEARED SOLID. THE CLUB WALL WAS MADE OUT OF DRAPED CHIFFON, AND THE PLAY OF CIRCUS YELLOWS THROUGH THE CHIFFON EVOKED A CANVAS BY GEORGES SEURAT. IT WAS AN INTENTIONAL REFERENCE TO GIVE THE MOMENT RESONANCE. (EC)

"YETH, YETH"—SPOT GIRL'S COSTUME SKETCH WAS USED TO ADVERTISE THE SHOW GIVING THE MISTAKEN IMPRESSION *REUBEN REUBEN* WAS A GLITZY MUSICAL RATHER THAN A DARK AND DEEPLY PERSONAL WORK. (EC)

There were two deep full-stage sets that were problematic. The San Gennaro Street Festival was designed by the Eckarts as if it were setting up right before the audience's eyes. Actors became street vendors bringing in push carts and setting up their stalls while Enzio Stuarti, later a pop star, sang a Blitzstein Italian ballad. The final scene in the first act was also tricky. It took place in a nightclub called "The Spot." Blitzstein's libretto required that Reuben, played by Eddie Albert, make a twenty-five foot dive off the chandelier (Albert, an accomplished gymnast, practiced the stunt for months before rehearsals started). While Reuben is contemplating this dive, the theatre audience has to experience his flashback, a reliving of his father's suicide at the circus. The challenge for the Eckarts was to transform the full-stage nightclub The Spot into a circus before the audience's eyes and to do it in such a manner so the circus would seem to be an interior thought. They accomplished this effect through lighting changes that allowed a circus backdrop to bleed through the scrim drapes that lined the nightclub.

The Eckarts also created some incredibly sexy but seedy costumes for the nightclub dancers called "The Spot Girls." The sketches were so evocative that Crawford decided to use one of the renderings and make it the show's logo. The seediness disappeared, seemingly absorbed by the advertising copy. The result was a show placard that was even more girly-girly than the now famous *Damn Yankees* poster, certainly a disconnect from what Blitzstein's show was all about, and in Boston this had dire consequences.

FINAL SCENE OF *REUBEN REUBEN*—DAWN, THE WILLIAMSBURG BRIDGE BACKDROP (EC)

At the gypsy run-through in New York (the last rehearsal before the show left for its out-of-town tryouts), everyone was extremely moved. People in the audience were weeping, and Kaye Ballard, who had a major singing role, was so convinced of the merit of the musical that she decided to become a backer and invested her life's savings. But on opening night in Boston, it was another story. By the third scene, the audience started marching towards the doors. It was clear they weren't just bored, they were angry. Cheryl Crawford, in a valiant effort to stem the tide, stood in the middle of the aisle and tried to stare them down and was almost trampled to death. During the first act intermission, an irate patron cornered Blitzstein in the lobby, grabbed him by the lapels, and shouted into his face, "I wish I could make you suffer the way you've been making me suffer."

"What was remarkable is that no one involved with the production had seen it coming," Bill said. "We all knew we had work to do in Boston. The show was much too long, but we fully expected that Bobby Lewis and Cheryl would whip the show into shape." It was a natural expectation since the Eckarts had recently worked with Abbott on *Damn Yankees*. But after the opening, Blitzstein was confused, lacking a clear idea about what to change. He cut and cut deeply, throwing out whole numbers, including some of the best in the show. But he wasn't able to reshape the script. Leonard Bernstein, a loyal friend, came to see the show in Boston. He was so moved by the portrayal of the female lead, Nina, that he eventually named his third child

"MOVING PLATFORMS, PANELS AND DROPS, PLUS STRIKING COSTUME."

HOBE. *VARIETY*

MISTER JOHNSON RENDERING OF NATIVE VILLAGE—TWO THATCHED COTTAGES WERE FLOWN IN TO MEET THE WINCH-DRIVEN SCENERY AS IT SLID INTO PLACE. HERE THE ECKARTS DID AWAY WITH PAINTED DROPS. EVERYTHING WAS MADE FROM NATURAL MATERIALS: BAMBOO, THATCH, AND GRASSES. THE RESULT WAS FILIGREE SCENERY WITH A FULLY DIMENSIONAL USE OF SPACE. THE ENCROACHMENT OF THE WHITE MAN'S CIVILIZATION WAS INDICATED IN THE SCENERY BY THE USE OF BUILDING MATERIALS SUCH AS CORRUGATED TIN AND OTHER CAST OFF REMNANTS. (EC)

TO ACCOMMODATE THE SET CHANGES, THE ECKARTS BUILT THEIR FIRST DECK. IT SPANNED THE ENTIRE WIDTH AND DEPTH OF THE STAGE FLOOR. THEY CREATED A FALSE STAGE LEVEL TO SQUEEZE WINCH-DRIVEN APPARATUS BETWEEN THE STAGE AND THE DECK FOR INVISIBLY PULLING SCENERY ON AND OFF. IN MEETING THE SCENIC REQUIREMENTS OF *MISTER JOHNSON*, THEY HAD DEVELOPED A SUBSTANTIAL MOVE FORWARD IN STAGE TECHNOLOGY. THE TWO HUTS SHOWN MOVED OFF STAGE IN OPPOSITE DIRECTIONS. (EC)

LEFT TO RIGHT, MARJORIE JAMES (GIRL), JOSEPHINE PREMICE (BAMU), RUTH ATTAWAY (MATUMBI), JAMES E. WALL (ALIU), DAVID THAYER (GOLLUP), AND WILLIAM SYLVESTER (RUDBECK) (EC)

after Blitzstein's heroine. He was also struck by "The Rose Song," which was set in the *Romeo and Juliet* sequence in the play and this may explain some of the similarities between this song and "There's a Place for Us" in *West Side Story*. But Bernstein was not a play doctor. With a second show to do that season and Blitzstein as stymied as his hero, Crawford decided to save $30,000 of the $700,000 budget and closed the show early in Boston. On that final night with the hopelessness of the situation beginning to register, Kaye Ballard shrugged, "The trouble with Marc is that he *likes* living on East 12th Street!" The Eckarts always felt Kaye's comment was an astute observation.

Mister Johnson

After their experience with *Reuben Reuben*, Bill and Jean were wary about working with Robert Lewis again, but they had committed to a two-play deal. It was clear he lacked Abbott's dramaturgical sense. But they remembered an early backer's audition and being excited by the potential involvement of Arthur Miller through his wife, Marilyn Monroe. Earle Hyman, who played the title role, said, "This beautiful woman showed up and asked if it would make me nervous if she sat next to me while I read. I said to myself, 'Oh, my God! It's Marilyn Monroe.'" She was impressed and at Miller's prompting invested $10,000 of her own money in the show. Miller's interest stemmed from his close relationship with Norman Rosten who was adapting Joyce Cary's novel for the stage.

Set in the remote bush town of Fada, Cary's *Mister Johnson* follows the career of a Nigerian government clerk who wears his British patent leather shoes on a string around his neck as a symbol of his allegiance to the Crown. Good-humored and resourceful, Johnson succeeds against all odds in building the town's one major road, once the dream of his white superiors. He expects to be rewarded but instead is sacked. Unable to accept his unjust treatment, Johnson resorts to petty thievery. One night while he is helping himself to goods from the town's store, he is fired upon by the shopkeeper. In the dark, he stabs and kills his white assailant. Nothing can mitigate the punishment for this crime, which is a public hanging. In the

NATIVE CHILD'S COSTUME SKETCH—THE WAY IN WHICH THE NATIVES RECYCLED THE SCRAPS OF THE WHITE MAN'S WORLD WAS ALSO BROUGHT FORTH IN THE COSTUMES, TESTIFYING NOT ONLY TO THEIR POVERTY BUT TO THEIR INGENUITY AND IRREVERENCE FOR THEIR SUBJUGATED STATUS. (EC)

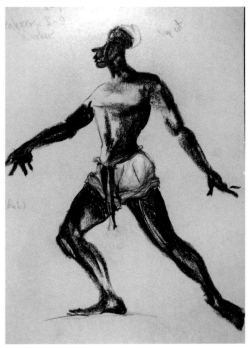

"WORKER IN THE FIELD" COSTUME SKETCH (EC)

WEDDING PROCESSION—JOSEPHINE PREMICE (BAMU) AND EARLE HYMAN (JOHNSON) AT EXTREME RIGHT. SHE IS WEARING A NIGERIAN WEDDING VEIL, AND HE IS CLAD IN A FORMAL WHITE LINEN WEDDING SUIT. (EC)

play's final moment, Johnson persuades the judge, his former boss, to break the law and shoot him instead, "You my frien'—you my father and my mother . . . shoot me yourself." His request granted, Johnson dies with dignity.

During the rehearsals of *Reuben Reuben,* Bill and Jean, looking ahead to their next project with Lewis, borrowed his *Mister Johnson* script. They were alarmed to find Lewis had plotted out all of the stage blocking in advance of rehearsals. "That told Jean and me he wasn't going to make any changes on that show either." And one thing the Eckarts were sure of was that the show needed changes. The first draft the Eckarts received required more than forty set changes. Rosten's adaptation simply stated, "The entire action of the play takes place within the 'landscape' of the Nigerian town of Fada—in or outside of several mud or bush huts . . . The scenes are indicated by backdrops or

suggested by the most fragmentary props, so that the *action will be entirely fluid and blending*." When the Eckarts spoke to Rosten, he assured them he would discuss changes in the script with Miller. What they didn't realize was that Miller was going to confine himself to being a dialogue coach. He was not going to help reshape the script and that proved tragic.

With forty set changes, a radical new approach to scene shifting was necessary. *Mister Johnson* was not a musical where the Eckarts could rely on music for bridges to cover set changes. What Bill and Jean came up with was their most significant technical innovation. They built a deck to span the entire width and depth of the stage floor and placed winch drives under it. Doing *Reuben Reuben,* they had learned that having hidden stage hands or even visible actors roll on large set wagons meant that each night the exact position of each wagon would

vary. Since they were also the lighting designers, they found it intolerable that each night their lighting design was off. These variances in wagon placements also altered audience sightlines. If they could control the movement of the set by anchoring it to the floor, they might overcome the problem. Bill and Jean then came up with the notion of putting the set pieces on tracks and propelling them into place by a series of cables and winches. To cover the mechanism, they built a false stage floor (deck). Grooves were cut into the floor and drivers were attached to set wagons, which then could be drawn effortlessly into place. A proscenium of bamboo and thatch helped to hide the mechanics of the system while also framing the action. Roofs and backing were flown-in to meet the wagons as they slid into place. Today, the use of a deck and winch system has become commonplace, but in 1956, it was virtually unknown. Since Bill and Jean had to raise the floor up to accommodate the winch apparatus, they also decided to make the deck part of the visual picture. According to Earle Hyman, "They got something that was very beautiful to look at. You knew you were climbing upwards in certain places on stage and going down small hills in others. There was even a suggestion of a pool or river from which you could drink water."

In December 1955, Rosa Parks had refused to give up her seat on an Alabama bus to a white person. *Mister Johnson* opened in New York three months later. Bill and Jean thought of *Mister Johnson* as a play that would challenge American attitudes about race. *Mister Johnson* was not just flawed dramatically but ahead of its time. The photographer Carl Van Vechten, a prominent figure in the Harlem Renaissance, wrote to African American writer Chester Himes, "Earle Hyman has been hailed as the actor of the century (white or Negro), but in the audiences who go to see him one seldom sees a Negro face." *Raisin in the Sun* was still two years down the road, and eight years would pass before the Civil Rights Act of 1964. In spite of the outstanding performances and the major technical innovations of the Eckarts, the subject matter and the play's down-beat ending proved too difficult for the predominantly white audiences of the 1950s. *Mister Johnson* closed after six weeks. The London production fared no better.

NATIVE WOMAN'S COSTUME SKETCH—THE USE OF LIVELY AND BATIK PRINTS CREATED AN ELEMENT OF AUTHENTICITY AS WELL AS COLOR TO THE LOOK OF THE SHOW. (EC)

A Year of Losses and Disappointments

As the Eckarts looked back at 1955–1956 season, they couldn't help but be sobered by the losses. Not only had their two shows closed prematurely, but they had also lost a friend and colleague when twenty-nine-year-old Jerry Ross, who had composed the music for *Pajama Game* and *Damn Yankees,* died in November.

The following June, they spent a week at Martha's Vineyard. "When we arrived," Bill remembered, "we found out that John LaTouche was living nearby and was working with Lillian Hellman and Leonard Bernstein on *Candide*. LaTouche asked me about Bernstein, and I told him that he (Bernstein) was a prodigious talent, and he had to work with him. That night, LaTouche brought us to Lillian's. The atmosphere was supercharged and Bernstein and Hellman were intent on being the best at charades. The rest of us, including Lenny's wife (Felicia), were quickly sidelined and watched in awe. I don't remember who won, but Lenny was full of tricks. He asked us if we had ever seen anyone play the piano upside down and backwards. He then sat at the stool, put his hands over his head positioning them on the opposite keys, and proceeded to play. It was such a great stunt that when I returned to New York I mentioned it to Marc Blitzstein. Marc was indignant, 'That's my trick. He stole it from me!' That June evening, we had no idea we would never see Touche again. He died in August at the age of thirty-eight, his work on *Candide* incomplete."

The fall was equally bleak with no shows in the offing. NBC organized an opera company to play forty-seven cities and hired the Eckarts to design *The Marriage of Figaro* and *Madam Butterfly*.

MAKING SADIE HAWKINS DAY ZING

AL CAPP INTRODUCED THE SADIE HAWKINS DAY RACE INTO HIS COMIC STRIP IN 1936. THE IDEA HAS BECOME SO MUCH A PART OF AMERICAN CULTURE THAT MANY PEOPLE ARE UNAWARE OF ITS ORIGINS IN CAPP'S CARTOON.

ALMOST EVERYTHING IN THE STAGE PRODUCTION OF LI'L ABNER RELATED TO FILM. THERE IS AN INHERENT SIMILARITY BETWEEN FILM AND THE COMIC STRIP'S STOP ACTION CELLS. THE LI'L ABNER CARTOON WAS CONCEIVED BY AL CAPP AS AN ACTION STRIP. THE ECKARTS' JOB WAS TO BRING THE ALMOST FILMIC MOVEMENT OF THE CARTOON TO THE STAGE SETTING. (© CAPP ENTERPRISES, INC. 1998, ALL RIGHTS RESERVED.)

MICHAEL KIDD'S CHOREOGRAPHY EXPLODED ACROSS THE STAGE AT THE START OF THE SADIE HAWKINS DAY RACE. FROM LEFT TO RIGHT: APPASSIONATA VON CLIMAX (TINA LOUISE), DAISY MAE (EDIE ADAMS) LEAPING IN PURSUIT OF LI'L ABNER (PETER PALMER), ALREADY AIRBORNE. SET PIECES MOVED IN OPPOSITION TO THE ACTORS ACCELERATING THE RACE AND MAKING THE FORWARD MOVEMENT AS SEAMLESS AS A MOVIE CHASE. (GJON MILI, GETTY IMAGES)

Li'l Abner

1956—The Chase

BASED ON THE POPULAR AL CAPP CARTOON, THE TOWN OF DOGPATCH BECOMES A CANDIDATE FOR AN ATOMIC BOMB TEST WHEN WASHINGTON DECIDES IT IS THE MOST USELESS SPOT IN AMERICA. BEFORE THE FINALE, THE FOLKSY RESIDENTS MANAGE TO SAVE THEIR TOWN AND THEIR HOME BREW OF YOKEMBERRY JUICE WHILE DAISY MAE CATCHES LI'L ABNER IN THE SADIE HAWKINS DAY RACE.

"What made Li'l Abner *a difficult show to do was finding a style that was sufficiently realistic for the stage which would still retain the spirit of Al Capp's cartoon."*

William Eckart

The impetus for the production of the *Li'l Abner* musical came from screenwriters and producers Norman Panama and Melvin Frank. Bill and Jean knew of Panama and Frank by reputation for their Danny Kaye films: *Knock on Wood* and *The Court Jester*. The successful Hollywood writing team had broken with the traditional means of raising money for a Broadway musical by taking their *Li'l Abner* concept to Paramount Pictures for financing. Paramount bankrolled the entire New York Broadway production as a tryout for what they believed would eventually be a hit film.

Michael Kidd was signed to both choreograph and direct *Li'l Abner* as well as share producing credits along with "Panama and Hattie," the affectionate nicknames the Eckarts gave Panama and Frank. Kidd had choreographed *Knock on Wood* for Panama and Frank, yet Kidd's Hollywood reputation for choreography really rested on his work for director Stanley Donen on MGM's *Seven Brides for Seven Brothers*. On that film, Gene De Paul composed the music with lyrics by Johnny Mercer. De Paul and Mercer were also signed on for *Li'l Abner*. Panama and Frank would write the book. Michael Kidd was no stranger to Broadway, having previously choreographed *Guys and Dolls*, but being both choreographer and director was something which hadn't happened on Broadway since Agnes de Mille's double duty on Rodgers and Hammerstein's *Allegro* and, more recently, Jerome Robbins' combo effort on *Peter Pan*. The Eckarts admired Michael Kidd's energetic work. His involvement meant *Li'l Abner* would be high on physicality. The show would thump, kick, and stomp its way across the stage.

"WE USED A LOT OF PROPS," SAID MAUREEN HOPKINS, ASSISTANT DANCE DIRECTOR. "EVERYBODY THAT CAME ON HAD A PROP. THEY WERE EITHER WIELDING A CLUB, SWINGING A NET, OR CATCHING A RABBIT."

A GIRL WITH A CLUB TAKES UNFAIR ADVANTAGE OF HER PREY WHO IS ALREADY CAUGHT IN A BEAR TRAP. (GJON MILI, GETTY IMAGES).

A GIRL WITH A BUTTERFLY NET RUNS AFTER A FRANTIC BOY WHO JUST BARELY ESCAPES. (GJON MILI, GETTY IMAGES).

FOR THE SADIE HAWKINS DAY RACE, SCENERY CHANGED ON AN OPEN STAGE IN FRONT OF THE DOGPATCH BACKDROP OF SCRAPPY HILLS. (EC)

Li'l Abner was not a book-driven musical that needed a George Abbott. The satire, what little there was of it, wasn't subtle. Under Kidd's direction, the production would be a chorus-driven show with the emphasis on dance and movement. The job for the designers was not only to provide locations for scenes but continuity so that the physical thrust of the show could keep moving forward. Bill and Jean knew what Kidd needed was unencumbered space, especially for the almost twenty-minute, non-stop, bring-down-the-house Sadie Hawkins Day Race Ballet, which capped Act One. In this number, chicken coops, sign posts, fences, and even whole groves of trees moved on and off during the dance. Rather than impeding the movement, the mobile scenic elements the Eckarts designed enhanced the entertainment. The units were changed in full view of the audience, in the middle of a dance number, without slowing down the action or compromising the reality of the show.

The Eckarts felt very good about the producers' choice of Alvin Colt to design the costumes. They had worked well with Colt on *The Golden Apple* and Colt had collaborated successfully with Michael Kidd on *Guys and Dolls*. Colt remembers "One thing I learned from the Eckarts was using tracing paper and water colors. I can't remember if it was Bill or Jean. You never knew who did what, but it didn't matter. I learned an overlay technique that saved me a lot of time, and I've been doing it ever since." "We worked closely with Alvin Colt," Bill said. "So whatever solution we came up with would be consistent in style and palette." Colt's costume scheme consisted of having all of

"THE ECKARTS BUILT A GROVE OF TREES THAT CAME ON DURING THE MIDDLE OF THE SADIE HAWKINS DAY RACE," SAID DEEDEE WOOD, ASSISTANT CHOREOGRAPHER. "THERE WAS NO STOP IN THE ACTION. THE GROVE CAME ON, THE LIGHTS WENT DOWN, AND WE WENT INTO THIS SLOW MOTION DANCE AMONG THE TREES. WE CALLED IT THE 'SNEAKY PETE.'" THE MOVING SCENIC ELEMENTS SUGGESTED THE CHASE THROUGH THE COUNTRYSIDE. (EC)

the clothes outlined in black; buttons, patches, every detail had a black outline. It was all done with appliquéd tape. This was the first time this approach had been attempted and because of its success, it has been frequently copied since. The movie studio's involvement meant a number of pluses for the production. For instance, Paramount's bankroll was substantial enough to make it possible for Bill and Jean to hire an assistant for the first time. They chose their Yale classmate, Tharon Musser. Musser, who went on to become one of the theatre's foremost lighting designers, had not been able to break into United Scenic Artists, which at that time did not have a separate exam for lighting designers. During *Li'l Abner*, Bill and Jean tutored her on her painting skills. Musser was then able to pass the exam and get into the Union as a set designer.

There was a certain degree of risk associated with bringing a comic strip to life on stage, as the last successful musical based on comic strip characters had been *Mutt and Jeff* in 1911! Since then, there had been a number of notable failures and the conventional wisdom was that readers of the "funnies" were not inclined to pay Broadway prices to see their favorite comic strip characters recreated by actors. The creative teams' approach was not to make fun of the cartoon but to treat the characters like real people.

"The first day, when everybody came together for the reading," dancer Maureen Hopkins said, "I was fidgeting near the elevator, and as people got off in their street clothes, I knew who they were going to be in the show. Julie Newmar had to be Stupefin' Jones and Tina Louise had to be Appassionata." Terry Little, the Stage Manager, agreed, saying "Michael Kidd took cartoon characters and didn't make them into caricatures. They were real people even though they were the characters from the comic strip." Charlotte Rae, who played Mammy Yokum, was leery about the role at first. "I didn't want to do the show because I thought 'who wants to do a cartoon?' But then I realized I could make Mammy a caring human being. I saw her as the leader of the town. I thought of special stylized ways of doing her so she would be strong." The humanism in Capp's well crafted strip translated well to the stage. *Li'l Abner* had over forty million fans in his comic strip heyday and his daily mishaps ran in over 700 newspapers. According to Al Capp, *Li'l Abner's* popularity was due to his painful case of girl shyness, which was hardly less-

ANIMAL PROBLEMS

MARRYIN' SAM (STUBBY KAYE), JULIE THE BURRO, AND MEMBERS OF THE CHORUS. THERE WAS AN ENTIRE MENAGERIE OF BARNYARD ANIMALS ON THE STAGE, INCLUDING FOUR GEESE, TWO DOGS, A PINK PIG, AND A BURRO NAMED JULIE. (EC)

ened by his marriage in 1952 to Daisy Mae. "Li'l Abner," said Capp, "never knows what to do about a succession of eager, luscious girls who throw their juicy selves at him. That makes every male who reads *Li'l Abner* feel . . . compared with *Li'l Abner*, he is a Don Juan."

The Eckarts helped carry the realism needed to make the show work into their design concepts. Even real animals played a part. "The Eckarts were such good sports about all those animals," said Deedee Wood, Kidd's assistant. "At one point, there were chickens as well, but they had to be taken out because one of them flew into the audience." Edie Adams (Daisy Mae) also remembered the animals in her autobiography *Sing A Pretty Song*, "The animals were always running around onstage, doing what animals always do. The Sadie Hawkins Day dance was particularly perilous. As we were running across the stage, we nearsighted folks had to be told what places

FROM LONG SHOT TO CLOSE UP ON STAGE

"PANAMA AND FRANK WANTED LOTS OF CABINS WITH SMOKE CURLING OUT OF THE CHIMNEYS," JEAN SAID. "THEY EVEN WANTED TO OPEN WITH DOGPATCH AS SEEN FROM THE AIR. I THINK THEY WOULD HAVE LIKED TO BUILD THE TOWN OF DOGPATCH AND THEN DONE A MOVIE IN IT."

STUDY FOR THE YOKUM CABIN (EC)

THE OPENING LONG SHOT—THE BARN ON THE SHOW CURTAIN ESTABLISHED THE PLACE "DOGPATCH" AND DEFINED THE LOOK OF THE REST OF THE SHOW. TO ACCOMMODATE THE FILM SENSIBILITIES OF THE PRODUCERS, THE OPENING SEQUENCE OF THE PLAY WAS CONSTRUCTED AS A PANORAMA OF DOGPATCH WHICH GRADUALLY PULLED IN FOR A CLOSE-UP OF THE YOKUMS IN FRONT OF THEIR CABIN. TO ACCOMPLISH THIS, THE ECKARTS USED THREE SETS. THE FIRST NUMBER, "A TYPICAL DAY IN DOGPATCH USA," STARTS WITH THE SHOW CURTAIN TRAVELER. THE TRAVELER ANNOUNCED THE PLAY'S PRIMARY LOCATION ON THE SIDE OF THE BARN, AS SEEN FROM A DISTANCE. A LIGHTING CHANGE MADE THE CURTAIN, WHICH WAS PAINTED ON SCRIM, DISSOLVE INTO THE FIRST SCENE. (COLLECTION OF THE MCNAY ART MUSEUM, GIFT OF ROBERT L.B. TOBIN)

to avoid. They'd shout, 'Upstage left, downstage right,' so we altered our course and tried to avoid not only what was on the floor but other dancers coming at you."

Each show has its special problems, but *Li'l Abner* had one that was exceptionally unique. "We've done a lot of things for our art," Jean said, "but we had never measured rear ends for a set before. For *Abner* we had to. Posterior dimensions were necessary for constructing Pappy Yokum's bathtub. It had to not only fit him but be as small as possible in order to fit into the set." It was probably the only bathtub ever to be tailor-made. In the Philadelphia tryouts, however, Pappy's tub went down the drain when the scene it appeared in was cut from the play.

Although knowing *Li'l Abner* would become a film helped keep the pace of the show up and moving at high speed, planning for the eventual film caused drawbacks as well. One problem was that Panama and Frank's book called for twenty-two scenes. The writing/producing team was adamant about needing all twenty-two sets. The Eckarts were required to build much more scenery than they knew was necessary.

When the show reached the National Theatre in Washington, the first stop in its out-of-town tryout tour, Bill recalled, "We found we just had too many pieces. The show was too cumbersome. Some of the pieces we never even put on stage. We just left them in the theatre alley. Of course, we didn't tell the producers what we were doing. Coming from film, they wouldn't have understood the concept of requiring less."

The biggest challenge for the Eckarts, however, was finding a style to capture the essence of Capp's comic strip and the place "Dogpatch." Bill and Jean turned to Capp's strip for inspiration but found he had not established a scenic dimension in his drawings. "When it came to Dogpatch," Bill said, "we found that almost everyone had a conception of what the town looked like, yet seldom did these conceptions agree. Naturally, we went to Capp's cartoons to find a definitive answer only to find that there were almost no indications of background scenery. There were one or two log cabins and the occasional pine tree and rocks, but nothing on which to rest the look of the show. Dogpatch and its environs had to be totally invented. We did hundreds of drawings trying to find a way in. We began to notice in looking at Capp's strip

ONCE THE TRAVELER DISSOLVES, A LEANING CABIN IS REVEALED, AS THE CHARACTERS ENTER. A LINE STRUNG FROM THE CABIN PORCH LEADS OFF STAGE RIGHT. IT SEEMS AS IF THE WEIGHT OF LAUNDRY HUNG ON THE LINE WAS ABOUT TO PULL THE CABIN INTO THE RAVINE, BUT INSTEAD, THE CABIN MOVES OFF STAGE LEFT. AS IT MOVES, IT APPARENTLY PULLS THE YOKUM CABIN ATTACHED TO THE SAME LINE ON FROM STAGE RIGHT, BRINGING THE YOKUMS WITH IT. BY STRINGING THE TWO CABINS TOGETHER, NOT ONLY HAD THE ECKARTS SUCCEEDED IN BRINGING THE AUDIENCE CLOSER TO THE YOKUMS, BUT BY CLEVERLY USING THE LINE TO CONNECT THE CABINS, THEY ALSO GOT A LAUGH. (EC)

that a great deal of the feeling of it came from the printed word, the hand-lettered signs that seemed to pop out at the reader." The Eckarts decided to use hand-lettered block print wherever possible, and their use of rural graffiti helped to relate the Eckarts' designs back to the hand-lettered comic strip itself. The Eckarts had used signage in numerous plays, but in *Li'l Abner*, they used even more, partly to stop the producers from ordering more scenery. As Tharon Musser said, "The producers kept saying, 'We don't know where we are,' so Bill and Jean made up little signs and used them throughout the play on curtains, banners, and freestanding." "We also decided," said Bill, "to take the 'patch' in Dogpatch quite literally. Everything on our set had patches, everything was worn out and beat up and held together in the flimsiest of ways." The Eckarts even created a Rube Goldberg shower stall that rolled on and off stage and was patched in various places. As Deedee Wood said, "Who knew what was behind that shower curtain? Maybe it was geese or chickens. It was a great reveal," for when it opened, there was Julie Newmar as outlined, patched, and shapely Stupefyin' Jones. Keeping with this sense of invention and unlike Capp's Dogpatch, where the cabins and pines stand erect as a protective bulwark against civilization, the Eckarts' version of the town was a series of compromises and reckless gestures. Cabins teeter atop their foundations; telegraph lines slump to the ground weighed down by tiny birds; and

THE YOKUM CABIN—THE BACKGROUND REMAINED IN PLACE WHILE HIDDEN STAGEHANDS MOVED THE HOUSE ON CASTERS FROM THE LEFT OF THE STAGE SO THAT IT APPEARED TO BE PULLED ON BY THE CONNECTING CLOTHESLINE. "THERE WERE NO TRACKS ON THE STAGE TO GUIDE IT," BILL SAID. "IT WAS AN EARLY ATTEMPT TO GIVE CINEMATIC MOVEMENT TO A SHOW." THE ECKARTS INVENTED A YOKUMBERRY TREE, AT RIGHT, FROM WHICH MAMMY YOKUM MADE THE YOKUMBERRY TONIC, WHICH GAVE LI'L ABNER HIS REMARKABLE SIZE AND STRENGTH. (EC)

CHARLOTTE RAE (MAMMY YOKUM), JOE E. MARKS (PAPPY YOKUM), AND PETER PALMER (LI'L ABNER) IN FRONT OF THE YOKUM CABIN. (FRIEDMAN – ABELES, BILLY ROSE THEATRE COLLECTION, NYPL)

DOGPATCHERS

THE ECKARTS' COMEDIC POINT OF VIEW WORKED NICELY WITH THE MUSICAL'S PLOT, A SATIRICAL ATTACK ON AMERICAN MATERIALISM AND WASHINGTON POLITICS. AL CAPP ADMIRED THE ECKARTS' WORK AND IN A NOTE TO THEM ON OPENING NIGHT HE EXPRESSED HIS APPRECIATION, "YOU'VE MADE IT THE PRETTIEST SHOW IN TOWN. THANKS."

A COMPOSITE SKETCH OF THE JUBILATION T. CORNPONE STATUE PROPPED UP BY A CAR JACK IN THE CENTER OF DOGPATCH. THE ECKARTS BUILT SETS FORWARD TOWARDS THE PROSCENIUM, WITH WING PIECES SILHOUETTED AGAINST THE BACKDROP OF THE HILLS IN THE REAR. (EC)

fences wander precariously in every direction. Time has forgotten this Dogpatch; even the fishing hole is surrounded by dead logs and densely hung willows. The Eckarts' depiction tells us this secluded town's inhabitants are living on the remnants of urban civilization. We don't know if it is simple-mindedness or superior wisdom. It is the uncertainty of these two attitudes—one naïve, the other shrewd—that made Al Capp's strip amusing and provocative. The Eckarts set up a similar physical contrast between the lush, bucolic landscape of the fishing hole and distant fields and the ramshackle world of the small town. Much of the humor and charm of *Li'l Abner* worked off the contrast between country people and sophisticated Washingtonians. The satire was generally aimed at bombastic politicians, and it was fairly non-partisan. The exception was a jibe at the Eisenhower Administration in which General Bullmoose, the villain of the play, declares, "If it is good for General Bullmoose, it is good for the country." Bullmoose's remark parroted an Eisenhower cabinet member who said, "If it's good for General Motors, it's good for the country."

"There was a big scene when the Dogpatch people go to Washington and disrupt an elegant diplomatic party," Alvin Colt, the costume designer said to Lynn Pecktal (*Costume Design, Techniques of Modern Masters*). "I had the Washington Society people very done up. They were all in grays, in contrast to the colorful, outrageous Dogpatchers, and looked beautiful, chic, and expensive."

SKETCH OF SET FOR "IF I HAD MY DRUTHERS"—"THE FISHING HOLE IS IDYLLIC RUSTICITY," BILL SAID, "NOTHING TO DO BUT LAZE AND FISH." (EC)

THE CORNPONE SQUARE BACKDROP (EC)

...MEET THE SOPHISTICATES.

ALVIN COLT AND THE ECKARTS WORKED CLOSELY TOGETHER TO CREATE THE ELEGANCE OF WASHINGTON SOCIETY. "IN THE MOVIE VERSION THEY DIDN'T USE MY HIGH-SOCIETY DESIGNS ," SAID COSTUME DESIGNER ALVIN COLT. "THEY JUST BOUGHT DRESSES AND IT LOOKED LIKE IT." (EC)

THE ECKARTS' STUDY FOR ELEGANT WASHINGTON PARTY IN GRAYS. (EC)

THE ECKARTS' SET RENDERING FOR THE WASHINGTON PARTY SCENE (EC)

"*Abner* was running long in Washington," Bill said. "This meant cuts and changes in Philadelphia and Boston before the New York opening in mid November (1956)." Since the Eckarts were responsible for the lighting as well as sets on *Abner*, and since the Eckarts' first job in Hollywood, *The Pajama Game* (Warner, 1957) began while *Li'l Abner* was in out-of-town tryouts, the decision was made to have Jean fly out to Los Angeles while Bill remained behind to prepare the show for New York. For the next six weeks, they each commuted back and forth on eight-hour flights through New York. "In those days," Bill said, "the airlines never thought anyone would fly directly from Los Angeles to Boston or Philadelphia. It was a red-eye and all steerage. They called it 'the flying Dutchman' and they gave you a box lunch. Fortunately, I don't remember very much about it."

The trip to Dogpatch was an up-tempo but exhausting journey.

FOLLOWING A COMPLICATED PLOT, THE FINAL PRODUCTION NUMBER ("THE MATRIMONIAL STOMP") INVOLVED MOVING THE ENTIRE TOWN, INCLUDING THE STATUE. THE ROPES THAT OPENED THE SHOW WERE REPRISED IN THIS SEQUENCE TO SHUFFLE THE SCENERY ON AND OFF. "WE DECORATED CORNPONE SQUARE WITH KNOTTED FABRIC," BILL SAID. "WE FLEW IT IN TO PROVIDE CONTRAST... WHITE ON BLACK." FROM LEFT TO RIGHT, JOE E. MARKS (PAPPY YOKUM), CHARLOTTE RAE (MAMMY YOKUM), PETER PALMER (LI'L ABNER), EDIE ADAMS (DAISY MAE), AND, OF COURSE, THE STATUE OF JUBILATION T. CORNPONE (FRIEDMAN – ABELES, MUSEUM OF CITY OF NEW YORK)

AS IN CAPP'S COMIC STRIP, THE GIRLS WERE ALL VERY BUSTY.
ALVIN COLT'S COSTUMES DID THE MOST WITH WHAT THE
ACTRESS' NATURAL ENDOWMENTS WERE AND WHERE THESE
WERE LACKING, HE AND KARINSKA, WHO BUILT THE COSTUMES,
IMPROVED UPON NATURE SO THAT THERE WAS NOTHING LEFT
TO THE IMAGINATION. JEAN SAID, "ALVIN KNEW HOW TO MAKE
WOMEN LOOK MARVELOUS IN A FIFTIES KIND OF WAY."

PETER PALMER (LI'L ABNER) AND EDIE ADAMS (DAISY MAE) "IN-
ONE," IN FRONT OF THE ROADSIDE TRAVELER CURTAIN
(PHOTOFEST)

INSIDE THE PATCHWORK SHOWER STOOD
STUPEFYIN' JONES, PLAYED BY JULIE NEWMAR.
NOT ONLY DID HER COSTUME HAVE PATCHES,
BUT THERE WERE PATCHES ON THE SHOWER
CURTAIN AS WELL. NOTE THE BLACK OUTLINES
AND PATCHES. (PHOTO: FRIEDMAN – ABELES,
BILLY ROSE THEATRE COLLECTION, NYPL)

Fate of the Show

What the evening might have lacked in subtlety, it
more than made up for in energy, charm, and
panache. Kidd's incredible dance sequence for the
Sadie Hawkins Day Race, De Paul and Mercer's
rousing "Jubilation T. Cornpone," Edie Adams' performance as Daisy Mae (which won her a Tony),
Peter Palmer's appealing Abner, Stubby Kaye
(Marryin' Sam), Howard St. John (Gen. Bullmoose),
Charlotte Rae (Mammy Yokum), and Joe E. Marks
(Pappy Yokum) all came together to make *Li'l Abner*
a hit. Although there were obvious problems of construction in the plot-heavy second act, *Li'l Abner*
was the kind of crowd-pleaser that didn't need critical assent in order to succeed. Kidd's choreography
beat down any objections.

The show was a big hit for everyone involved. It
ran for 693 performances. The Eckarts' genius was
recognized by the out-of-town press. "The Eckarts
have done wonders with the settings, some dozen of
'em, swinging from the idiocies of Dogpatch to the
grandeur of a Washington ballroom, which flow into

THE ECKARTS' ROADSIDE
TRAVELER CURTAIN WAS USED
TO "WIPE" THE STAGE DURING
SET CHANGES. THE TRAVELER
MOVED IN ONE DIRECTION
WHILE THE AUTOMOBILE
MOVED IN THE OTHER. THE
EFFECT PRESERVED THE
SHOW'S MOMENTUM. (EC)

each other without a hitch," wrote R. E. P. Sensenderfer of the *Philadelphia Bulletin*. In Boston, Elliot Norton of the *Post* wrote, "The settings of William and Jean Eckart are inspired. The crazy hillbilly characters of Al Capp's Dogpatch come noisily to life against hilarious backgrounds of crazy huts and crazier mountains and the lunatic statue of General Jubilation T. Cornpone who was, in his own confederate day, crazier than anyone." In New York, the press was no less enthusiastic. Walter Kerr of the *Herald Tribune* wrote, "William and Jean Eckart have splashed termite ridden shacks and hairpin hills clear across an obviously tilting planet," while Brooks Atkinson of *The New York Times* wrote, "It is amusing to see Dogpatch come to life in the Eckarts' good-natured scenery." John Chapman of the *Daily News* concluded, "William and Jean Eckart . . . must have been born and bred in the hillbilly community of Dogpatch."

THE ENSEMBLE SINGING "JUBILATION T. CORNPONE." AT CENTER IN THE SECOND ROW STANDS STUBBY KAYE (MARRYIN' SAM) WEARING A BROAD BRIMMED HAT AND VEST. THIS PHOTOGRAPH WAS TAKEN USING SPECIAL NON-THEATRICAL LIGHTING. (PHOTOFEST)

Even though Al Capp's comic strip is now only a memory, the show is regularly revived with success. Robin Wagner (designer of *A Chorus Line, Dreamgirls,* and *The Producers*), who was then a young designer said, "*Li'l Abner* was sensational. I tried to imitate what they did when I was working in summer stock, but it was so fresh and so original I couldn't do it."

Ironically, the Paramont film (1959) made from the show of *Li'l Abner* didn't work. In the theatre, the audience was ready to suspend disbelief and accept larger than life characters. But film demands greater realism. The heightened *Li'l Abner* characters which worked on stage became grotesque and unacceptable. This was true of other devices used to translate the show to the big screen. When Kidd's Sadie Hawkins Day Ballet was filmed, Bill and Jean's scenic inventions were not appreciably changed except that the dance was shot cut-to-cut, breaking up the action into little pieces. This weakened the impact of the ballet. In fact, the film borrowed so much from the Eckarts' stage designs that the studio's attorneys decided to contact the Eckarts and offer them a small payment. As Bill recalled, "We said, 'No.' We demanded instead that they duplicate our New York design fee, and give us on screen credit for designing the New York stage production." The Eckarts could have asked for more credit, but neither Bill nor Jean wanted their names associated with what they considered a botched effort to translate their work to the screen.

A FAIRY TALE ON A VERTICAL SET

THE ROYAL STAIRWAY. DANCERS WAIT FOR "THE GRAND WALTZ" WHILE A TECHNICIAN LISTENS FOR THE CUE TO START. (PHOTO: GORDON PARKS, GETTY IMAGES)

IN ORDER TO KEEP ACTION CONSTANTLY FLOWING, THERE WERE THREE CAMERAS AT THE CENTER OF THE STUDIO. A FOURTH CAMERA (ON A CRANE) WAS USED AROUND CORNERS AND COULD BE RAISED AND LOWERED AT WILL. SCENERY WAS CONCEIVED SO THAT THE ACTION WOULD CONTINUOUSLY FLOW WITHOUT MOVING THE THREE HEAVY CAMERAS FROM THEIR POSITIONS AT THE CENTER OF THE STUDIO. THE EARLY COLOR TELEVISION CAMERAS WERE COLOSSAL AND COST $100,000 A PIECE, A FORTUNE AT A TIME WHEN THE ENTIRE PRODUCTION COST LESS THAN FOUR CAMERAS. THE SET FOR CINDERELLA HAD FOUR SPIRAL STAIRCASES WHICH WERE NOT ONLY WONDERFULLY ATMOSPHERIC, BUT WERE A NECESSITY GIVEN THE CONSTRICTIONS OF SPACE IN THE STUDIO. THE ECKARTS' USE OF SPIRALS AND ARCHES CREATED A SENSE OF DEPTH. THE PALACE'S LONG STAIRCASE CREATED A SENSE OF GRANDEUR AND OPULENCE.

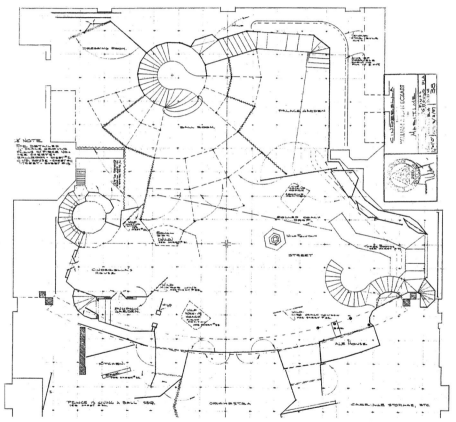

ECKARTS' FLOOR PLAN OF CBS' SMALLEST COLOR STUDIO. IN TYPICAL LIVE TELEVISION FASHION, THE SETS WERE ARRANGED IN A CIRCLE AROUND THE CONVERTED THEATRE, SO THAT THE THREE CENTRAL CAMERAS DID NOT HAVE TO MOVE VERY FAR TO GET TO THE NEXT SHOT. THE FOURTH CAMERA WAS CALLED THE "HOUSTON FEARLESS" AND WAS SPECIALLY RIGGED TO POKE AROUND CORNERS AND BE RAISED AND LOWERED AT WILL. REVEAL SEQUENCE AT LEFT TAKES PLACE IN THE AREA SHOWN IN THE TOP RIGHT OF THE FLOOR PLAN.(EC)

Cinderella

1957 Big Show—Small Screen

A SOPHISTICATED LOOK AT A DOWNTRODDEN GIRL WHO IS TRANSFORMED BY MAGIC AND LOVE INTO A PRINCESS.

"In the theatre you move the sets, in TV you move the camera." William Eckart

REHEARSAL PHOTO—BROADCAST IN COMPATIBLE COLOR, *CINDERELLA* ONLY SURVIVES IN BLACK AND WHITE ON KINESCOPE (A FILM TAKEN FROM A TELEVISION MONITOR). TWO RECENTLY DISCOVERED REHEARSAL KINESCOPES ALSO SURVIVE. IN THE ABOVE PICTURE, CAMERA STARTS WITH A SHOT OF THE PRINCE (JON CYPHER). AS HE TURNS TO LEAVE, IT PULLS BACK AND PANS LEFT TO CATCH CINDERELLA (JULIE ANDREWS) HIDING BEHIND A PORTICO IN THE PALACE GARDEN. THE STORY HAD TO BE RESTRUCTURED SO THAT THE *CINDERELLA* REVEAL COULD TAKE PLACE WITHIN A TEN-BY-TWELVE-FOOT AREA COVERED BY TWO LARGE, FAIRLY IMMOBILE CAMERAS OPERATING WITHIN A CIRCULAR SET. (EC)

*C*inderella was conceived as a musical for television, but everything about its production values would be on a par with a Broadway show. The possible exception, as Edie Adams (the Fairy Godmother) noted, was that there was no understudy for Julie Andrews (Cinderella). Part of the preparation was two "out-of-town tryouts"—actually filmed rehearsals, which Richard Rodgers nicknamed Boston and Philadelphia. The show was called a "spectacular" and the producers, CBS, and Rodgers and Hammerstein, wanted a fully integrated approach to the costumes and the sets. Bill and Jean Eckart were a natural choice for the assignment for a number of reasons: they had worked in live TV, they knew the limitations of the medium, and they were designers of costume as well as sets. Based on their previous experience in television, Bill and Jean were eager to avoid the kind of last minute rush that marred so many small screen efforts. The work the Eckarts had done on *The Golden Apple* and *Li'l Abner* had shown they had the imagination to create light, whimsical shows, and Rodgers in particular wanted a fairy tale without evil, which would stress comedy.

They completed the complex set before the cast or the technical crew ever moved into the theatre.

The twenty-one-year-old star Julie Andrews was the production's reason for being. As Richard Rodgers later wrote in his autobiography, *Musical Stages*, "There wasn't a composer or lyricist who didn't start dreaming of songs for her to sing or roles for her to play . . . Casting (Andrews) as Cinderella was like casting Ethel Merman as Annie Oakley. It was right from the start."

NO APOLOGIES—IT'S A MUSICAL

A STEEP AND TREACH-EROUS STAIRCASE WAS CREATED SEEMINGLY TO TEST CINDERELLA'S BALANCING ACT WITH A PILE OF PACKAGES. FROM THE TOP OF THE STAIRS, THE HERALD ANNOUNCED THE BALL WHILE THE TOWN'S PEOPLE ARRANGED THEMSELVES IN A VER-TICAL LINE. THE SCENE PROVIDED A PLACE TO DISPLAY THE FULL RANGE OF OCCUPA-TIONS AND CLASSES OF THE FAIRY TALE KING-DOM'S POPULACE. BILL AND JEAN STOCKED THE FLOWER MARKET WITH OVER 800 BLOSSOMS.

REHEARSAL PHOTO, "THE PRINCE IS HAVING A BALL" (EC)

Both Rodgers and Hammerstein saw *Cinderella* as an opportunity for Broadway talent to get national recognition, and the cast included some of the brightest stars in the American theatre, both in front of and behind the cameras. Ralph Nelson, the Emmy Award-winning director of *Requiem for a Heavyweight*, had worked with Rodgers and Hammerstein as a production assistant on *Oklahoma!* and *Carousel*. He was signed on to direct. Howard Lindsay and Dorothy Stickney were cast as the King and Queen, having been established as the quintessential Father and Mother from *Life with Father*, the longest-running straight play in Broadway history. The stepfamily would have Ilka Chase as the Mother, and Kaye Ballard and Alice Ghostley as the stepsisters. Richard Rodgers wanted Vic Damone, a popular crooner, for the part of Prince Charming, but Ralph Nelson vetoed him as not having the "regal" look (too short) to play opposite the five-foot-eight inch Julie Andrews. On the first day of rehearsals, because of Andrews' height, all men under six feet were eliminated from the cast. The tall tenor, Jon Cypher, was selected by the CBS casting office. The big contention was over who would play the Fairy Godmother. Richard Lewine, the CBS producer, wanted Mildred Natwick for the role, but Rodgers had his heart set on Edie Adams. Rodgers felt he had discovered Adams years before at an open audition but he couldn't find the appropriate vehicle for her. By 1957, she had won a Tony for *Li'l Abner,* and he was determined

HERALD

NUN

STREET PEASANT

FLOWER GIRL

APPLE CART MAN

STREET PEASANT

VAGABOND

EGG LADY

JULIE ANDREWS (CINDERELLA) IN THE OPENING SEQUENCE WEARING THE COSTUME
SKETCHED AT RIGHT (EC)

BILL AND JEAN LOWERED THE PACKAGES ELIMINATING THE SIGHT GAG WHILE THE
STREET TOOK ON AN ANIMATED FESTIVE QUALITY WITH THE SONG "THE PRINCE IS
GIVING A BALL." LITTLE CHILDREN DANCED AROUND CINDERELLA AND TOWNS
PEOPLE CELEBRATED. (EC)

she would be his glamorous Fairy Godmother. Nelson objected on the grounds that the Fairy Godmother should be old, to which Rodgers replied, "If she has magical powers, why couldn't she make herself beautiful?" Rodgers signed Edie Adams before Nelson could fly in from the Coast. Since both Andrews and Adams had starring roles on Broadway at the time, Adams in *Li'l Abner* and Julie Andrews as Eliza Doolittle in *My Fair Lady*, full-run-throughs of the show could only be rehearsed on Sundays in New York City.

There was one hitch: CBS didn't have a large stage available in New York City. They had moved their production facility to Los Angeles. All they had in New York was a converted theatre on 81st Street and Broadway. It turned out to be the smallest network color television studio in the country. What the facility lacked in floor space, though, it made up for in height, leaving Bill and Jean with the job of devising a vertical scheme for the sets. They had to find and create room for: a palace, a ballroom, a street scene, the interior of Cinderella's home, a

EVIL TO COMEDY

TWO FULL RUN-THROUGHS WERE FILMED IN PART TO SERVE AS BACK UP SHOULD DISASTER STRIKE DURING THE LIVE BROADCAST. AFTER WATCHING THE KINESCOPES, HAMMERSTEIN DECIDED TO ADD A NEW NUMBER FOR THE STEPSISTERS. HE TOOK THE MUSIC RODGERS HAD WRITTEN FOR THE ORIGINAL OPENING. THE "WHERE IS CINDERELLA" MARCH BECAME "THE STEPSISTERS LAMENT" AND WAS USED TO ADD HUMOR TO THE HALF-HOUR-LONG ROMANTIC BALLROOM SCENE.

ILKA CHASE (STEPMOTHER), FOLLOWED BY KAYE BALLARD (STEPSISTER PORTIA), AND FOLLOWED BY ALICE GHOSTLEY (STEPSISTER JOY), WEAR ECCENTRIC MILLINERY AS THEY ENTER ON THE GENTLY CURVING TOWN SQUARE STAIRCASE. (EC)

palace garden, as well as a limbo area for isolated shots, not to mention a space for a thirty-three-piece orchestra. Not only would the sets be narrow and of necessity laced with spiral staircases, but because of the verticality of the space the traditional fairy tale gowns would have to be rethought in favor of high-waisted Empire silhouettes. The vertical look had to be maintained in all aspects of the design.

CBS compensated for the size of the studio with the size of the budget—$385,000, an astounding amount in 1957 for ninety minutes of television. Not only were Rodgers and Hammerstein paid as creators and producers but the budget also covered fifty-six actors, forty-four production technicians, thirty-six stage hands, thirty-four musicians, eleven musical numbers orchestrated by Robert Russell Bennett, a waltz ballet choreographed by Jonathan Lucas (*The Golden Apple*), three weeks in CBS's Studio 81, four television cameras (one of which flew), two mobile microphone booms, eight hanging mikes, a mile and a half of cable, six dozen huge flood lights plus 115 costumes, and six full sets designed by William and Jean Eckart.

The opening of the show originally followed the traditional story of Cinderella's servitude to her oppressive stepfamily. The stepmother and step-sisters berated Cinderella as they walked across the town after a shopping trip. An attempt to liven up the browbeating by turning the sisters into buffoons while Cinderella balanced a huge load of packages didn't work. After seeing this

FROM THE OPENING SEQUENCE OF *CINDERELLA*, THE STEPFAMILY'S STREET COSTUMES. ABOVE LEFT: STEPSISTER JOY, CENTER: STEPSISTER PORTIA, AND RIGHT: STEPMOTHER. (EC)

"A LOVELY NIGHT."
LEFT TO RIGHT:
ALICE GHOSTLEY
(JOY), KAYE BALLARD
(PORTIA), JULIE
ANDREWS
(CINDERELLA) AND
ILKA CHASE
(STEPMOTHER), THE
MORNING AFTER
THE BALL. (EC)

COSTUMES FOR THE STEPFAMILY IN THREE DIFFERENT SCENES. LEFT TO RIGHT: STEP-
MOTHER, SISTER PORTIA, AND SISTER JOY. TOP ROW—THE BALL; MIDDLE ROW—THE
MORNING AFTER; AND BOTTOM ROW—THE WEDDING. (EC)

approach played out in the first filmed rehearsal, Rodgers and Hammerstein made a major decision: they shifted "The Prince is Giving a Ball" from the third scene of the show to the first. When the script was first conceived, they had wanted to begin as if it were a fairy tale and not open with a big musical number, but once the play was mounted, it became clear that the opener had to be a musical number. "Up until then," Bill said, "everyone thought they were creating a fairy tale with songs, but after they moved 'The Prince is Giving a Ball' to the top, *Cinderella* became a true musical."

As costume designers, the Eckarts took advantage of the stepfamily's first entrance to make a comedic fashion commentary for grown-ups, not just a series of amusing costumes for children. Their vision took in the entire production, which they decided should have a "Never Never Land" storybook appeal without resembling either Disney or the illustrated Brothers Grimm.

In keeping with Rodgers and Hammerstein's decision not to modernize the story for psychological significance and to make the villainous characters comedic, the Eckarts created a period style of clothes for the stepfamily, which were take-offs on some of the latest couture creations but which were also plausible as correct period clothing. They played these creations off the more traditional period costumes they created for the royal family,

COMEDIC CUTAWAYS: "THE PRINCE IS GIVING A BALL"

A SIGHT GAG, A GIRL GETTING DRESSED FOR THE BALL (EC)

WINE STEWARD AND CHEF—THE PAIR APPEARED SAMPLING A ROASTING PIG (EC)

COMMENTARY: A GIRL IRONING AND NO LONGER ELIGIBLE TO ATTEND INTERJECTS "I WISH I HADN'T MARRIED SAM." (EC)

BILL AND JEAN HAD WANTED "WHISTLER'S MOTHER" TO APPEAR IN A CUT-AWAY SHOT DURING "THE PRINCE IS GIVING A BALL." IT WAS ANOTHER ONE OF THEIR MODERN ART SIGHT GAGS. A HEADSHOT WAS RETAINED, BUT THE FULL FIGURE SHOT WAS OMITTED FROM THE BROADCAST. (EC)

townspeople, and the other members of the kingdom. "The Eckarts had a marvelous time devising outrageous costumes for my stepfamily," Julie Andrews remembers. "My sisters (Kaye Ballard and Alice Ghostley) were early fashion victims. Ilka Chase as my stepmother was truly in a world of her own wearing a hat that looked like a lampshade and which bobbed up and down as she walked. It was great visual comedy." According to *Women's Wear Daily*, the production featured, "The funniest hats ever assembled for stage, screen or a women's club tea party."

The technical constraints of live television were tremendous and to vary the look of the show as well as to buy time, a number of isolated (reaction) shots of unspecified characters were added to the script. These small vignettes were used to cover costume changes, camera resets, lighting changes, and general cast movement. The cutaways also became comic comments on age, social position, vanity, and taste.

The Eckarts' sets also struck a middle ground between reality and fantasy. Cinderella's house was imbued with a quality of hominess. Although she was at the mercy of her step relations, Cinderella still had her own little place by the fire where she could dream. The Eckarts designed a fireplace that was accessible to cameras so that the television audience could observe her in her reveries. They also designed windows that automatically sprang open. The Eckarts' springing mechanism popped the windows open as soon as Cinderella closed them, and she was constantly ordered by her stepfamily to close the windows. The Eckarts windows helped show the futility of Cinderella's existence as well as her subservience. Only when Cinderella was alone did the windows behave. Animating the set to reflect Cinderella's plight made it seem as if the house itself, and by extension, the world at large, were protesting the injustice of her condition. It was one of the few planned special effects that worked.

CINDERELLA'S CORNER SHOWING THE FIREPLACE AND THE CURVED STAIRWAY (EC)

Other special effects planned for the broadcast were more problematic. The Fairy Godmother originally entered with a magical broom. The Eckarts had equipped the broom with flashing electric lights, but the television camera made the lights appear as if the broom were on fire. With time for experimentation unavailable, the broom was cut and replaced by a superimposed shot of a sparkler.

The script also called for the Fairy Godmother to appear outside Cinderella's window as if by magic but the blue screen matting flared around the edges making the Fairy Godmother's form seem to peel and flicker in both color and black and white. Instead of this effect, Cinderella exited to the street to greet her Fairy Godmother and, while out of sight of the camera, Edie Adams scooted around the edge of the set. The low-tech substitution made it look as if the Fairy Godmother appeared inside the house by magic, surprising Cinderella.

The costume change, which turned Cinderella, the scullery maid, into Cinderella, the belle of the ball, was another bit of magic that proved difficult to execute for live television. As Jean described it, "Julie goes to the window; looks out at the pumpkin. Then the viewing audience saw a coach, and in the next shot Cinderella had to be ready for the ball. Since this was live, there was no time to get Julie into a dressing room and changed into her ball-gown. We had her stand right at the window and dressed her on the set. We improvised a cloak to cover the fact that she had not yet changed her costume."

JULIES ANDREWS (CINDERELLA)—THE ECKARTS POSITIONED A CAMERA TO SHOOT THROUGH THE FIREPLACE. (BILLY ROSE THEATRE COLLECTION NYPL)

MAGICAL CHANGES "IMPOSSIBLE"

FAIRY GODMOTHER'S FIRST COSTUME, ENTERING WITH THE ELECTRIFIED MAGIC BROOM (WHICH REALLY WAS "IMPOSSIBLE") AND HAD TO BE CUT. ALTHOUGH RODGERS WANTED A CONTEMPORARY FAIRY GODMOTHER, AFTER VIEWING REHEARSALS, DECISIONS WERE MADE TO CHANGE ADAMS' COSTUME AND DELIVERY TO A MORE TRADITIONAL FAIRY GODMOTHER AND AWAY FROM A JOAN BLONDELL LOOK ALIKE. (EC)

THE ECKARTS GAVE SEXY EDIE ADAMS A BILLOWY COSTUME OF GOLD CHIFFON FOR THE BALL. (EC)

FOOTMAN FOR MAGIC COACH, ONCE A RAT.

THE FIRST CLOAK DESIGNED TO COVER CINDERELLA'S CHANGE INTO HER BALL GOWN DIDN'T WORK. THE CHIFFON FABRIC WILTED UNDER THE INTENSE LIGHTS AND LOOKED LIKE DRAPERY.

"I had a very quick change," Julie Andrews said, "when my Fairy Godmother makes it possible for me to go to the ball. Since this was a live broadcast, I had to do the change on stage. I can still remember the scary excitement as the TV camera panned up from my feet while the hairdresser was restyling my hair and placing a tiara in it. There really was no room for error."

Most of the Eckarts' time and effort were devoted to costumes. Because of a shortened pre-production schedule, the costume fittings for the production were done on schedules so precise that the singers, dancers, and principals followed each other at five-minute intervals. Mme. Karinska coordinated the staffs of three costume houses to accomplish the execution of the entire wardrobe, which included satins, Japanese silks, ermines, gold braid, jeweled trimmings, and plumes—all in nine days.

"The only other problem we had was Jonathan Lucas' choreography," Bill said. "He had planned ballet lifts in the waltz sequence, which required a fitted bodice for the dancers. However, we had designed Empire clothes for the women. When we got to the first rehearsal, Mme. Karinska turned to Jean and said very loudly in her thick Russian accent, 'This choreographer, how could he do that with these kind costumes?' We couldn't change the costumes at that point, but somehow the dancers made the lifts work without having the girls slide out of their dresses."

BILL AND JEAN WERE AWARE OF THE TECHNICAL LIMITATIONS OF 1950s TELEVISION. THE FIRST COLOR CAMERAS LACKED SENSITIVITY TO LIGHT AND COLOR. TELEVISION SCREENS WERE SMALL AND EVEN THOUGH THE SHOW WAS BROADCAST IN COLOR (AS FAR WEST AS CHICAGO), MOST PEOPLE WATCHED IN BLACK AND WHITE. THE HEAVY ROYAL FABRICS USUALLY USED IN FAIRY TALES WOULD HAVE BEEN SEEN AS DARK GRAY OR BLACK. CUT BROCADES, DEEP PURPLES, AND VELVETS ALL ABSORB LIGHT AND OBSCURE DEFINITION OF LINES. WITH THE LOW-RESOLUTION TELEVISION OF THE TIME, THE SHOW WOULD HAVE BEEN MURKY AND DEPRESSING. "BRIGHT COLOR LOOKED HORRIBLE IN EARLY COLOR TEL-EVISION," BILL SAID. "GRAY, BLACK, AND WHITE LOOKED FABULOUS. WE MADE THE COSTUMES IN A MUTED PALETTE OF GRAYS AND PASTELS, WHICH SHOWED FLESH TONES BETTER ON TV. THEN WE ADDED TOUCHES OF BRILLIANT COLOR. MANY OF THE LADIES' COSTUMES WERE DONE IN TRANSPARENT FAB-RICS, ONE COLOR OVER ANOTHER, TO CREATE SHIFTING COLORS AND SHIMMERING HIGHLIGHTS." THE RESULT WAS A PRODUCTION WITH A DREAM-LIKE QUALITY.

THE ECKARTS REDESIGNED A PINK SATIN CLOAK TO HIDE THE FACT THAT JULIE ANDREWS DIDN'T HAVE TIME TO CHANGE INTO HER BALL DRESS. (EC)

REHEARSAL SHOWING GOTHIC ARCHES AND PALACE STAIRWAY—IN THE FOREGROUND JEAN ECKART CONFERS WITH PRODUCER RICHARD LEWINE. (EC)

EARLY SKETCH OF THE BALLROOM SHOWING CINDERELLA CENTER—IN THE ORIGINAL ECKART DESIGN FOR THE BALLROOM, THERE WERE THIRTY COLUMNS. SEVERAL COLUMNS HAD TO BE REMOVED TO PERMIT ENOUGH ROOM FOR THE DANCERS AT THE BALL. (EC)

DREAMY COSTUMES FOR A TELEVISION BALL

TO ASSURE THE CONNECTION BETWEEN ANDREWS' GOWN AND HER SURROUNDINGS, THE ECKARTS HUNG 500 YARDS OF LAVENDER CHIFFON AROUND THE BALLROOM. THE CHIFFON WAS COMPLIMENTED BY THE SPIDERY GOTHIC DESIGN, WHICH GAVE THE SHOW LIGHTNESS AND EMPHASIZED VERTICALITY RATHER THAN DEPTH. LAYERING THE CUT-OUT FORMS ONE UPON THE OTHER SUGGESTED RECEDING PLANES AND CREATED DEPTH.

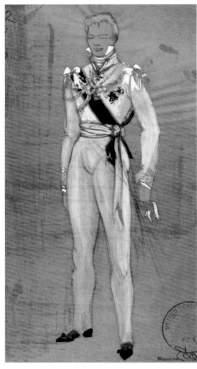

HOWARD LINDSAY AND DOROTHY STICKNEY, IN REAL LIFE MR. AND MRS. HOWARD LINDSAY, WERE THE KING AND THE QUEEN. (EC)

PRINCE CHARMING'S FULL DRESS UNIFORM

DANCERS AT THE BALL (EC)

CINDERELLA'S BALLGOWN—"MY WHITE EMPIRE BALL GOWN," JULIE ANDREWS SAID, "HAD A DREAMY QUALITY. THE LINE WAS CLASSIC AND SIMPLE, AND IT WAS MADE OF CREAMY WHITE CHIFFON, A FABRIC THE ECKARTS USED LIBERALLY THROUGHOUT THE PRODUCTION." (EC)

"TEN MINUTES AGO," THE WALTZ AT THE BALL. IN BALCONY: HOWARD LINDSAY (KING) AND DOROTHY STICKNEY (QUEEN) FOREGROUND: JULIE ANDREWS (CINDERELLA) AND JON CYPHER (PRINCE CHARMING) AT BACK: KAYE BALLARD (PORTIA), ILKA CHASE (STEPMOTHER) AND ALICE GHOSTLEY (JOY) (CBS PHOTO ARCHIVE)

SKETCH OF A FLOWER GIRL'S COSTUME FOR THE BRIDAL FINALE—THE FLOWER GIRL WAS NECESSARY TO PREVENT THE TRAIN OF ANDREWS' DRESS FROM CATCHING ON THE STAIRCASE. (EC)

Fate of the Show

Rodgers and Hammerstein's *Cinderella* was a tremendous success. Two hundred and forty-five stations carried the telecast, the largest number ever to carry a live television show. Ratings benefited from an extensive pre-production publicity drive orchestrated by sponsor Pepsi Cola in which there were *Cinderella* contests and give-aways. An estimated audience of 107 million watched the show, enough people to fill a Broadway theatre seven days a week for 165 years. At the time, the ratings were a network record. The broadcast proved that CBS could compete with NBC, which had pioneered color television. Julie Andrews received her first big national audience and won an Emmy (1958) for the Best Single Performance Lead or Support.

The reviews for *Cinderella* were outstanding. *The Chicago Tribune* summed up what critics all across the country wrote, "The lavish costumes, the fabulous scenery . . . (were) dazzling . . . making it TV's most expensive and wonderfully colorful show to date." *Women's Wear* headlined, "Chiffon for *Cinderella*" and ran a line drawing of Andrews in her ball gown. For those who cared to notice, there were nearly five hundred yards of the filmy lavender fabric hung about the ballroom as well. John Crosby in the *Herald Tribune* noted, "The Eckarts' soft gray and pastel colors were stunning." The Rodgers and Hammerstein songs were judged "just right" for Andrews' clear-as-a-bell delivery. Ethan Mordden describes it as Rodgers' "most infectious score." "Do I Love You?" "In My Own Little Corner," and the waltz "Ten Minutes Ago" were recorded by popular singers such as Vic Damone and Peggy King and were promptly picked up by disc jockeys across the country.

A young Tony Walton, later the designer of *Pippin* (1972) and *The Will Rogers Follies* (1991), was employed by Rodgers and Hammerstein to do caricatures of the company. As a British subject, he did not have an American union card and expressed his frustration to Bill and Jean. They volunteered to help him prepare for the union examination by lending him drawings of their work. "I studied the Eckarts' drawing to try to teach myself American drafting techniques," Walton said. "It was a revelation as to the delicacy and imagination they brought to their design and drafting. My strongest memory of *Cinderella* is how pretty it was in color."

Cinderella's popularity continues. In 1997, ABC broadcast a Disney production starring: Brandy, Whitney Houston, Whoopi Goldberg, Bernadette Peters, and Jason Alexander, which retained a few elements of the Eckarts' humorous approach to costuming. But like its immediate predecessor, the CBS television revival of 1965 starring Lesley Ann Warren, it lacked the Eckarts' sophisticated adult approach. The designs seemed to retread the clichés of traditional children's fairy tales. The Rodgers and Hammerstein organization expanded the show to create a theatrical property, a version of which recently toured with Eartha Kitt as the Fairy Godmother, and the Rodgers and Hammerstein Library records at least 250 productions of the show annually in the United States. After many years, the original kinescope of *Cinderella* is now available on home video.

ONCE IT WAS CLEAR THAT CINDERELLA HAS HER PRINCE, THE STEP-FAMILY, LED BY THE STEPMOTHER, DO AN ABRUPT ABOUT FACE AND BECOME CINDERELLA'S MOST FERVENT SUPPORTERS. THE ECKARTS' COSTUMES FOR THE FAMILY BECAME MORE RESTRAINED AND TASTEFUL. HOWEVER, IN THE WEDDING SCENE, ADDED AS A KIND OF CURTAIN CALL, BILL AND JEAN COULD NOT RESIST GIVING THE STEPMOTHER A FEELING OF BEING "NOUVEAU RICHE" CHIC BY CROWNING HER WITH A BOUFFANT TURBAN AND PLUME AND DECKING HER NECK WITH A FOUR-TIER PEARL NECKLACE.

REHEARSAL PHOTO OF JULIE ANDREWS (CINDERELLA) IN HER WEDDING DRESS—WHEN THE SHOW AIRED, A CAMERA ON A FORK LIFT EQUIPPED WITH A MICROPHONE CAPTURED ANDREWS FROM ABOVE ASCENDING THE STAIRS. SIMILAR HIGH VERTICAL SHOT WAS ALSO USED IN "TEN MINUTES AGO." (CBS PHOTO ARCHIVE)

CINDERELLA'S WEDDING DRESS (EC)

DORIS DAY WEARING ONE OF THE MANY PANTS OUTFITS THE ECKARTS DESIGNED FOR HER WITH CO-STAR JOHN RAITT. THOUGH DAY WAS AN OUTSIDER (BEING THE ONLY NON-THEATRE PERSON AND A MAJOR STAR), THE ECKARTS FOUND HER A PLEASURE TO WORK WITH. (PHOTOFEST)

THE SLIGHTLY SCANDALOUS FINAL SCENE OF *THE PAJAMA GAME*, IN WHICH DORIS DAY AND JOHN RAITT SHARE A PAIR OF HEART PATTERNED PAJAMAS. (PHOTOFEST)

Hollywood

No Brass Band

"It was the end of the Big Studios and people were staking out their turf. Everyone was afraid of losing their jobs, so as theatre people from New York we were not greeted by a brass band."
                    William Eckart

The Eckarts would work on two films in Hollywood, both during the late 1950s and both based on hit Broadway musicals. (At the end of the 1960s they'd work on a film shot in New York, *The Night They Raided Minskys*.)

Jerome Ross and Richard Adler's *Damn Yankees* and *The Pajama Game* were done with the same teams behind the camera: George Abbott and Stanley Donen co-directing, Bob Fosse choreographing, Hal Prince, Bobby Griffith, and Freddie Brisson associate producing, and William and Jean Eckart designing costumes. Both movies were based on Broadway hits originally done by George Abbott and featured most of the original Broadway casts. *The Pajama Game* came first and shortly afterwards, *Damn Yankees*. Bill and Jean, avid moviegoers since childhood, eagerly anticipated working in film. They wanted to find new ways of translating an author's words into pictures. Their early days in television had been frustrating because of the primitive quality of the medium and the networks' general lack of interest in artistic product.

They hoped when they went to Hollywood it would be different. The experience turned out to be an anti-climax.

The Pajama Game (Warner Bros.)

"We were in New Haven opening the road company of *Damn Yankees*, when Hal Prince and Bobby Griffith asked us to meet Stanley Donen," Bill said. "As much as we wanted to do movies there were plenty of costume designers in Hollywood already. Then they also offered us the unique position of color consultants, which they told us would have more to do with the look of the entire film. We accepted."

"We had expected Hollywood to be the way it was depicted in the movies. At lunch hour, Jean and I trekked over to the Warner Brothers commissary ready to see everyone decked out and in costume, but there was hardly anyone there. They had recently started filming television series and only *Maverick* and *Cheyenne* were shooting on the lot."

SKETCH FOR DORIS DAY COSTUME (EC)

SKETCH FOR DORIS DAY COSTUME (EC)

As co-director, Abbott was coaching the actors in an already established Broadway hit. Abbott's position on the set left Stanley Donen with little to do but stand behind the camera, according to the Eckarts. With the exception of Doris Day, who starred in the film, the entire cast had been imported from New York. Day later complained of feeling like an outsider on the set, but she gave one of the best performances of her musical career. The Eckarts enjoyed designing a casual yet enticing wardrobe for her. "She was a lovely person and very easy to work with," said Jean.

The budget constraints for the entire production were severe. The Warner brothers, with the exception of Jack, had sold their shares in the studio a year earlier. With Jack Warner in charge of production and the company's largest shareholder, the studio would record its first revenue-losing year since 1938.

For the Eckarts, the penny-pinching made designing costumes very frustrating. "We had done a lot of costume sketches for *The Pajama Game* in New York, many of which were for costumes for the chorus," Jean said. "But when we arrived at Warner Brothers they couldn't understand why we wanted to have costumes built. They had intended on pulling the chorus costumes from stock." The Eckarts didn't think that was right. As color consultants, they wanted the whole film to have a particular look. "We thought in theatre terms of an ensemble," Bill said. "That's when we found out in Hollywood designers are only supposed to do the stars. We wouldn't give up. We went over and over our ideas with the head of wardrobe. Begrudgingly, he looked at the sketches and finally agreed that our chorus costumes would have to be built."

Their biggest disappointment was in their job as color consultants. Warners was using a Technicolor process, but the film was printed in Warner Color. "We would get fabrics and have them filmed and then projected but none of the colors turned out to be true. We had very little control," said Bill. "We found out that the lighting conditions made all the difference. You could have the same colors in one shot and they would look one way, and another shot from a different direction would be completely different. Also, in each screening room the color would look different depending on the age of the bulb in the projector. It turned out that being a color consultant was pretty much of a joke." The Eckarts began to realize that the Hollywood they'd dreamed of no longer existed.

Disappointed even years later, Bill said, "I saw a print of the film not long ago, and I did not recognize anything. Everything had turned orange and blue." That was the way with Warner Color. But recently, when the film of *The Pajama Game* was cleaned up and released on videotape and then to DVD, the original colors came through brilliantly and the Eckarts' intensely bright palette lit up the small screen.

What the Eckarts really enjoyed about filming *The Pajama Game* was its exuberant cast, with performers like dancer Carol Haney, who did outstanding work in such numbers as "Steam Heat" and "Once A Year Day." As Jean said, "What I love about dancers is they work so hard, and they're such professionals. They're grateful for anything you as a designer can give them. They're really my favorite people." Carol Haney was quite sick by the time shooting began. "She was diagnosed with diabetes, and she wasn't taking very good care of herself," said Jean, "but she still gave it her all." Bill remembered George Abbott holding Haney up off-camera so they could get finished.

Still, *The Pajama Game* was well received by the critics. William K. Zinsser of the *Herald Tribune* wrote, "It has color… and the costumes are dazzling. You will be amazed to see that pajamas come in such a variety of gaudy patterns." Jean-Luc Goddard, the French

GWEN VERDON RECREATED HER SHOW-STOPPING "WHATEVER LOLA WANTS" IN THE FILM OPPOSITE TEEN IDOL TAB HUNTER. (PHOTOFEST)

"STANLEY DONEN THOUGHT THAT LONG HAIR WAS THE ONLY WAY I COULD LOOK SEXY," GWEN VERDON SAID. "ONLY ON ME IF IT'S JUST A LOT OF HAIR HANGING DOWN AROUND MY SHOULDERS, I LOOK LIKE A MAN IN DRAG."(EC)

director and film critic, wrote glowingly about the film (in Stephen M. Silverman's *Dancing on the Ceiling: Stanley Donen and His Movies*, 1996), "Donen (the film's director) is the master of the musical. *The Pajama Game* exists to prove it." Goddard particularly admired the "Once-a-Year Day" number and marveled how the kaleidoscope of colors contributed to its frenzied tempo.

Damn Yankees (Warner Bros.)

One year and three months after *The Pajama Game* finished shooting, the Eckarts were once again headed to Hollywood with the same creative team behind the cameras. The Eckarts' duties this time had been expanded to include production design (sets) as well as costumes. Knowing they would need to stay for three months, they brought their dogs and rented a house in Toluca Lake. "It was a nice house," Jean said, "except that when we put artichoke leaves down the garbage disposal, they ended up in the washing machine."

The cinema version of *Damn Yankees* would follow the pattern established with *The Pajama Game* except the budget was even tighter as the studio was in worse shape by then. Partly in the interest of cost containment, the entire New York cast was once more assembled with the sole exception of Joe Hardy. "In *The Pajama Game*, Doris Day was brought in. She was box office," Bill said, "but why Tab Hunter for *Damn Yankees*?" Evidently, Stanley Donen opposed giving the role to Hunter and blamed George Abbott for selecting him, but Hunter was a Warner Brothers contract player at the time and the decision to use him was made by Jack Warner (the man responsible for casting Audrey Hepburn instead of Julie Andrews in the film version of *My Fair Lady*).

In Hollywood, singing roles didn't have to be played by singers because post-production could take care of all shortcomings. Although Tab Hunter had recorded a couple hit singles during the 1950s, his pop voice wasn't up to the demands of a Broadway score. Using him meant having to cut several songs from the original production for the movie version. The new song, "There's Something About an Empty Chair," by a solo Adler (Ross had tragically died by then), was not on par with the rest of the score. "Donen said of Hunter, 'He couldn't act, couldn't sing and couldn't dance. He's a triple threat.' But Stanley also didn't want to use Gwen Verdon," Bill said. "He wanted someone more glamorous, like Rita Hayworth. So we were faced with trying to make Gwen Verdon look like Rita Hayworth."

The shooting script contained a scene near the beginning when the character of Lola wakes up in bed and answers the telephone. "Donen insisted Gwen wear a long wig," Bill said. "She looked terrible in it. Gwen had the right to demand that it be re-shot with her short hair. It was the only re-shooting ever done on *Damn Yankees*."

The filming was plagued by the threat of a musicians' and a directors' strike. The picture, therefore, was shot in a near-record forty-three days: forty at the Warner Studio, two days for travel, and one day on location at Griffith Stadium in Washington, D.C.

"The art director on the film was Stanley Fleischer," Bill said, "but he followed our Broadway production very closely. If you look at the locker room, you can see that it was all our ideas even down to using the same colors. For the exteriors, with the exception of the ballpark, we were told to use the backlot. The exterior of Joe and Meg's house was located on a set called 'the mid-western street'. We got to choose which house. There was a scene where Applegate walked up an alley. This was shot on 'the New York street.' The theatre was a pre-existing theatre façade. We did some minor decoration on it. Applegate's bedroom was a redecorated standing set. We used a photomural of Washington, D.C. in the window and added some plaster cast decorations. Even the molds we used for the decorations were pre-existing molds that Warner Brothers owned. We got to choose the ones we liked. I think the word that best describes what we achieved is serendipitous." The budget crunching at Warners made it impossible for the Eckarts to open up the play the way they had in the "Once A Year Day" number in *The Pajama Game*. Instead the camera work was up-close and tight, which made everything look flat and two-dimensional.

BOB FOSSE AND GWEN VERDON "WHO'S GOT THE PAIN" FROM THE FILM OF *DAMN YANKEES*, PERFORMING THE BEST DANCE DUET FILMED IN THE 1950s. BOB FOSSE AND GWEN VERDON WERE ALREADY ROMANTICALLY INVOLVED WHEN AT THE LAST MINUTE DURING FILMING, HE DECIDED TO PARTNER HER IN THE DANCE. (PHOTOFEST)

They were able to make only a few improvements in the costumes. They had not been happy with Gwen Verdon's vamping outfit on Broadway. During the out-of-town tryouts, they had had to add a strap in the center of the bodice to keep Verdon from popping out periodically during her dance. At Warner Brothers, they got a chance to redesign the bodice so it fit better, and they eliminated the center strap.

There were other costume catastrophes. In the mambo number, the studio refused to pay for a back-up pair of capris, and the dance pants ultimately became a problem. "Whenever Bob and I were back to back and sat down during the dance, the pants split," Gwen Verdon said. "Bill and Jean at one point had to run up to Malibu and get my original pants from the Broadway show." "We had to hold up production," Bill said. "It wound up costing Warner Brothers a bundle."

Damn Yankees came in under budget, a minor Hollywood miracle for a musical, and although it cost more to put in the can than *The Pajama Game,* it didn't do nearly as well at the box office. Warner Brothers, however, still made money.

GWEN VERDON AND RAY WALSTON IN THE WARNER BROTHERS' MOVIE VERSION OF APPLEGATE'S BEDROOM (PHOTOFEST)

The loss of control the Eckarts experienced on their first film was even more trying on *Damn Yankees.* "Stanley Donen was a horrendous creature and very destructive to Bob Fosse," Jean said. "If you look at the 'Shoeless Joe' number, you'll notice that what we called the baseball ballet, Fosse's best work in the stage version, was just hacked up in the final print. The entire number was filmed, but because it was long, someone left big pieces of it on the cutting room floor. The music ends abruptly, they cut away, and then come back, and the music picks up and ends a second time. It makes no sense."

Having helped to create the Broadway hit, the Eckarts' involvement with the show was that much more intense. "The artists are never consulted," Bill said. "You don't find out what happened to your work until you see the film in a theatre."

On top of everything else, watching George Abbott coach Tab Hunter was just too frustrating. Finally, the Eckarts decided it might be better if they were not present. "We wandered off and looked around the lot," Bill said. The only other film being shot at Warner Brothers was *Auntie*

Mame. "We loved Rosalind Russell, whom we knew through her husband Freddie Brisson (Brisson was also associate producing *Damn Yankees*). We went over to the *Auntie Mame* set. Roz had wanted us to be involved with the film. One of Hollywood's grand old men, Orry-Kelly, was designing Roz's clothes. He had worked on Broadway in the early 1920s and then on such films as *Busby Berkeley's 42nd Street*, *Casablanca*, *Now, Voyager*, and *An American in Paris* (one of his two Academy Awards, *Some Like It Hot* was the other). We got to be friendly with him. Harry Stradling, who was the cinematographer for *The Pajama Game*, was working for Morton DaCosta (who was directing Russell in *Auntie Mame*)."

"Bill and I felt more at home on their set. We had no idea then we would wind up designing the Broadway musical *Mame*. It turned out to be great research."

Ironically, the only two films shooting at Warner Brothers, *Damn Yankees* and *Auntie Mame*, had both been hit Broadway plays. Even the screenwriters on *Auntie Mame*, Betty Comden and Adolph Green, were Broadway babies. So, naturally the Eckarts never felt very far away from their old haunts. "Things kept happening in Hollywood which brought us back to thinking about New York," Bill said. Richard Bissell, who had worked on *The Pajama Game* and *Damn Yankees*, had written a novel about his Broadway experiences. It was called *Say, Darling*, and it was turned into a play with music. "There was a character in the play named Snow, a producer, modeled after Hal Prince. Bobby Morse acted the role and made the character incredibly funny by exaggerating all of Hal's idiosyncrasies. Reading the reviews in Hollywood, Hal was fit to be tied. He was carrying on that he could never go back to New York, but, of course, he got over that pretty quickly. You had to look at what Bissell and Morse did as a kind of a left-handed compliment. At any rate, nothing was about to stop Hal Prince. And then, too, we were getting calls for jobs. One call we remember was from the producers of *Bye Bye Birdie*. Michael Stewart (Rubin) was the author of the book. We had done his first musical at Yale. It bothered us to have to say no, but we were unavailable to do *Bye Bye Birdie* because of the filming of *Damn Yankees*. Things like that kept happening, that's how we knew we belonged back in New York."

Damn Yankees was a less successful film than *The Pajama Game*. Newspaper reviews were positive but not enthusiastic. Much of the blame was laid upon Tab Hunter. However, Warner's budget cutting was also a factor. As Gerald Mast wrote (*Can't Help Singin'*, 1987), "The decor of the film is surprisingly flat, which resulted in the film looking more like a filmed stage show than like a film musical."

The Eckarts had come to Hollywood full of anticipation, but when they arrived, they found Hollywood had changed. "It was the end of the Big Studios," Bill said. "And people were staking out their turf. Everyone was afraid of losing their jobs, so as theatre people from New York, we were not greeted by a brass band." They were daunted by the loss of artistic control. In New York, they were a part of every major creative decision. In Hollywood, they were no more than high paid extras there to fill out the shots.

LIVIN' THE LIFE SHOW CURTAIN ON BURLAP. THE ECKARTS CHOSE THE FABRIC TO CREATE THE RUSTIC LIFE OF MARK TWAIN'S RIVER STORIES. (EC)

"You can have a very successful set that is evocative, but if the play doesn't live up to it, it just doesn't work."

William Eckart

Riding the Broadway Roller Coaster

1957–1959 Youths, The Rebellious Stage

LIVIN' THE LIFE

THE DOCK—SIMPLE, MODEST, AND IMAGINATIVE. MOBILE PIECES FLOWED BACK AND FORTH DURING THE ACTION WITH ALMOST AS MUCH FLUIDITY AS THE DANCERS. (EC)

SKETCH OF HEAVILY ATMOSPHERIC GRAVEYARD (EC)

Tin Pan Alley and its near-neighbor Broadway were already rocking from the explosive gyrations of Elvis Presley and the new generation of popular music called rock and roll. In January 1956, RCA released Elvis' "Heartbreak Hotel," which skyrocketed to the top of the charts paving the way towards his first movie, *Love Me Tender*, premiering in the fall of the same year. By January of 1957, the King had made his third and final appearance on the *Ed Sullivan Show,* making it clear that rock and roll and all it stood for was the dominant force in American popular music. There were still Broadway show tunes on the charts, but they were becoming fewer and fewer as a youth culture led by teenage passions took over the industry. Following the music, stage and film images of the new culture were ones of rebellion and promiscuous sexuality.

Eager to climb on the bandwagon, Broadway producers sought after projects in which the new culture could show its impact. *West Side Story* is perhaps the best known example of this growing trend. Before 1957, it would have been an impossible show. Cheryl Crawford, who had optioned it initially, let it go because she did not feel it could find an audience. Suddenly, a musical about Huck Finn and his gang seemed worthy of production, if for no other reason than it lent credence to the idea that youthful rebellion had a historical precedent.

Livin' the Life, an adaptation of Mark Twain's Mississippi River stories, by Dale Wasserman (book) and Bruce Geller (lyrics) was the Eckarts' next project. Although the play never transferred to Broadway, it helped to launch the careers of Wasserman (who would go on to do the book for *Man of La Mancha*) and Geller (who would become the producer of the TV series, *Mission: Impossible*).

"We had one gimmick in the show that Marshall Barer (lyricist for *Once Upon a Mattress*) always liked to tell about," Bill smiled. "We had to fly a tree out in full view of the audience in order to set up the next scene. We decided to make roots out of rope, which were hidden behind the tree on the floor during the scene. When the tree flew out, the roots hung down. The effect was like a real tree being uprooted by the hand of God. It had nothing to do with the show, but it got a nice laugh and kept people amused during a dull set change."

COPPER AND BRASS OLD POLICE HEADQUARTERS AT 240 CENTRE STREET. "WE CHOSE TO SHOW THE HEADQUARTERS WITH SCAFFOLDING AND IN THE PROCESS OF RECEIVING A NEW PAINT JOB," JEAN SAID. (EC)

Livin' the Life opened April 27, 1957. The reviews were lackluster for the show, but there were raves for the production. Walter Kerr in the *Herald Tribune* wrote, "the rumor that Mark Twain's Mississippi River stories had been turned into a musical comedy was, like certain other rumors about Mr. Twain, exaggerated. No one, with the possible exception of designers William and Jean Eckart, has come even close...." Brooks Atkinson in *The New York Times* wrote, "Working on an austere budget, the designers have accomplished more than the writers. William and Jean Eckart have provided scenery that catches the pleasant simplicity of the town, the fecundity of the river flora, and the black mystery of the caves." Unfortunately, an audience doesn't leave a theatre humming the scenery. It closed after its Phoenix run of twenty-five performances.

ONE OF THE FUNNIEST BITS IN THE SHOW WAS NANCY WALKER DIRECTING TRAFFIC IN THE HOLLAND TUNNEL, WHICH PROMPTED JOHN CHAPMAN OF THE *DAILY NEWS*, "NOTHING LIKE IT SINCE W.C. FIELDS HAD A GRIM TUSSLE WITH A CELLO." (EC)

NEW YORK CONSTANTLY UNDER CONSTRUCTION—NOTE THE TYPICAL BARRIER WITH PORTHOLES FOR SIDEWALK SUPERINTENDENTS. (EC)

Copper and Brass

Copper and Brass was an old-fashioned star vehicle created for Nancy Walker by her husband David Craig, vocal coach and lyricist. Walker was then in a transitional phase of her long career which spanned fifty years on stage, screen, and television (today, she is best known for television appearances as Rhoda's mother on *Rhoda* and the "quicker-picker-upper" paper towel commercials). She had always been typecast as a rough-and-ready comedienne and she felt she desperately needed a makeover role, and this was her chance to play a romantic lead. Cast as a rookie cop (the *Copper* of the title), she falls in love with Dick Williams, a musician (the *Brass* of the title), but her persona, like TV's Lucille Ball (*I Love Lucy*), had a knack for finding trouble. The romantic plot was overshadowed by broad comic episodes of Walker as O'Shea in distress.

When the Eckarts were asked to design *Copper and Brass*, set in New York City, they were enthusiastic. The most enticing aspect of the show for Bill and Jean was recreating colorful locations from all over the metropolitan area: the Holland Tunnel, the Staten Island Ferry, an underground rock club, and police headquarters. Their take on the City was that like Nancy Walker, it too was involved in a makeover. "We had done a number of shows set in New York," Jean said, "and I can't remember which one of us came up with the notion that the City is always in the process of being rebuilt, but that became our springboard."

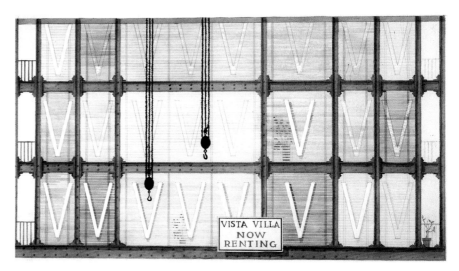

VISTA VILLA BACKDROP—A NEW BUILDING RISES IN THE BAUHAUS STYLE MADE POPULAR BY MIËS VAN DER ROHE. (COLLECTION OF THE MCNAY ART MUSEUM, GIFT OF ROBERT L. B. TOBIN)

The Eckarts' concept—that old forms were constantly giving way to new ones—would add a note of visual novelty. It was a clever idea but one that went unexploited.

For the producers there was nothing timely or compelling about this simple story. Sensing the uncertainty of a novice playwright, they got to work. "Draft number one," book writer Ellen Violett said, "did not have juvenile delinquents in it. The story was about the junior league, but the producers were adamant, 'It is too waspy … There ought to be a gang.' 'What about *West Side Story*?' I said, knowing that show was rehearsing out-of-town. They replied, 'Oh, it'll never come in.' Well, not only did it come in, but when we arrived in Philadelphia for our try-out, we discovered *West Side Story* (which preceded us at the same the-atre) had even taken the floor with them."

In Philadelphia, the creative floor of *Copper and Brass* fell out as well: the costar, the director, and the choreographer were replaced. Bob Fosse was brought in to restage, but it wasn't enough. Opening in New York less than three weeks after *West Side Story*, *Copper and Brass* seemed to tread lightly upon a subject which the Bernstein/Sondheim/Laurents musical had made hallow.

The critical onslaught against *Copper and Brass* was devastating, although the Eckarts' work was praised. "William and Jean Eckarts' settings are expansive and devilishly clever," wrote John Chapman in the *Daily News*, "as they picture today's Manhattan, from its cellar dives and police stations to its new half-pint-size apartments and its buildings under construction." "The physical production is luxurious and colorful, and flexible as well," wrote Henry Murdock in the *Philadelphia Inquirer*. "William and Jean Eckart share the credit for what is, at the moment, the most certain of the show's attributes." *Cue* magazine summarized the majority opinion, "funny-woman Walker needs more than the gifted Eckarts." *Copper and Brass* melted away after only thirty-six performances.

TV Personalities . . . Never

At Dorothy and Richard Rodgers' Annual Christmas Party, the Eckarts met Lee Guber (who later produced *Happiest Girl in the World*) and his wife, Barbara Walters, hostess on NBC's *Today* show. "We had no idea who she was because we never watched television, but when someone at the party mentioned Dave Garroway, we made the connection. We were to do a segment for Garroway with a Sunday show called *Wide Wide World* in March 1958. Our part was entitled 'American Theatre '58' with Helen Hayes, Robert Preston, Arthur Laurents, Peter Ustinov, and Melvyn Douglas. There were actors, playwrights, and composers—one of each. Jean and I represented designers. We went to Sardi's on a Sunday and sat around a table. Charles Van Doren hosted the segment that led into ours which originated on the campus of Northwestern University. He was then a celebrity having won $129,000 on the TV game show *Twenty-One*. Garroway, who anchored the show, greeted us on a monitor. The whole thing was supposed to look spontaneous, but of course, it wasn't. We had all been interviewed in advance from which they had prepared a written script which we then read off the teleprompter." Bill appeared nervous and Jean, as usual, calm. They stressed training, versatility, and perseverance.

In less than a year, Van Doren's status as a national icon would topple when a congressional investigation revealed that the quiz shows were also scripted. In fact, they were rigged. It was a part of that quintessential American saga which might be entitled lost innocence. "It would have been nice to think that we were picked simply on the basis of our merit, but Robert Whitehead who produced the segment for

NANCY WALKER (OFFICER O'SHEA) PROVES SHE CAN SHAME A GANG OF REBELLIOUS TEENS COMICALLY IMPROVING HER OWN FORM OF ROCK AND ROLL. (EC)

NBC, selected us because we were then being considered to design a show he was to produce on Broadway called *Goldilocks* which starred Don Ameche and Elaine Stritch. The book was by Walter and Jean Kerr whom we admired greatly. But, in the end, we turned it down. The book kidded old-fashioned movies, musical comedies, and dance fads. It was weak. The critics agreed. That was one choice we were right about."

The Body Beautiful

The Eckarts, who had designed *Damn Yankees*, the first successful sports musical in fifty years, were a natural choice for the high-spirited, noisy tuner called *The Body Beautiful*. What was *The Body Beautiful?* For starters, a "misnomer," since the subject of the play was about prizefighting, a sport where beautiful bodies were hardly the primary attraction. The idea for *The Body Beautiful* originated with librettists Joseph Stein and Will Glickman. The show, although not a hit, has historical significance because of the people associated with it. It was the first collaboration of the composer and lyricist team of Jerry Bock and Sheldon Harnick. (Sheldon Harnick's account of *The Body Beautiful* appears in his Preface to this volume.) *The Body Beautiful* would be the first rung on a ladder that would eventually lead Bock and Harnick to create *Fiorello! Tenderloin, She Loves Me,* and *Fiddler on the Roof*. The creative team also included director George Schaefer (known for his TV films with actresses such as Kate Hepburn, Bette Davis, and Ellen Burstyn) and choreographer Herb Ross (who went on to direct many films including *Pennies from Heaven, The Turning Point, Nijinsky,* and *Steel Magnolias*).

The Eckarts built upon their experience designing *Damn Yankees*, by bringing a series of industrial looking landscapes to life: a gym, an arena, and a playground, all of which had a rugged, masculine quality. Much of the inspiration for their settings came from the linear compositions of American artist Ben Shahn, who imbued his subjects with a strong element of social conscience.

Critical reception for the show was mixed. Since there was a youth gang in this play as well, critics naturally compared the show unfavorably to the hit *West Side Story*. *The Body Beautiful* couldn't secure the box office figures needed to run. The reviews of the sets, however, were all positive. Kerr in the *Herald Tribune* was so impressed by Bill and Jean's boxing arena that he began his Sunday column as an admonishment to designers of musicals to learn from the Eckarts how to embellish a production, not confound it with scenery. In several columns, the operative word to describe the visual impact of the show was "staggering." Even the hard to please Walter Winchell took up the cause and touted the Eckarts' sets in his national column under the guise of what "New Yorkers are talking about." But after a valiant struggle, *The Body Beautiful* was knocked out in sixty performances.

Summer Camp

"That summer we received a phone call from Mary Rodgers (Richard Rodgers' daughter)," Jean said. "We had met Mary a year and a half earlier when we were working on *Cinderella* with Rodgers and Hammerstein. Summer was a time when theatrical projects took shape; Mary invited us up to Camp Tamiment in the Poconos to see her show."

"The Camp was a place for the 'having a wonderful time' crowd," Bill said. "Moss Hart had begun his career there, and it was the setting for Herman Wouk's bestseller *Marjorie Morningstar*. It was the kind of place where an idea for a new production might be born. Mary wanted us to see the one-act musical she and Marshall Barer had written together. It was called *The Princess and the Pea*. We found it very amusing. We did not pursue it at the time, though, because we never had any idea of becoming producers."

THE BODY BEAUTIFUL PLAYGROUND—THE HANGOUT FOR A REBELLIOUS GANG. THE ECKARTS USED A BOLD ORANGE TO ACCENTUATE THE RAWNESS OF THE URBAN LANDSCAPE, GIVING THE PLAYGROUND SET A RUGGED AUTHENTICITY. (EC)

Once back in town the Eckarts did pursue a project Hal Prince had mentioned to them. It was a musical based on the life of Gypsy Rose Lee, entitled *Gypsy*, with lyrics by Stephen Sondheim and a book by Arthur Laurents. In one of their meetings with Laurents, the Eckarts were dismayed to learn that David Merrick was going to produce the show on his own and Prince had withdrawn. The Eckarts would not get to design *Gypsy*.

It was then that George Abbott called. He had a farce in which Elsa Lanchester, the British star of *The Bride of Frankenstein*, would play a moneyed older woman confined to a hospital. It was called *The Soft Touch*. Bill and Jean took it on as their next assignment.

"We were in rehearsal and the show was in the shop being built," Bill said, "when Abbott decided to have a run-through to see how things were shaping up. George insisted that everyone associated with the show attend. After the rehearsal, as was his practice, he solicited opinions from each of us." In the dimly lit auditorium, Abbott listened patiently and dispassionately. As the discussion wound down, Abbott announced he could not see his way clear to spending any more money on *The Soft Touch*. "'When all current obligations are met, any funds remaining will be returned to the investors,' he said. It left us all gasping, but that was it. It wasn't as if we didn't know there were shows that closed in rehearsal, but we just never expected something like that to happen with an Abbott production."

What appealed to the Eckarts in their next show, *Far Away the Trainbirds Cry*, was the director, John Frankenheimer. They knew of his work at CBS. His episode for the TV series *You Are There*, "The Plot Against King Solomon," had caused a stir and Frankenheimer had already taken one of his *Playhouse 90* scripts, *Deal A Blow*, to the big screen as *The Young Stranger* starring, in his first film role, James MacArthur (*Hawaii Five 0*). Frankenheimer would go on to become legendary as the director of such film works as *The Manchurian Candidate, Seconds, 7 Days in May, Ronin*, and others too numerous to mention. But try as they could in 1958, the money just couldn't be raised for *Far Away the Trainbirds Cry*. "We designed the show," Bill said, "and while it was in the shop, we learned that it was not going ahead."

"Then Mary Rodgers invited us to her apartment for dinner," Bill said. "It was six months after we had been to Camp Tamiment. We asked her, 'What's happened to *The Princess and the Pea*?' And Mary said, 'Nothing.' We knew Marshall had written the part of the Princess in the play for Nancy Walker. We had recently done *Copper and Brass* with her so we asked if we could make a few phone calls. We had nothing formal or in writing but we went ahead and called Hambleton and Houghton at The Phoenix. The season before, they had done a revue with Nancy. We said, 'We've got this little musical. Do you want to do it for Nancy?' They thought that was a fine idea. For Jean and me, getting George Abbott to direct was crucial. We set up an audition. George came, listened politely and said, 'Well, it's amusing, but it's only one act, and I don't think you can expand it.' We could tell that he thought it was too campy, but we said, 'If we expand it, and get it to you by such-and-such a date, would you look at it again?' 'Sure,' he said. Honestly, he didn't have much faith in it as a project, but by that time, we did."

THE BODY BEAUTIFUL EXTERIOR OF THE BOXING ARENA—THE ECKARTS USED ORANGE AGAIN TO ACCENTUATE THE MASCULINITY OF THE STRUCTURE. (EC)

A STORYBOOK IN TWO DIMENSIONS

THE SHOW CURTAIN WAS MADE UP OF PANELS HUNG ON ALTERNATING LINES. IT COULD BE BROKEN UP INTO SECTIONS AND EACH SECTION COULD BE USED SEPARATELY OR TOGETHER TO REPRESENT DIFFERENT LOCATIONS. THE PANELS WERE PLACED IN FRONT OF A SERIES OF BACKGROUNDS: A BLACK CURTAIN, A LIGHT CURTAIN, AND A DRAPED CHINA SILK HALF-CURTAIN SO THAT EACH ARRANGEMENT COULD CREATE ANOTHER CASTLE CORRIDOR. THE CURTAIN SERVED AS AN APPROPRIATE INTRODUCTION INTO THE WORLD OF FAIRY TALES. IT USED A COMBINATION OF TAPESTRIES AND HERALDIC SHIELDS, WHICH BILL AND JEAN EXAGGERATED DEPICTING MEDIEVAL STYLE BY BEASTS IN COMIC POSES. THEY COULD ALSO REVERSE THE PANELS SO THE IMAGES LOOKED LIKE PHOTO NEGATIVES, CREATING A MODERN SUBTEXT. THIS VERSATILE SHOW CURTAIN WAS A STYLISH REFINEMENT OF THE OLD-FASHIONED TRAVELER CURTAIN AND SERVED TO HIDE SET CHANGES. (EC)

"We wanted the texture of the show to be flat as if you were looking at an illustration in a children's book come alive."
William Eckart

Once Upon a Mattress

1959 A Children's Book Musical

A MUSICAL FAIRY TALE ABOUT AN OUTLANDISH PRINCESS WHO IS TESTED FOR HER DELICACY BY AN OVERBEARING QUEEN. A SINGLE PEA IS PLACED UNDER THE PRINCESS'S MATTRESS. IF SHE IS ROYALTY, SHE'LL FEEL IT. WITH THE HELP OF THE ENTIRE COURT, THE PRINCESS MANAGES TO WIN THE PRINCE.

CAROL BURNETT (PRINCESS WINIFRED) AND JOE BOVA (PRINCE DAUNTLESS) IN THE STUDY SCENE—THE ECKARTS' FAUX TAPESTRY BACKGROUNDS WERE PAINTED DIMENSIONALLY AND GAVE THE ACTION ON THE STAGE A POP-UP BOOK APPEARANCE. (FRIEDMAN-ABELES, BILLY ROSE THEATRE COLLECTION, NYPL)

DETAIL OF PAINTED FAUX TAPESTRY PANEL (EC)

The Eckarts had unprecedented artistic control over their work in *Once Upon a Mattress*.

"Without really thinking about it, we had become producers," Bill said. Not only did they design the scenery and the costumes, but they collaborated on the script and as producers raised the money for the show as well. In association with The Phoenix Theatre, they even helped to invent the slightly naughty title. "The show was a fairy tale for adults based on *The Princess and the Pea*," Bill said. "We considered other titles, but we never deviated from the idea of keeping the feeling of a children's book alive in the production."

The Eckarts' townhouse in the Washington Mews became the production office for the show. "The writers were Dean Fuller, Mary Rodgers, Marshall Barer, and Jay Thompson," Jean added, "with Bill, Tharon (Musser) and me manning typewriters. The re-writes began. We were scattered all over our townhouse. I'd take scene two, act one and say, 'Who's got scene 3?' and then read through it and say, 'Wait a minute, we've got to fix this here so we can make such and such a transition.' And Tharon, who was the best typist, would be typing away, trying to get it all together. I guess you could say she typed her way into her first musical."

CREATING AN ANTI-CINDERELLA KINGDOM

IN *CINDERELLA*, THE CHIFFON AND TRANSLUCENT MATERIALS GAVE THE WHOLE PRODUCTION A DREAMY QUALITY. THIS HAD AS MUCH TO DO WITH THE CHARACTER OF THE HEROINE AS IT DID WITH THE MAKE-BELIEVE OF THE STORY. IN *ONCE UPON A MATTRESS*, THE FAIRY TALE PRINCESS IS AS TOUGH AS NAILS. THE BACKDROPS EMPHASIZED HER CHARACTER AND ARE UNAPOLOGETICALLY SOLID AND DECORATED WITH GARGOYLES. THE COLORS ARE EARTH TONES AS OPPOSED TO *CINDERELLA'S* ETHEREAL, PASTEL PALETTE. THE *MATTRESS* STORY IS ALSO FULL OF FAIRY TALE REVERSALS: THE QUEEN IS IN CHARGE, THE KING IS SILENT, AND PRINCE DAUNTLESS IS A DUNCE.

THE CASTLE CORRIDOR (EC)

ANOTHER PART OF THE CASTLE (EC)

"We would arrive at 9:00 a.m. at the Eckarts' home," Mary Rodgers recalled, "to be received by three fabulous standard poodles. Then we'd work until 2:00 a.m. the next morning. We worked around the clock for six weeks. Everyone of us had a place to work in the townhouse. We didn't know anything about advances. The Eckarts fed us and took care of us. When the show went into previews, we were summoned to The Phoenix to get our first checks. I was so surprised. I had completely forgotten about royalties or that we were going to be paid for this show."

The expanded script, now called *Once Upon a Mattress*, built up the part of the Princess, making hers the starring role. Her first act entrance, soaking wet from swimming a moat, is trumpeted by an ear-splitting tune humorously entitled, "Shy." This number was followed by a mock sentimental ballad entitled, "The Swamps of Home." There was also a hilarious dance number for the Princess called "The Spanish Panic."

When George Abbott read the new script, he liked the changes. "George agreed to direct the play for $100 per week for rehearsals," Bill said. "This was about enough to cover his cab fares and lunches. He also agreed to become one of our first investors although the investment was made in the name of his grandchildren. Another stipulation he made was that one of us would have to eat lunch with him everyday. We knew that when you lunched with George Abbott, he never offered to pick up the tab. In fact, to make certain everyone knew his preferences, he'd announce to the waiter, 'Separate checks,' which Jean and I thought should have been the title of his autobiography. But on *Mattress*, which was his first Off-Broadway show, he didn't like the idea of having to fend for himself on East 12th Street, which was not an upscale neighborhood."

THE BACKDROP OF THE FIELDS AND CASTLE DIVIDED THE STAGE INTO TWO NATURAL PLAYING AREAS. THE INFLUENCE OF PAINTER GRANT WOOD IS EVIDENT IN THE STYLE OF THE HILLS. IN THE CASTLE PORTION OF THE DROP, PERSPECTIVE WAS ACHIEVED BY CREATING RECEDING, FLAT PLANES. THESE CONTRIBUTED TO THE POP-UP BOOK STYLE OF THE DESIGN ELEMENTS. (EC)

Having Abbott on board was a great relief both artistically and financially. But a few days later, after re-reading the script, Abbott made a startling declaration. He didn't want to direct Nancy Walker. "Abbott said that Nancy was wonderful," Mary Rodgers recalled, "but he would rather not do the show with her because Nancy was already a star. He wanted someone who wasn't known. Abbott suggested we take a vote on it. 'How many people want Nancy Walker? If everyone wants Nancy Walker, then I suppose that's the way it has to be. But I'm not going to like it.' We all knew what that meant. Poor Marshall went crazy. After the meeting, Abbott said, 'Who was that unpleasant person?' Jean told him he was the lyricist. And Abbott said, 'I don't care who he is, I don't want him at meetings.' But Jean handled it. She was good at getting the political thing done."

The Eckarts were stunned. They were also in a bind. They had received the backing of The Phoenix Theatre with the understanding that the star of the new musical would be Nancy Walker. The Phoenix

"WE WANTED TO TAKE THE SHOW A STEP AWAY FROM REALITY, SO THAT THERE WAS NOTHING ORDINARY ABOUT IT," BILL SAID. THE ACTORS, FROM LEFT TO RIGHT: HARRY SNOW (MINSTREL), ANNE JONES (LADY LARKEN), JACK GILFORD (KING), MATT MATTOX (JESTER), HAVE GREATER PRESENCE AND VITALITY IN FRONT OF THE ECKARTS' PAINTED CASTLE BACKDROP. (FRIEDMAN–ABELES, EC)

CUTOUT CONSTRUCTION

CHILDREN'S STORYBOOKS USE A THEME, A PALETTE, AND A DRAWING STYLE TO MAINTAIN A LOOK THROUGHOUT A NARRATIVE. THE ECKARTS' DESIGNS USED INCREMENTAL CHANGES IN THE SETS, COLOR TONES, AND COSTUMES. THE REPETITIVE USE OF ARCHES ON THE PORTICO, WHICH FRAMED THE ENTIRE PLAY, ESTABLISHED A PICTORIAL UNITY.

CASTLE CORRIDOR (EC)

THE THRONE ROOM. THE BANISTERED SMALL PLATFORM AT LEFT SERVED AS AN INTERROGATION CHAMBER. IT WAS ALSO A VISUAL JOKE BORROWED FROM TELEVISION QUIZ SHOWS OF THE 1950s. (EC)

had only agreed to do the show because they thought Walker's name would sell tickets. But Abbott's logic (and muscle) were compelling. According to Bill, Abbott said, "Remember you are putting the show on Off-Broadway. The lead should be someone the audience discovers." Bill and Jean had to take the bad news to Nancy Walker.

"The idea to cast the then-unknown Carol Burnett came from Joe Harris, a theatre manager," Bill said. "Joe had seen Burnett on television and in her nightclub act at the Blue Angel. Carol was getting quite a lot of attention for a piece of special material she performed called, 'I Made a Fool of Myself Over John Foster Dulles.'" (The story of Carol Burnett's casting and subsequent triumph is theatrical legend, which she has described at the beginning of this volume in the Foreword.)

Other casting decisions for the *Mattress* were equally unusual. Jack Gilford, who had refused to talk during the McCarthy era and was blacklisted, was cast in the role of the silent king. Jane White, an African-American actress, was cast against type in the role of Queen Aggravain. "Two people were replaced in rehearsal," Bill said. "One was a tenor named Robert Rounseville. Abbott decided he was too stiff. The role of the Wizard had to be recast as well. Abbott had chosen Jack Goode, an old vaudevillian, but he soon tired of his shtick. There were also problems with the Stage Manager chosen by The Phoenix. His name was George Quick. Unfortunately, he wasn't. A couple of days into rehearsal, Marshall came up with, 'Goode is bad, White is black, Quick is slow, and Rounseville is square.'"

THE PRIMARY COLORS FOR THE SHOW WERE BEIGE, YELLOW, AND BLACK. LEFT TO RIGHT: BOBBY WEIL (WIZARD), JOHN BAYLIS (SIR LUCE), STUART HODES (SIR STUDLEY), JANE WHITE (QUEEN), JOE BOVA (PRINCE DAUNTLESS), WILL LEE (KING), JERRY NEWBY (JESTER), CARLA HUSTON (LADY MERRILL), ANNE JONES (LADY LARKEN), ELLIE ZALON (LADY LUCILLE), HARRY SNOW (MINSTREL). PHOTOGRAPHED AT THE ST. JAMES THEATRE. (ROBERT A. WILSON, BILLY ROSE THEATRE COLLECTION, NYPL)

THE ACTORS CHANGED THE SET

THE ECKARTS DESIGNED A CLEVER COMBINATION SET FOR THE THE BEDCHAMBER AND THE BREAKFAST ROOM.
FOR THE FINAL SCENE OF THE SHOW, THE ACTORS MADE A QUICK CHANGEOVER IN FRONT OF THE AUDIENCE.
THE BED SLID OUT LIKE A DRAWER AND WAS PIVOTED 180 DEGREES. THE HEAD OF THE BED BECAME THE CHAIR-
BACKS FOR THE THRONES WHILE DIMENSIONALLY PAINTED DRAPES ON FLAT PANELS WERE FLOWN IN. (EC)

DETAIL OF
MOTIF -
NOT TO
SCALE.

BEDCHAMBER

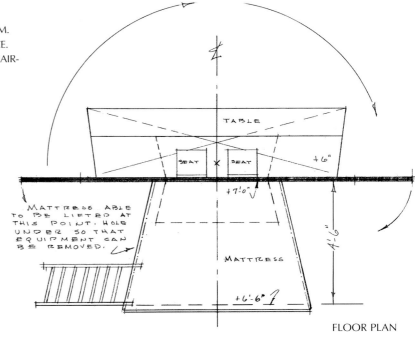

FLOOR PLAN

MATTRESS ABLE
TO BE LIFTED AT
THIS POINT. HOLE
UNDER SO THAT
EQUIPMENT CAN
BE REMOVED.

BREAKFAST
ROOM

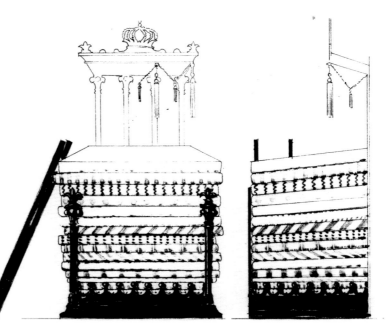

SIDE VIEW OF
MATTRESS

THE NO-REST MATTRESS

THE ECKARTS CONSTRUCTED A STACK OF MATTRESSES IN BEAUTIFUL FEMININE COLORS AND FANCIFUL MATTRESS TICKINGS TO DISGUISE THE BIG SIGHT GAG AT THE END OF THE PLAY. BY MAKING THE BED SO ELEGANT, THEY WERE ABLE TO SURPRISE THE AUDIENCE WHEN THE TOP MATTRESS WAS REMOVED. A TRAPDOOR OPENED AND THE REAL REASON THE PRINCESS COULDN'T SLEEP WAS REVEALED. A SERIES OF POINTED OBJECTS—DEER ANTLERS, PITCH FORKS, ETC.—WERE PULLED OUT FROM INSIDE THE BED.

CAROL BURNETT (PRINCESS WINIFRED) AND GINNY PERLOWIN (THE NIGHTINGALE OF SAMARKAND)—THE SCRIPT CALLED FOR A HUMAN-SIZED BIRDCAGE THAT AN ACTRESS COULD ACTUALLY SIT IN. (FRIEDMAN–ABELES, EC)

THE REVEAL OF THE CONTENTS OF THE MATTRESS

JOE BOVA LEAVES AN EXHAUSTED CAROL BURNETT WHILE THE CHORUS CELEBRATES.

As was his practice, Abbott made a great many changes during rehearsal. It was his idea to begin with the then-popular 1950s format of a television quiz show. "What didn't change was the way we conceived of the show," Bill said. "Since we were involved in the writing of it, and we knew we didn't have a lot of money, we saw to it that it remained a show that could be done with 'close-ins' and 'travelers.' There were no special shifting mechanism, no decks, or winches or anything like that. A scene would play 'in-one' while a change would be accomplished manually upstage behind a traveler. We did make one concession to stage mechanics. We used the fly system." Given the future production history of *Once Upon a Mattress*, the simplicity the Eckarts achieved proved to be extremely wise.

"Having Tharon do the lighting gave great cohesiveness to our designs," Bill said. "She was like one of the family and had an intuitive grasp of what was needed."

The key word for the Eckarts' concept was simplicity. Their emphasis was on line, color, and texture. "Costumes were simplified," Jean said. "We devised a scheme so that each member of the chorus had only one basic costume. Adding pieces to each costume or taking something away, such as a glove, a petticoat, or accessories, changed the look of the garment. As producers, we saw to it that everything was very economical. The shops that we worked with for so many years were pleased to put in very low bids. If we needed something additional, it just somehow turned up, even though it wasn't in the bid. Everyone got hooked on the idea of this joyful little show and being a part of it."

In their work for television, the Eckarts sought to hide scene changes. On stage, the Eckarts worked openly à vista, choreographing the set changes to make them part of the show. Like *The Golden Apple*, *Once Upon a Mattress* had that quality of dancing scenery. "Their contribution," Mary Rodgers said, "was something—well, let's say minimalist with charm. Their sets seemed so light you felt you could blow them away."

"We decided *Mattress* should not look like a cartoon and not at all

POETIC LICENSE WITH 15th CENTURY COSTUMES

AFTER SWIMMING THE MOAT AND CLIMBING THE CASTLE WALL, CAROL BURNETT (CENTER) SINGS "SHY." THE WET LOOK WAS ACHIEVED BY USING SHINING JERSEY FOR THE DRESS. BILL AND JEAN CUT THE GARMENT TOO LARGE SO THAT THE DRESS HUNG DOWN IN HUGE FOLDS. IT WAS ALSO DRAPED WITH SEAWEED AND GLASS THAT LOOKED LIKE BEADS OF WATER. BURNETT APPEARED TO THE AUDIENCE TO BE SOAKED. MEMBERS OF THE ENSEMBLE, FROM LEFT TO RIGHT: GINNY PERLOWIN (LADY IN WAITING), DAVID NEUMAN (SIR HAROLD), DOROTHY AULL (LADY ROWENA), DAN RESIN (SIR DANIEL), JIM STEVENSON (SIR STEVEN), MARY STANTON (LADY IN WAITING), PATSI KING (LADY MERRILL), AND JERRY NEWBY (SIR STUDLEY). (FRIEDMAN–ABELES, EC)

THE TRAINS ON THE WOMEN'S DRESSES WERE VERY LONG, AND CAROL BURNETT'S ATTEMPTS TO DEAL WITH HERS BECAME A FUNNY BIT IN THE "FRED" NUMBER. (EC)

ONE BASIC COSTUME: LOTS OF ADD ONS AND TAKE AWAYS

"THERE WAS ENOUGH IMAGINATION AND WIT IN THE SCRIPT THAT WE COULD HAVE GONE INTO ALL KINDS OF STYLE AND STILL SUPPORTED IT," BILL SAID. "IT'S MUCH BETTER THAN AVERAGE FROM A DESIGN POINT OF VIEW. THE TRICK IS TO LISTEN TO THE MATERIAL. IT'S VERY GENTLE, RATHER SWEET, SATIRE. THE CHARM OF THE SHOW IS IN THE SIMPLICITY. SIMPLICITY IS RIGHT FOR THE FAIRY TALE IT IS."

ENSEMBLE COSTUME SKETCHES. ACCESSORIES CHANGED THE LOOK OF THE GARMENT AND VARIED THE NEUTRAL PALETTE. "TO CONVEY THIS IDEA TO THE COSTUME HOUSES, WE CREATED A UNIQUE POSE FOR EACH CHARACTER IN OUR DRAWINGS," JEAN SAID. (EC)

Disney, but something much more sophisticated," Jean said. "We wanted it to have style and what this meant to us was basing everything we did on our research of 15th century costumes. The costume that Carol Burnett wore in 'Shy' came right out of tapestry, even the hat. The crown on the derby was also 15th century French. Where we took liberties was in combining French and German or mixing early and late. We called it poetic license, but it was all based on research."

Another area where the Eckarts' sense of style was evident was in their color pallet. "There was nothing naturalistic about a show in which everyone in the kingdom wore beige, black, and yellow," Bill said. "I think what people expected were a lot of velvet costumes, instead we made all the women's dresses of wool chalee. We didn't want heavy fabrics or satins or that kind of thing. We wanted the texture of the show to be flat as if you were looking at an illustration in a children's book come alive. Where we were faced with creating traditional ermine trim, we substituted materials. We had white fur stitched on the costumes, but instead of black ermine tails, we used jet-black beads. It made the white borders look extraordinary."

"The show had an incredible, chic look," writer Jay Thompson said. "It was gorgeous. I still remember the opening vividly—a dark blue stage with three white dancers, a burst of color. It was so alive. It didn't have that cartoon feel to it. The actors looked like real people. The Eckarts managed to maintain the idea of twentieth century people even though the show was authentically in period."

CROWNS AND HATS

COSTUME SKETCHES FOR DANCERS. THE ECKARTS USED LIGHTWEIGHT CONE-SHAPED MEDIEVAL HEADWEAR (HENNINS) ONLY IN THE BEGINNING SCENE OF THE PLAY. (EC)

Fate of the Show

Once Upon a Mattress opened at The Phoenix's 12th Street Theatre on May 18, 1959. It was standing-room-only from the beginning of the run. But again, as with *The Golden Apple*, The Phoenix had another show to run right behind it. *Mattress* had to move, and it just kept on moving. Before closing after 460 performances, *Mattress* played in no fewer than five theatres. (See Foreword for the full story.)

Yet the reviews of the initial production were not all raves. In fact, Douglas Watt in the city's largest circulating paper, the *Daily News,* was openly dismissive. Walter Kerr in the *Herald Tribune* and Brooks Atkinson in *The New York Times* agreed that Mary Rodgers and Carol Burnett were major theatrical discoveries. Atkinson closed his review, "*Once Upon a Mattress* is a small show, (but) it has not economized on craftsmanship... the musical theatre has acquired a genuine new composer and a funny new clown. April may be a cruel month, but May is kind." *Variety* concurred, "In a season of not-too-fresh musicals, this is a little

THE COSTUME DESIGNS FOR THE KING AND QUEEN—BOTH CROWNS WERE BASED ON HISTORICAL RESEARCH, BUT THE OVERSIZED QUEEN'S CROWN WAS CHANGED TO A SMALLER ONE FOR THE SECOND ACT. (EC)

gem." *Newsweek* best summed up the tone of the press, "New talent Broadway must reckon with."

Since the Eckarts were now part of the producing team, their design contributions received less specific notice except in *Cue* magazine, "[The Eckarts'] scenery and costumes for *Once Upon a Mattress* should be required viewing for all students of the theatre arts. . . There is a growing number of theatre buffs who go to musicals primarily to see the Eckarts' sets." Thomas Nash in *Women's Wear Daily* wrote: "William and Jean Eckart in their setting and costumes of kings and queens, jesters, knights, and wizards have whipped together a resplendent production and gotten tremendous chromatic mileage out of simple props and ingenuity with the blending of colors on their stage palette."

It was miraculous that in spite of five moves that cost as much as the show's entire capitalization, not only did *Once Upon a Mattress* recoup its investment, but it made a one hundred percent profit. The show made Carol Burnett a major star. She was only committed for one year though, and at the end of that time, there were many new opportunities available to her. When she decided to pursue them, George Abbott said to Bill and Jean, "You won't be able to replace her. As soon as she leaves, the show will close in two weeks."

"It was small satisfaction to us," Bill said, "that we stretched it out to three."

In a recent interview, Mary Rodgers said, "Jean and Bill made my career for me so I really owe them everything. As producers, they were responsible for the first show I did in the theatre."

Once Upon a Mattress was the only show the Eckarts ever produced, but they won high praise for their efforts. Hal Prince said, "*Once Upon a Mattress* was terrific. The Eckarts kept it from being cute, campy, and fake sophisticated. Casting Carol was a stroke of genius, and George was the perfect director. It was well produced, and they were wonderful designers for it." Designer Tony Walton

CAROL BURNETT (PRINCESS WINNIFRED) AND GINNY PERLOWIN (THE NIGHTINGALE OF SAMARKAND) (EC)

commented, "*Once Upon a Mattress* had the quality of dancing scenery. I was conscious of their work when I was working on *Pippin* (1972). It had the lightness I was trying to employ and that came from their imaginative approach to scene changing." Jay Thompson said, "No one could have produced this play as well as the Eckarts. Since they were also the designers, they did a little grander job. I remember in the final scene, there was a long table. I thought Jean could have used a less expensive fabric than white velvet to cover it. When I asked her about it, she said, 'We know it's there. Like the gargoyles on the top of the cathedral, not everyone can see them, but God knows they are there.'"

CAROL BURNETT (PRINCESS WINNIFRED) (EC)

THE FIRST RENDERINGS OF THE NEW YORK BACKDROP USING CRAYONS, WHICH THE ECKARTS FOUND CAPTURED THE "AMIABLE CRUDITY" OF THE CHARACTER OF FIORELLO LA GUARDIA. (EC)

Fiorello!

1959 Crayons Capture the Essence of Character

THE LIFE OF THE CHARISMATIC MAYOR OF NYC, FIORELLO LA GUARDIA, AS HE LOVES, MARRIES, AND CRUSADES FOR SOCIAL JUSTICE, WHILE AT THE SAME TIME OVERCOMING NEW YORK'S CORRUPT POLITICAL MACHINE

"Bill went out to the five-and-ten and came back with two boxes of children's crayons . . . we found that the crayons helped to express the quality we were seeking."

Jean Eckart

"Sometimes the essential quality of a show can be very elusive or at least the means of communicating it can be," Jean said. "We wrestled with that problem for a long time in the case of *Fiorello!* What is the essence of the story of the early life of Fiorello LaGuardia? It takes place in a lot of offices and apartments, mostly in New York City. But then so do a lot of other shows; locale wasn't the answer. Our search for the essence of *Fiorello!* ended with Fiorello himself. Obvious, of course. But it took us a long time to arrive at what seems so obvious now. Then how to convey what we felt about him? Our early designs for *Fiorello!* could have been used for any show; they were characterless, too limp for *Fiorello!* We were having a terrible time until one afternoon, Bill went out to the five-and-ten and came back with two boxes of children's crayons. When we began sketching with them, we found that the crayons helped to express the quality we were seeking. They gave the sketches a forcefulness, a kind of crudity—not a cartoon look but a childlike directness and vigor. The crayons provided the springboard we needed."

PRELIMINARY SKETCH OF THE OPENING SCENE—LA GUARDIA SITTING IN RADIO STUDIO UNDER THE "ON THE AIR" SIGN, READING THE SUNDAY FUNNIES TO THE CHILDREN OF NEW YORK DURING A NEWSPAPER STRIKE (EC)

TOM BOSLEY: "HE *IS* LA GUARDIA"

JOHN CHAPMAN (*DAILY NEWS*)

FIORELLO H. LA GUARDIA AS HE REALLY WAS (MUSEUM OF THE CITY OF NEW YORK)

TOM BOSLEY AS LA GUARDIA IN *FIORELLO!* (GETTY IMAGES)

"THE NAME'S LA GUARDIA"—TOM BOSLEY (FIORELLO) STUMPS THE LOWER EAST SIDE IN HIS FIRST ELECTION FOR CONGRESS. (GETTY IMAGES)

At seventy-two, George Abbott loved working with unknowns and Tom Bosley, the actor he found for the role of Fiorello, qualified. After ten years of waiting to be discovered, Bosley was about to quit show business when Abbott cast him. Bosley was so unnerved by getting the role that he spent the first week terrified and unable to perform. The Eckarts and other collaborators were asked to attend a rehearsal. "After seeing the rehearsal," Bill recalled, "George asked for our advice about keeping Bosley. We said, 'Get Eli Wallach.'" That feeling was universal. The only problem was that Wallach couldn't sing. Abbott took it all in, sorted it out, and decided to keep Bosley. "He had found something in Tom that none of us had seen," Bill said, "and it turned out to be the right decision."

Mister Abbott was both directing and co-writing the show. *Fiorello!* was more cinematic than his earlier shows. *Damn Yankees* and *Once Upon a Mattress* demonstrate his mastery at shifting from full-stage scenes to transition scenes "in-one." But in *Fiorello!* Abbott, with some prompting from producers Hal Prince and Bobby Griffith, changed his technique so one full-stage scene shifted directly to another full-stage scene. This approach made it possible to interpolate filmic material at a crucial point in the first act showing Fiorello serving in World War I. The decision to include film changed the look and feel of the surrounding play. The challenge of simulating newsreel style gave the Eckarts a rationale for creating a scene shifting mechanism capable of moving full-

COSTUME SKETCH 1914 (EC)

DOUBLE DONUTS

THE ECKARTS DECIDED TO EMPLOY TWO TURNTABLES, ONE STAGE RIGHT AND THE OTHER STAGE LEFT. THEY REFERRED TO THE PAIR AS "DOUBLE DONUTS."

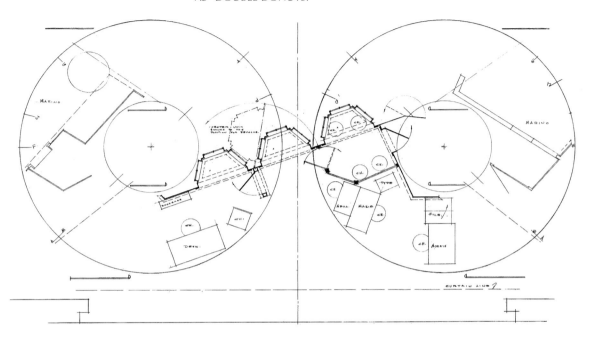

SKETCH FOR "POLITICS AND POKER" (EC)

"POLITICS AND POKER"—THE ECKARTS CREATED A SMOKE-FILLED ROOM THROUGH THE USE OF LIGHTING. AROUND THE POKER TABLE ARE THE POLITICIANS. ON THE FAR RIGHT IS HOWARD DA SILVA (BEN MARINO) WHO GIVES LA GUARDIA THE NOMINATION BUT BETS HE'LL LOSE THE ELECTION. SHELDON HARNICK'S LYRICS STATE THE SITUATION SUCCINCTLY: "POLITICS AND POKER, PLAYING FOR A POT, THAT'S MEDIOCRE. POLITICS AND POKER, RUNNING NECK AND NECK. IF POLITICS SEEMS MORE PREDICTABLE THAT'S BECAUSE USUALLY YOU CAN STACK THE DECK!" (PHOTOFEST)

stage sets. They decided to employ two turntables. A "double donut" approach enabled scenery together with actors to be loaded on from the wings from both sides and revolved into view at the same time as the on-stage set revolved off. The stationary center sections or "donut holes" were used for masking and hiding stagehands. In order for the effect to work, the general size and shape of the sets that swept on and off stage had to be shallow. Flying set pieces were used to fill in at the apex of the inverted "V" shaped area center stage. While attending Yale, they had seen Oliver Smith's production of *Beggar's Holiday,* which employed a similar device. What differed in the Eckarts' approach was their self-conscious adaptation of film technique while Smith relied more heavily on graphic metaphors drawn from William Hogarth's etchings. The Eckarts made composite sketches of the backstage areas of all the theatres *Fiorello!* played, designing the mechanism so it would work in the smallest one. Through carefully established lighting effects, the scenery imitated the dissolve technique used in the cinema. The cinematic equivalent is the montage, a series of dissolves of progressive intensity restating a theme or image until it establishes itself as an indelible icon. It was a method appropriate for an historic epic covering a quarter century of the hero's life.

CHANGING SIGNS: THE CITY AS A MELTING POT

"THE NAME'S LA GUARDIA"—BILL AND JEAN SUCCESSIVELY CREATED FOUR DIFFERENT NEIGHBORHOODS ON ONE SET BY USING A PINWHEEL DEVICE TO RAPIDLY CHANGE THE STOREFRONT SIGNS. THEY DID THIS BY ATTACHING FOUR DIFFERENT SIGNS TO A ROTATING WHEEL. THERE WERE SIGNS ON EACH WHEEL IN THREE LANGUAGES: ENGLISH, ITALIAN, AND YIDDISH. ONLY ONE SIGN WAS VISIBLE AT A TIME. AS THE NUMBER PROGRESSED, AND THE ETHNICITY OF THE NEIGHBORHOODS CHANGED, THE SIGNS ROTATED TO SHOW THE APPROPRIATE LANGUAGE. (FRIEDMAN–ABELES, BILLY ROSE THEATRE COLLECTION, NYPL)

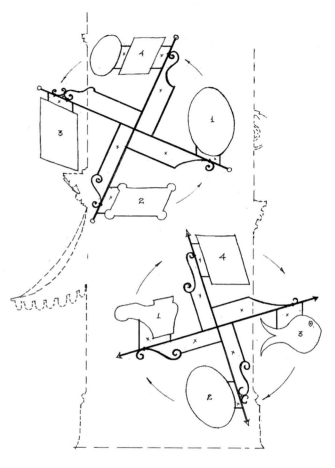

WORKING DRAWING SHOWING THE OUTLINE OF THE CENTRAL FLAT UNIT AND PINWHEEL DEVICE MOUNTED ON THE UPSTAGE SIDE OF IT (EC)

LIGHT FOR SHIFTING SCENES

"TILL TOMORROW"—THE GARDEN DANCE WITH MEMBERS OF THE COMPANY, ELLEN HANLEY (THEA), AND TOM BOSLEY (FIORELLO) ON THE EVE OF THE FIRST WORLD WAR, 1917. (EC)

"One of the really important things that light can do," Jean said, "is to isolate a moment on stage. You can use light to engrave an image. In *Fiorello!* we dimmed out one set into what we called a 'key light,' which was used to start the scene shift. That would allow the set to look as if it were a rose unfolding as it traveled off stage. Then as the new scenery appeared we would focus the lights so that the audience got an initial impression of the new set. We would hold that light for just a second before feeding in what we called 'the playing light' for the actual scene. We wanted to imprint that first impression in the audience's mind. We needed to make the most of that first impression because later in the scene we would have to add a lot of front light to make the actors visible. Abbott used to call the lights on the balcony rail 'his string of pearls.' He'd reach over and put his hand on your knee and say, 'It's time for my string of pearls,' which was French for, 'It's too dark to see their faces, Jean.' I remember on *Fiorello!* I was lighting away, doing marvelous things, I thought, and our old front lighting man, Larry Cochran, put his arm around my shoulder and said, 'Jean, will you please get some light downstage? I've had two spots flooded and covering you for two days.' I think that any time a lighting designer announces him or herself by creating too much 'atmosphere.' that's a form of self-aggrandizement. We always tried to avoid that."

But in "Till Tomorrow" the Eckarts created such a fantastic moonlight effect that fifty years later the impression was still vivid in choreographer Peter Gennaro's mind, "I've never seen anything like it since." The city was festively interlinked with the party. As critic Walter Kerr (*Herald Tribune*) wrote, "The ladies in lavender waltz and begin to languish; the gentlemen in puttees embrace them soberly. No one is spotlighted: no sharp sentimental focus is given to the scene. A graceful and rueful 1917 gathering is simply suspended for a moment, like an enchanted memory, in a pale blue monochrome that drifts in from the portals; a faded photograph stirs, and the world is younger and more innocent than it will ever be again."

CHANGING TIMES
1914: "UNFAIR"

COSTUME 1914 (EC)

COSTUME 1914 (EC)

"UNFAIR"—SKETCH FOR THE NIFTY SHIRTWAIST FACTORY. THE CITY BACKDROP IS VISIBLE BEHIND THE FACTORY. (EC)

Simulating lap dissolves was not the biggest problem facing the Eckarts with *Fiorello!* Because Marie LaGuardia was involved with the show as an advisor, *Fiorello!* had to be historically accurate in every way. In *Mattress*, the Eckarts had used essentially one costume for each member of the chorus, but *Fiorello!* needed entirely different silhouettes for each period. The action began in 1914, and went through four distinct periods: pre-war, post-war, the 1920s, and the 1930s. The script also called for several quick changes. All the women's party dresses worn in "Till Tomorrow" had to be changed for street clothes in the few minutes it took to project newsreel footage of LaGuardia at war on a screen lowered across the full stage. At the same time the full set change was taking place, a returning troopship with gangplanks, bunting, and flags was readying to unload its cargo for "Home Again," the number that closes Act I.

The most time-consuming element of *Fiorello!* proved to be the costumes. Selecting materials, shopping for fabrics, supervising work in the shop, and the various fitting sessions added up to a full-time commitment. Work on dance costumes had to be done with the choreographer and the director present. With *Fiorello!* the Eckarts decided to hire on Patton Campbell to assist with the men, while Katie Feller—whose husband, Pete Feller, built the sets in his shop—helped with the women's. In order to meet the deadlines, Peter Harvey was hired on to assist with the scenery. "It was a huge undertaking," Bill said, "and when we made the decision to have a family, our son Peter was born that year, we knew we could no longer do big shows and do all the elements: sets, lights, and costumes. There simply wasn't enough time to do it all and have a life."

1917: "TILL TOMORROW"

COSTUMES 1917 (EC)

TOM BOSLEY (FIORELLO) IN HIS ARMY UNIFORM AND ELLEN HANLEY (THEA), FIORELLO'S FIRST WIFE, 1917. (PHOTOFEST)

1919: "HOME AGAIN"

"HOME AGAIN"—SKETCH OF TROOPSHIP IN NEW YORK HARBOR. FIORELLO RETURNS FROM WAR, 1919. THE SET WAS INSPIRED BY THE FLAG PAINTINGS OF CHILDE HASSAM. (COLLECTION OF THE MCNAY ART MUSEUM, GIFT OF ROBERT L. B. TOBIN)

COSTUME 1919 (EC)

"HOME AGAIN"—THE ECKARTS CREATED A SHIP WHICH UNLOADED THE RETURNING SOLDIERS DOWN GANGPLANKS, TO FLAG-WAVING LOVED ONES. ELLEN HANLEY (THEA) AND TOM BOSLEY (FIORELLO), WITH MEMBERS OF THE ENSEMBLE (PHOTOFEST)

1920s: "GENTLEMAN JIMMY"

"GENTLEMAN JIMMY." EILEEN RODGERS (MITZI), CENTER, LEADS THE FLAPPER ENSEMBLE IN A CHARLESTON CELEBRATING THE VIRTUES OF MAYOR JAMES J. WALKER, LA GUARDIA'S OPPONENT. (PHOTOFEST)

SKETCH FOR THE PENTHOUSE TERRACE, DONE IN ART DECO STYLE. THE SKYLINE UPTOWN CONTRASTED TO THE WORKING CLASS NEIGHBORHOOD IN "TILL TOMORROW." (EC)

1920s FLAPPERS (EC)

1930s: "THE VERY NEXT MAN"

SKETCH FOR MARIE'S COSTUME 1930 (EC)

ROUGH SKETCH OF FIORELLO'S OFFICE—THE SKETCHES WERE KEPT ROUGH SO THAT THERE WOULD BE ROOM FOR LATER DEVELOPMENT. TO ACCOMMODATE THE ACTION IN THE OFFICE, THE ECKARTS CHANGED THE THREE WINDOWS TO BAY WINDOWS. SEE THE DOUBLE DONUT DRAWING. (EC)

"I LOVE A COP"

Fate of the Show

Fiorello! opened at The Broadhurst Theatre on November 23, 1959, to rave notices. Seven dailies covered the opening. There were no mixed or unfavorable reviews. Atkinson's review in *The New York Times* read like a love letter to George Abbott. Walter Kerr's review for *The Herald Tribune* read like a love letter to the Eckarts. In his Sunday piece, he was particularly responsive to the Eckarts' lighting, "I keep remember-ing the lights … Quite a few of the scenes take place in LaGuardia's not especially affluent law office, tucked away in one of the seedier corners of World War I New York. Designers William and Jean Eckart have not tried to glamorize this minor Mecca to which the insolvent and the indicted come. Yet there is a time in the second act, a time when every-thing is not coming up roses for the Little Flower, when the sun and air that seem to pour through a second-story window somehow wash the premises with glory. LaGuardia is in trouble, all the lovely and lovelorn girls are in trouble, the skyline is bleak with spidery black chimneys,

and still you believe it's a beautiful day. As, in a musical, you should." Without pulling focus away from the "amiable crudity" of Abbott's bustling show or detracting from the high-energy performances of its ensemble, the Eckarts had managed to create a time for reflection.

The show went on to become only the third musical to be honored with the Pulitzer Prize, and it won both the New York Drama Critics Circle Award and the Tony for best musical (tied with *The Sound of Music*). *Fiorello!* ran for 795 performances. It could have run longer, but as Hal Prince said, "The 1960s actors' strike cost *Fiorello!* six months on Broadway."

The show made a star of Tom Bosley, who created such an indelible impression in the title role that John Chapman (*Daily News*) wrote, "He IS LaGuardia. His voice has the same squeak, he has the same temper, he moves like LaGuardia, always scurrying, always gesturing, always the bantam rooster ready to take on anybody of any size."

Those who were close to the Eckarts couldn't help notice the stylistic differences between *Once Upon a Mattress* and *Fiorello!* Mary Rodgers, who was partial to *Mattress* and loved its airy lightness, felt the Eckarts had designed a boxy, brown show, sacrificing wit to spectacle. Up until this time, the Eckarts had sought to isolate specific qualities by finding the essence of the show, striving always for minimalism. For them, the musical form was enchanting, magical, and flowed effortlessly as a bird in flight. But *Fiorello!* driven by the engine of history, left little room for imaginative constructs. For Prince, this nostalgic musical had to be grittier, and that meant a more substantial form of realism. Although it wasn't their métier, the Eckarts willingly obliged. If other shows in their repertoire suggested parallels to film genres, *Fiorello!* was their documentary.

"I LOVE A COP"—MARK DAWSON (FLOYD), AND PAT STANLEY (DORA)   (PHOTOFEST)

CALIFORNIA LIVING ROOM *TAKE HER, SHE'S MINE*, (LEFT TO RIGHT) JUNE HARDING, PHYLLIS THAXTER, ELIZABETH ASHLEY, AND ART CARNEY—SELECTIVE REALISM MOVING TOWARDS MIN-IMALISM, THE ECKARTS DID AWAY WITH SOLID WALLS CREATING THE IMPRESSION OF A FULLY DIMENSIONAL ROOM BY USING SCREENS OF FABRIC AND THE ANGULAR WALL SECTION AT THE BOTTOM OF THE STAIRCASE. THE OTTOMAN, THE SOFA, AND THE END TABLE ARE ATTACHED TO THE PLATFORM AND ARE NOT FREE STANDING. EVERYTHING WAS DESIGNED FOR RAPID SCENE SHIFTING. (PHOTOFEST)

Feast or Famine

1960–1962

"It's a feast-or-famine business. In theatre, there are great periods of idleness, great periods of frenzy."

Jean Eckart

RENDERING *TAKE HER, SHE'S MINE* LIVING ROOM—MANY OF THE SCENES INVOLVED TELEPHONE CALLS BACK AND FORTH FROM CALIFORNIA TO THE DAUGHTER'S COLLEGE IN NEW ENGLAND. THE AREA AT RIGHT WAS DESIGNED TO ACCOMMODATE THE TELEPHONING DAUGHTER. THE TELEPHONE LINES HANGING DOWN FROM THE PROSCENIUM WERE THERE FOR THE MORE LITERAL MINDED. (EC)

Fortunately, *Mattress* and *Fiorello!* were running on Broadway and income from these shows sustained Bill and Jean through the 1960–61 season. One show did come their way, *Viva Madison Avenue*, a semi-autobiographical script about the advertising industry written by George Panetta. "We never had any illusions about the play," Bill said. "We felt that kind of play had been replaced by television sitcoms. We took the job to pay the rent."

Viva starred Buddy Hackett playing an Italian-American television director. The fact that he was such a well-known Jewish comedian contributed to the production's air of unreality. By the time the play opened in New Haven, everyone knew they were in trouble, and in Philadelphia, Aaron Frankel replaced Ira Cirker as director. "I can't think of one occasion," Bill said, "when a new director has turned a show around and made it a success." Panetta's play had three acts, but it lasted on Broadway for only two performances.

"The most amusing thing about *Viva Madison Avenue* was the party at Buddy Hackett's house in New Jersey," Bill recalled. "Buddy had just moved into this house built by a Mafia godfather. There were these pretentious religious murals on the walls so that the place resembled an Italian restaurant. When we drove back to the City, all we could talk about were the 'muriels.'"

BILL, JEAN, AND PETER AT WORK ON *HAPPIEST GIRL*—AT RIGHT, THE RENDERING OF MT. OLYMPUS (OPPOSITE PAGE) (EC)

RENDERING *VIVA MADISON AVENUE*, THE ADVERTISING AGENCY (EC)

Famine 1960–61

An entire year would pass before the Eckarts' next Broadway show. During the interim Bill and Jean sought to capitalize on their *Once Upon a Mattress* producing success. Teaming up with *Mattress* writer Marshall Barer, they approached the widow of Eric Knight, author of *Lassie* and *Lassie Come Home*. Columbia Pictures, however, controlled the short stories they were interested in developing. They then pursued Emlyn Williams to make a musical from *The Corn is Green*. They wanted to shift the story from Wales to Louisiana and give the story an interracial relevance. The Eckarts wanted Ossie Davis to adapt the play, but Williams refused, insisting he had to do it himself. Sensing potential disaster, Bill and Jean withdrew. Emlyn Williams took the project to Joshua Logan, and the result was the musical *Miss Moffat* starring Bette Davis, which closed after one week in Philadelphia in 1974. There were several other attempts to produce, but none came to fruition.

At ages thirty-nine and thirty-eight, Bill and Jean took the time to start a family. Their first child, Peter, was born in October 1960. Making room for the baby meant closing in the open balcony, the Eckarts' workroom, and turning it into a nursery. The workroom moved to the cellar. "There were problems with the light," Bill said, "and we also had to install air conditioning." Their concern over interiors also extended to

power boats. Producer Hal Prince's partner Bobby Griffith hired the Eckarts to do the interior of his thirty-three-foot cruiser. Griffith then took the designs to Boothbay Boats and theatrical personalities cued up to order. Nineteen-sixty also witnessed the nation's first televised presidential debate between Richard Nixon and John F. Kennedy. For Bill, this event prompted a series of amusing encounters. "When I was in Washington, a cab driver addressed me as 'Mr. Nixon.' It was very upsetting to be told that I looked like Nixon. If there were a resemblance, I never saw it."

The Happiest Girl in the World

Lee Gruber was mounting his first Broadway musical, *The Happiest Girl in the World*. The book was based on *Lysistrata* by the ancient Greek playwright Aristophanes, and "Yip" Harburg was on board to write the lyrics. "Yip Harburg was a wonderful little man, who Jean and I felt, was the leprechaun from his own *Finian's Rainbow*," Bill said. "*The Happiest Girl* was his idea." The music was by Jacques Offenbach, who got the nod from beyond the grave. The great French composer wrote 101 musicals, and *The Happiest Girl in the World* contained music from a dozen Offenbach scores including *Orpheus, La*

AN OPEN SHIFT FROM AN ATHENIAN HOUSE TO A CLOUD-COVERED MT. OLYMPUS

Belle Helene, Genevieve de Brabant, Tales of Hoffman, La Vie Parisienne, La Perichiole, Bluebeard, and *The Grand Duchess.* The cast was headed by the multi-faceted Cyril Ritchard (forever immortalized as Captain Hook in NBC's *Peter Pan* opposite Mary Martin). At age sixty-two, Ritchard was in spirit the youngest person on stage. He energetically acted a total of seven roles while also directing the show. "Cyril was the kind of actor/manager who appeared in vehicles designed to show off his extraordinary talents," Bill stated. "As a director, he was nothing like George Abbott or Jerry Robbins. He didn't work on the libretto and he wasn't a book doctor, but he was extremely clever and full of surprises." Ritchard's playfulness inspired the Eckarts as they designed Mt. Olympus. "Olympus followed a scene set in General Kinesias's bedroom," Bill said, "We did an open shift. Instead of using wagons, we flew in the entire mountain. The gods were seated on clouds, which were actually platforms that descended from the grid. Each platform was scalloped at the edges to resemble clouds.

While these units descended, fog machines filled the entire stage with mist. No flat edges were visible and the hard edges of the platforms disappeared when the platform reached stage level. The script called for a late entrance by Pluto, one of Cyril's roles. We contrived to have him brought up from underneath the stage through a trap, with a devilish red light and a blast of smoke." The effect on the audience was sensational. The Eckarts had culled the idea from Renaissance stagecraft and had given a new twist to what the ancients meant by the term *deus ex machina*.

RENDERING *HAPPIEST GIRL IN THE WORLD*—GENERAL KINESIAS' HOUSE, A BEDROOM AND A PATIO, WAS MADE UP OF TWO INTERLOCKING WAGONS WHICH CAME ON TOGETHER PULLED BY WINCHES, PIVOTED IN THE MIDDLE OF THE SCENE, AND, AT THE END, BROKE APART TO TRACK OFF IN OPPOSITE DIRECTIONS. (EC)

THE OPEN SHIFT FROM GENERAL KINESIAS' BEDROOM TO MT. OLYMPUS WAS DONE IN FULL VIEW OF THE AUDIENCE. THIS RENDERING SUGGESTS THE ECKARTS' DEBT TO RENAISSANCE STAGE DESIGNERS. (EC)

CYRIL RITCHARD DIRECTED *HAPPIEST GIRL* AND PLAYED MORE THAN A HALF DOZEN ROLES. (PHOTOFEST)

RENDERING *LET IT RIDE* SHOW CURTAIN—A COLLAGE MIXING GREETING CARDS WITH *THE DAILY RACING FORM* AND *THE WALL STREET JOURNAL*. ALL OF THESE PUBLICATIONS FIGURE PROMINENTLY IN THE PLOT OF THE PLAY. ONE CHALLENGE OF THIS SHOW WAS PUTTING FOURTEEN SETS IN THE EUGENE O'NEILL THEATRE, A THEATRE NOT DESIGNED FOR MUSICALS. (EC)

RENDERING *LET IT RIDE*—OFFICE OF THE GREETING CARD WRITER GEORGE GOBEL (THROWBRIDGE), ANOTHER OF THE ECKARTS' MONDRIAN INSPIRED SETS. (EC)

The Happiest Girl in the World received generally favorable notices and two raves. Ritchard was praised, but the book and the old-fashioned sound of Offenbach were not. The critics praised the "brilliant production job [and] great sets" (John McClain, *Journal American*). Taubman (*The Times*) called them "spectacular" and "ingenious." *Happiest Girl* ran for ninety-seven performances. It was overshadowed by *Carnival*, however, which opened the following week and walked away with all the awards, running for 700 performances.

Feast 1961–62

Carnival (1961) was only the second musical to be drawn from a film script; *Destry Rides Again* (1959) was the first. Traditionally, stage comedies were the main source of musical librettos, and the Eckarts' next show followed this tradition. Based on George Abbott's (with John Cecil Holm) 1935 hit comedy *Three Men on a Horse*, *Let It Ride* is the story of a greeting card salesman who picks winning racehorses until exploitive gangsters lock him in a hotel room. *Let It Ride* was the second attempt at a musical version; the first was *Banjo Eyes*, a vehicle for Eddie Cantor. It ran until Cantor got sick of the New York winters and left for the sunny climes of California. The second version, *Let It Ride*, was a vehicle for television funny man George Gobel. Tellingly, neither effort involved the veteran, Mister Abbott. Two days after *Let It Ride* opened, *How to Succeed in Business Without Really Trying* hit the boards and sealed the fate of the Gobel show. It limped along for sixty-eight performances.

Take Her, She's Mine

Take Her, She's Mine, a generational comedy about a California girl who goes off to college in New England and her father who can't seem to let go, was important for a number of reasons: after the sudden death of Robert Griffith, Hal Prince was producing alone for the first time; actor Art Carney was breaking out of his character of Ed Norton on *The Honeymooners* to star as the father; and Elizabeth Ashley was playing his daughter in her Broadway stage début. For the Eckarts, the show

THE AIRPORT *TAKE HER, SHE'S MINE:* JUNE HARDING (LIZ), PHYLLIS THAXTER (MOTHER), ART CARNEY (FATHER) AND ELIZABETH ASHLEY (MOLLY). "THE SCENERY WENT ALL OVER THE PLACE," BILL SAID. "THE AIRPORT BECAME A SYMBOL OF THE FAMILY'S STATE OF TURMOIL. CHARACTERS TRAVELED BACK AND FORTH FROM THE HOUSE IN CALIFORNIA TO THE COLLEGE IN NEW ENGLAND. WE WANTED IT LIGHT AND SIMPLE SO THE CHANGE COULD TAKE PLACE IN FULL VIEW OF THE AUDIENCE AND ALMOST INSTANTANEOUSLY." (EC) was a challenge because the script was so cinematic. Like *Mister Johnson*, the script called for a number of short scenes in different locales. And no wonder, since *Take Her* was the brainchild of Henry and Phoebe Ephron, the successful screenwriters of *John Loves Mary, Daddy Long Legs,* and *Desk Set*. In their day, the senior Ephrons were almost as well-known as screenwriters as daughter Nora (*You've Got Mail, Sleepless in Seattle, When Harry Met Sally*) is today, the subject of *Take Her, She's Mine*.

RENDERING *OH DAD...,*—ONE OF THE MANY SCHEMES THE ECKARTS CREATED FOR HARD-TO-SATISFY JEROME ROBBINS (EC)

PRELIMINARY SKETCH FOR *OH DAD...,*—SHOWING THE OBVIOUS DEBT TO FRENCH FARCE. THE ECKARTS EXECUTED FLATS IN SCRIM FULFILLING ROBBINS' DESIRE "OF HAVING EVERYTHING TWO FEET OFF THE FLOOR." (EC)

With or without cinematic roots, contemporary comedy in 1960s had its own style: the zanier the characters and the more bizarre the situations, the more the design scheme had to be rooted in recognizable reality. The challenge, therefore, for the Eckarts in doing *Take Her, She's Mine* was to find just the right amount of realism to ground the play with enough stylization and lightness to keep the vehicle moving. Under the fast-paced direction of George Abbott, Bill and Jean decided to use the same kind of visual shorthand they used so successfully in musical theater.

Howard Taubman, writing for *The Sunday New York Times,* observed that the Eckarts had cleverly helped to end the tyranny of the single set play: "Thanks to William and Jean Eckarts' breezy designs the movement is so graceful that it contributes to the mood of this lightweight but occasionally amusing piece." For Hal Prince, the sets helped tell the story of the play in a clean, polished, and highly professional way. "The Eckarts' contribution," Prince said, "and the casting made a success of this otherwise conventional comedy." *Take Her, She's Mine* breezed on to play 404 performances before a national tour.

During this period, young Peter Eckart was present. The Eckarts took him wherever they went. "He was small," Bill stated. "We had a basket we could put in a taxi, and when we arrived at someone's house for dinner, we put the basket on the bed. Young children sleep a lot." Even so, Cyril Ritchard, who visited the Eckarts at the Mews, took to referring to Peter as "the diaper." "It was clear to us that our current living arrangement would have to change. Because of the late hours we kept, we needed a space that was large enough for our family and a sleep-in nanny." In addition to Peter, the Eckarts' household included three frisky French poodles: Spot, Ollie, and TUT. TUT was named after "Tulane University Theatre" where Bill and Jean first met.

"In 1961, we did *nothing* but buy a house, have a baby, and get kind of nervous," Jean reflected. "After ten years, you feel that people should know you're around if they want you, and it's an enormous temptation to pick up the telephone and offer your services when a new show is announced." But Jean knew the theatre was not that kind of a business. She lamented, "Either there's more work than you think you can wade through or there's not enough. And work is always against a deadline. I think you have to be a little nuts or tremendously secure. Fortunately, there are two of us. You don't tend to get so frightened as one person

AUSTIN PENDLETON (JONATHAN) FIGHTS BACK THE VENUS FLY-TRAP, AN ELABORATE PUPPET THE ECKARTS CREATED, WHICH TOOK FOUR ACTORS TO OPER-ATE. (BILLY ROSE THEATRE COLLECTION, NYPL).

SANDOR SZABO (COMMODORE) AND JO VAN FLEET (MADAME ROSEPETTLE) (PHOTOFEST).

might alone. There are no vacations. If you're unemployed, you stay home. The times we like best of all are when the producer or director says, 'We want you,' and when it's all over."

The Eckarts found a townhouse on East 75th Street between Madison and Park Avenues diagonally across from the construction site of the new Whitney Museum. "It was big: five stories in all with a tiny elevator," Bill recalled. "When we took it, the first floor was rented to a neurologist, the second to an ophthalmologist, and the fifth to a psychiatrist. This left the third and fourth floor for living apartments." The Eckarts reconfigured several of the spaces as the apartments became vacant and located their studios on the second floor in the rear of the building. They purchased the property for $62,000. Today, the same building is worth well over two million. "It was a good arrangement," Bill said. "We had rental income, but we didn't like being landlords."

From the Absurd …

The Eckarts were not alone when they moved uptown to the East Seventies. Coincidentally, The Phoenix Theatre, which had served as an early proving ground for their work, moved with them. With the growth of the Off-Broadway movement, several new and more radical theatres had emerged, forcing The Phoenix to seek a smaller house in a friendlier neighborhood. "We could walk there easily from our house on Seventy-Fifth," Bill remarked. "Norrie [Houghton] and T [Hambleton] called us, and asked us if we would be interested in working with Jerome Robbins on a new play by Arthur Kopit called *Oh Dad, Poor Dad, Mama's Hung You in the Closet and I'm Feelin' So Sad.*" *Oh, Dad…*, the abbreviated title, is set in a Caribbean resort. Edith Oliver of *The New Yorker* aptly described the play as "a perverse comic nightmare on the old theme of man-eating mother and unfortunate son—that is compounded of Surrealist pranks, Grand Guignol, sound and sight gags, and large dollops of symbolism."

"We read the script, and we liked it," Bill recalled. "We had never worked with Jerry [Robbins]. A half dozen years earlier, we had met him through Mary Hunter when we were being considered to design *Peter Pan.*" Since *West Side Story*, Robbins had been turning down opportunities to choreograph shows because he wanted to direct. *Oh, Dad…* was to be his first non-musical assignment. "We liked the idea of working with Jerry. We met practically everyday, and each day we looked at another scheme for *Oh, Dad…* I don't think we ever worked harder coming up with new approaches on any show. Jerry's way of working is one of discovery. What's fascinating is that sometimes he will make a very subtle change and that will make all the difference in the world. With *Oh, Dad…* he was searching for a way to do this absurdist play. I remember him saying, 'everything would have to be two feet off the floor.' He used wonderful images, not things that were practical. For awhile, we tried going at the play through contemporary art. One scheme was to do the show in the manner of Jackson Pollack with paint thrown over everything, actors as well as scenery."

In the end, Robbins and the Eckarts decided to take *Oh, Dad…* in the direction of French farce. "Jerry gave us wonderful books of photographs of French theatre at the turn-of-the-century. We discovered that French farces had a style of scene painting that was flat and a very particular style of detail work. Farces also made use of a semicircular ground plan, made up of at least five back wall segments, in each segment there was either a door, a window, a bed, or a piece of furniture." By using these traditional elements, the Eckarts achieved what at first glance looked to be a perfectly ordinary set, but since Robbins hated

the doors a farce would normally require, Bill had to come with another angle. "What made *Oh, Dad…* different was that we used scrim instead of muslin. The difference in materials made everything feel insubstantial, which is how we achieved what Jerry wanted, the idea of *everything two feet off the floor*." Jerome Weeks remembers Bill stating that even after the director had finally settled on an overall look, "Robbins could not accept the couch for Madame Rosepettle's hotel suite. With no explanation, at every rehearsal he would state that the couch didn't work. So each day, Bill went out and brought in another couch. Day after day, every style and size imaginable. But after each rehearsal, Robbins told Bill the new couch was wrong. After couch number seventeen was rejected, Bill got up, announced he'd had it and headed out the door. Robbins said, 'Oh, well. All right. It can stay.' When Arthur [Kopit] came to the theatre and saw the set, he hated it. 'This is not a French farce,' he said, but it didn't faze Jerome Robbins. He just said, 'This is it,' and that was the end of that."

Not a man to skimp on symbols, Kopit called for his scenery and props to perform as characters throughout the show. For instance, to underscore Madame Rosepettle's man-devouring nature, the playwright gives his leading lady a pet piranha named Rosalinda that must gurgle, spurt, spit, and ultimately die a-flapping center stage. In addition to this piscatorial scene-stealer, there is a clump of giant Venus fly-traps that attack passersby, a self-sliding chair that pins a man under a table, a trunk that sprays books, and Oh Dad himself, a corpse that swings out of a closet terrorizing young lovers in bed. "Our biggest problem was the new Phoenix Theatre, a converted movie house. There was just no room: no basement, no backstage space, no flies. So everything had to be operated manually which meant more people backstage than we can possibly fit." Somehow, the Eckarts managed to make it all work.

Robbins' conception of the play was so strong that it instantaneously took hold with

FOR *NEVER TOO LATE*, THE ECKARTS DESIGNED THE ORDINARY ROOM OF AN ORDINARY HOUSE IN THE ORDINARY TOWN OF CALVERTON, MA. TO ACCOMMODATE THE TUB SIGHT GAG, THEY PLACED THE STAIRS IN THE NOT SO ORDINARY POSITION OF CENTER STAGE. (EC)

the critics. Edith Oliver writing in *The New Yorker* stated, "Seldom can a production have more effectively carried out the ideas of a playwright than this one." Theatregoers in search of what was new and avant garde flocked to The Phoenix's new home and *Oh, Dad...* extended to well over a hundred performances before closing for the summer. The following season it moved to Broadway before beginning a national tour. The success of the show was due in no small measure to Robbins' casting. Jo Van Fleet headed the cast as Mme. Rosepettle. A member of the Actors' Studio, Van Fleet first came to prominence through her association with Elia Kazan. Her Oscar-winning performance as James Dean's mother in *East of Eden* was still fresh in the collective memory and no doubt helped pave the way for her theatrical tour de force in Kopit's play. Austin Pendleton, fresh from Yale, made his New York début as the browbeaten son, Jonathan. But far and away the greatest praises of the evening went to Barbara Harris for her hilarious portrayal

NEVER TOO LATE FEATURED FINE PERFORMANCES FROM (LEFT TO RIGHT) MAUREEN O'SULLIVAN, ORSON BEAN, PAUL FORD, AND FRAN SHARON SHOWN HERE IN TUB-INTERRUPTUS. (EC)

of the imperious nymph Rosalie who gives her all to seduce Jonathan. "I remember watching a rehearsal one day," Bill remarked. "Barbara was so laid back and low key, she drained the energy out of the scene. I said to Jean, 'If I were Jerry, I'd fire her.' But when she got in front of an audience something wonderful happened. She was riotously funny and gave what was the authoritative performance."

For a time *Oh Dad. . .* broke box office records for an Off-Broadway show. When The Phoenix was forced to close it for their coming season, it moved to Broadway, starring Hermoine Gingold, and then toured nationally. A London production followed using the Eckarts' designs. "We lost most of the visual record of this production when we sent our sketches to England," Bill said.

The Eckarts enjoyed working with Robbins, and they actively sought out other opportunities to collaborate. "It just never worked out although we came close to doing several shows with him." The list of almosts and maybes include three rather well-known musicals: *Peter Pan*, *Funny Girl*, and *Fiddler on the Roof*.

... to the Ordinary

In July, the Eckarts took time off to have their second child, a daughter named Julie. Ironically, their next assignment dealt with the subject of middle-aged parenthood from a humorous perspective. Bill, then age forty-three, and Jean, forty-one, did not find the subject particularly amusing. *Never Too Late* opened at the end of November 1962 and brought the Eckarts back together with George Abbott and Florence Klotz. "We thought the script was really awful, but we said we'd do it because George was doing it." *Never Too Late* called for an ordinary living room of an ordinary house in the ordinary town of Calverton, Massachusetts. "One of the play's sure-fire comedy bits consisted of carrying a bathtub up a flight of stairs. To maximize the gag, we had our stairs turn. *Never Too Late* was 'kitchen sink realism' which we did perfectly competently, but it was one of those shows we did to pay the rent." The Eckarts were so certain that the play would not run that they took twice the fee and gave up their royalties. "Well, we were so wrong. Why a play like that is so successful," Bill grimaced, "I'll never know. I must say mass taste constantly astounds me!"

"ICE CREAM" REPRISE. MARACZEK'S PERFUME SHOP—DANIEL MASSEY (GEORG), AND BARBARA COOK (AMALIA)—"FOR THE FINAL SCENE," BILL ECKART SAID, "WE BROUGHT ON AN ENORMOUS CHRISTMAS TREE, LARGE ENOUGH TO FILL THE ENTIRE STORE WINDOW. DURING THAT SCENE, THE SNOW BEGINS TO FALL. WHAT WE HAD IN MIND WAS ONE OF THOSE GLASS GLOBES YOU HOLD IN YOUR HAND AND SHAKE TO WATCH THE SNOW FALL." (PHOTOFEST)

She Loves Me

1963 Romantic Atmosphere

BASED ON ERNST LUBITSCH'S FILM *SHOP AROUND THE CORNER*, SET IN BUDAPEST BETWEEN THE WARS, THE SHOW REVOLVES AROUND A PAIR OF YOUNG LOVERS WHO CORRESPOND WITHOUT MEETING ONLY TO DISCOVER THEY ARE COWORKERS WHO HAVE CONSTANTLY CLASHED.

"We wanted our Budapest to be romantic, to have the kind of nostalgic quality you find in fairy tales. We sought for an idealization. Atmosphere was all important."
William Eckart

PAINTER'S ELEVATION: EXTERIOR FAÇADE OF THE SHOP. (EC)

Look around and see for yourself
The romantic atmosphere
That's what all our patrons demand
That's the reason why they're here.

They all come here just for the mood,
And if you don't believe me,
Try tasting our food.
That's why we have got to preserve
A romantic atmosphere.

These lyrics are sung by the hysterical head waiter of the Café Imperiale in the song, "Romantic Atmosphere," which appears near the end of the first act of *She Loves Me*. Up until this moment in the play, every movement on stage has reinforced the charm and romance of the evening. But this song radically departs from that atmosphere and humorously spoofs the reality of the Café Imperiale, where everything seems to go wrong — trays are dropped, dishes are broken and a gypsy violinist screeches crescendos. The jarring, humorous quality of the café scene makes us aware of just how well this musical was designed to flow seamlessly, emphasize charm, and create a romantic atmosphere. "The Café Imperiale has a special mood and feeling to it," Bill said. The Eckarts' evocation was so perfect the audience greeted its appearance with a round of applause every night.

LIKE THE COGS OF A WATCH

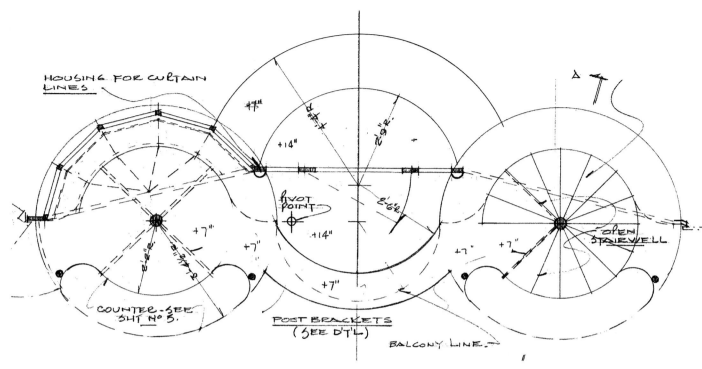

GROUND PLAN OF THE THREE INTER-
LOCKING REVOLVES, WHICH MAKE UP
THE INTERIOR AND EXTERIOR OF THE
PERFUME SHOP (EC)

Four years after *Fiorello!* Bill and Jean teamed up once again with Jerry Bock, Sheldon Harnick, and Harold Prince on *She Loves Me*. This time, the Eckarts concentrated their efforts on sets and lighting and Prince was also directing. "It was Hal's show," Bill remarked. "He made all the decisions. It was his first time directing a Broadway musical from scratch." *She Loves Me* drew its inspiration from Ernst Lubitsch's film *The Shop Around the Corner* (MGM, 1940), the same source Joe Pasternak tapped for *In the Good Old Summertime* (MGM, 1949) and, more recently, Nora Ephron in *You've Got Mail* (WB, 1998). All of these derived from a little-known Hungarian play, *Parfumerie* by Mikos Laszlo. The Lubitsch film, which starred James Stewart and Margaret Sullavan, was considered by Pauline Kael, critic for the *New Yorker,* to be "one of the most beautifully acted and paced romantic comedies ever made in this country" (in Samson Raphaelson's *Three Screen Comedies,* 1983). Lubitsch ranked the picture as one of his best. "Never did I make a picture in which the atmosphere and the characters

were truer than in this picture." To their credit, Prince and his collaborative team stayed true to the film's feeling of intimacy.

The Eckarts employed a variety of scenery-shifting devices, revolves for the larger units, and winch-driven wagons for the smaller ones. The winches, which the Eckarts had introduced as early as *Mister Johnson* (1956), were still being powered by hand and were considered innovative. Bill humorously referred to the winches as "early mechanization," but the effect on the audience was magical. Bill and Jean's quietly performing sets helped to make *She Loves Me* a style show that relied more on romance, nostalgia, and atmosphere than on brassy production numbers.

"It is a small show," Bill said, "even though there is more music in the show than in most musicals. The songs that Sheldon and Jerry wrote are very good, but there were no great big blockbusters, no great revelations. And the play really didn't provide opportunities for that kind of showiness. The music is integrated into the dialogue; it has a conversa-

INTERIOR OF MARACZEK'S PERFUME SHOP (COLLECTION OF THE MCNAY ART MUSEUM, GIFT OF ROBERT L.B. TOBIN)

EXTERIOR OF MARACZEK'S PERFUME SHOP (EC)

WHEN THE SHOPPING AREA OF THE PERFUME SHOP WAS ROTATED INTO VIEW, ACTORS COULD CLIMB A CIRCULAR STAIRCASE ON STAGE LEFT AND CROSS TO STAGE RIGHT ON A BALCONY IN FULL VIEW OF THE AUDIENCE. THE BALCONY PROVIDED FOR EAVESDROPPING WITHOUT WHICH PLOT INTRIGUES WOULD HAVE BEEN DIFFICULT TO COMPREHEND, WHILE IT ALSO HELPED TO REINFORCE THE PLAY'S SENSE OF INTIMACY.

"ILONA"—JACK CASSIDY (KODALY) APPEALS TO BARBARA BAXLEY (MISS RITTER). WATCHING FROM THE BALCONY: RALPH WILLIAMS (ARPAD), AND NATHANIEL FREY (MR. SIPOS) (PHOTOFEST)

tional tone. When you design scenery for a show like *She Loves Me*, you try to stay with this feeling of intimacy. You don't want to overwhelm what is happening on stage and so you concentrate on creating an atmosphere."

Perhaps because it was a small show, Prince booked the Eugene O'Neill Theatre, which with its small stage was never intended for musicals. Bill and Jean had previously designed another musical called *Let It Ride* (1961) for that theatre, and they knew its limitations well. The set the Eckarts felt was right for this show would have to be wound into the O'Neill tighter than the movements of a Swiss watch. The Eckarts used three interlocking revolving units for a fluid shift which "literally opened up the [perfume] shop's exterior like a wrapped present to reveal the inside," according to Ethan Morddan in *Open a New Window*. The central unit was designed to simulate a revolving door. To enhance the feeling of intimacy, Bill and Jean made the shop two stories high with one of the other revolves housing a spiral staircase.

"Although we grounded everything we did on research," Bill said, "we did not let it dictate to us. We wanted our Budapest to be roman-

OFF TO AN UNHAPPY START FOR BARBARA COOK (AMALIA), GINO CONFORTI (VIOLINIST), AND DANIEL MASSEY (GEORG) (EC)

tic, to have the kind of nostalgic quality you find in fairy tales. We sought an idealization. Atmosphere was all-important." To capture the feel of pre-war Budapest the Eckarts used gentle sloping curves identified with the Art Nouveau style popular in European capitals in the early part of the twentieth century. Curving patterns were used within the façade in the round, jewel-like windows, which together with the skeletal tracery of the supporting columns, echoed the trees that framed the composition. The roundness of the Art Nouveau style complimented the fixed, arching trees to the right and left.

The trees were an important storytelling element which let the audience know the action of the play transpired over an entire year. At first, the play was to have a series of ensemble dances to bridge scenes and to make evident the passage of time. "There would be a small dance number," Bill said. "And each dance signaled the arrival of a new season. Carol Haney (choreographer) worked out the dances, but they didn't fit. They halted the flow of the show and were intrusive. We discovered that having an actor say a single line and then changing the scenery was more effective. For instance, Arpad, the delivery boy, says 'Look! Autumn!' and with that the leaves, which we rigged to the trees with magnets, were released and fluttered to the floor." Arpad became the announcer of seasons, and the changes became instances of the set performing in concert with his announcements. Winter was ushered in with his statement, "Look! Winter!" The set responded and, magically, icicles clung to the over-arching tree branches. The transformations were always subtle and clever enough to be appealing. The audience accepted them immediately as appropriate shorthand stylizations. The transformations underscored not only the passage of time, but also the connection between the lives of the shop clerks and the natural world.

"A ROMANTIC ATMOSPHERE," CAFÉ IMPERIALE. THE ECKARTS SPOOFED EVERY PLACE OF ASSIGNATION THAT EVER EXISTED REPLETE WITH SWIRLING COLUMNS AND A GYPSY FIDDLE PLAYER.
THREE COUPLES DANCE, WOOD ROMOFF (WAITER), AND GINO CONFORTI (VIOLINIST) IN ONE OF THE SHOW'S TWO PRODUCTION NUMBERS. (PHOTOFEST)

AMALIA'S APARTMENT SHOWING THE ARCHING TREES AND THE ROOFLINE AGAINST THE SKY—THE ECKARTS ALSO INDICATED THE MAJOR LIGHTING FOCUS. (EC)

The Eckarts' Budapest was impressionistic and evocative. Realism was achieved in their handling of details and hand props. In New Haven, the orchestra pit was piled high with props such as perfume bottles, Christmas decorations, and boxes with paper and ribbons. "While that kind of dressing can be imagined or stylized in some musicals," Bill said, "a show like *She Loves Me* requires that these items be authentic. Outfitting the perfume shop drove the prop man crazy, and he literally quit the business after this show. As a designer, you can carry realism to extremes, but you don't want to burden the play with it. The way scenes follow one another is more important to maintaining the mood of the show. If you interrupt the flow of a delicate piece like this one, you can kill it." The Eckarts' scene changes were so seamless they were incorporated into the *mise en scene* (the stage directions) and are now part of the published script.

"ICE CREAM," AMALIA'S APARTMENT—DANIEL MASSEY (GEORG) COMFORTS BARBARA COOK (AMALIA). (PHOTOFEST)

Some of the play's most important scenes took place in the perfume shop's workroom. Here the audience saw the private side of the employees' lives. This is where the quarreling lovers, Amalia (Barbara Cook) and Georg (Daniel Massey) snipe at each other, their affection for each other as yet undiscovered. The workroom was also the site for one of the play's most memorable numbers, "Tonight at Eight," which sets up the lovers' meeting at the Café Imperiale. Yet the space on stage was so limited that the workroom set had to be hinged and accordion-folded out of view, creating major backstage traffic problems. Bill and Jean anticipated this problem and constructed special hidden doors in the walls of the set so that actors could navigate through it backstage. They also designed a sliding curtain wall, which traveled off stage to reveal the workshop when it came into view. The clearances at the O'Neill Theatre were so tight that a slight miscalculation by a stage-hand would have resulted in backstage gridlock.

Winched wagons were used to bring on sets for other locations out-side the perfume shop. To enable the passage of the wagons, the revolving stages had to be moved upstage behind traveler curtains, but the large over-arching trees on either side of the stage could not be struck. Because of this, Amalia's apartment, the setting for the number "Ice Cream," seemed to be almost a tree house hidden in the woods. The trees also provided a sense of protection, their gentle arches seem-ing to hover over Amalia as she took to bed following her heartbreak-ing experience at the Café. Here the Eckarts' trees combined with atmospheric lighting effects gave the set a folk tale quality. The folk art on the bed's headboard helped to make this connection apparent. They also deliberately elongated the headboard so that it would connect with the hovering trees in the natural world. As Hal Prince remarked, "It was very pretty and what fascinated me was that they were able, over and over again, to make pretty pictures without making them sentimental or gooey."

Another wagon had to be created for the hospital room. But in this instance, the setting was kept minimal: screens, bed, and nightstand. A neutral curtain hid the perfume shop set. The result was a variation of George Abbott's "down in-one" scene. Even so, the Eckarts gave this institutionalized setting an atmospheric quality. They used toned whites, which melded with the background and keyed tonally off the blanket. The subtle lighting removed the harshness from what could have been a sterile hospital room, the starkness of which threatened the romantic atmosphere of this urban fairy tale.

Fate of the Show

She Loves Me opened out-of-town to good reviews. In New Haven, *Variety* welcomed the show as a "change of pace from the brassy, rapid-fire musicals of recent vintage," and noted it was staged with "up to the second stage techniques…William and Jean Eckart have done an outstanding job of designing that has players and settings melding in a fluid manner that promotes smooth story flow." In New York, Howard Taubman (*The New York Times*) loved the show, and found the Eckarts' work had the "right period grace and flair." John Chapman (*Daily News*) admired "the frilly perfume shop and the overly-romantic Hungarian café," which is where Norman Nadel (*World Telegram and Sun*) found "the funniest scene in the play…designers

William and Jean Eckarts' spoof on romantic cafés."

A few days after the opening, the Eckarts received an enthusiastic letter from Mikos Laszlo, who had written the play *Parfumerie* so many years earlier in his native Hungary. He was then living in Long Island City:

> Thank you for making *She Loves Me* so beautiful. Your sets are ingenious and enchanting and so much of the success is yours. I shall always be grateful to Hal Prince for you.
> Please accept my heartfelt appreciation and gratitude for your artistry.

"TWELVE DAYS OF CHRISTMAS" (EC)

"In 1963, we were at the peak of the noisy heavy sell musical," Hal Prince wrote in *Contradictions, Notes on Twenty-six Years in the Theatre*, 1974. "A style piece (like *She Loves Me*) in which no one came to the edge of the footlights and 'gave it to you' … was soft sell." Although the Tony Awards singled out Jack Cassidy for best supporting actor, it was *Oliver!* and next season's *Hello, Dolly!* that garnered much of the attention and helped to shorten the run of *She Loves Me*. The fact that the Eugene O'Neill Theatre was too small to support it financially contributed to the show's commercial failure. Jean Eckart always felt the show missed having the classic status of Lubitsch's *Shop Around the Corner* because of the casting, "For all of Barbara Cook's voice and beauty [the show] would have been much more successful if it had someone like a Maggie Sullavan [from the film] who could sing. Barbara was a healthy girl-next-door who would have had plenty of boys. She didn't have that neurotic, schizoid quality that Maggie Sullavan had…Danny [Massey] was pallid—a nice man, but you weren't that interested in having them get together." Even so, *She Loves Me* ran for 320 performances and has been frequently revived, becoming a favorite in regional theatres and opera companies. A recent successful revival by the Roundabout Theatre on Broadway (1993), with sets by Tony Walton, paid homage to the Eckarts in its use of stage space.

"ICE CREAM," HAS BECOME A SIGNATURE SONG FOR BARBARA COOK IN HER CONCERT AND NIGHT CLUB CAREER. (EC)

HERE'S LOVE, THE OPENING SEQUENCE ASSEMBLY FOR THE MACY'S THANKSGIVING DAY PARADE. THE ECKARTS CREATED "BOZO THE CLOWN" AS A BALLOON FLOAT REPRESENTED BY A PAIR OF GIGANTIC INFLATED CANDY-STRIPED LEGS EXTENDED ON TO THE STAGE. LATER IN THE PARADE, THE CHORUS WOULD APPEAR ONLY WITH THE GRIP ENDS OF THE BALLOON GUIDELINES IN THEIR HANDS ANIMATING THEM AS IF THEY WERE WRESTLING WITH HUGE FLOATS. THEY MADE A VIRTUE OF THE FACT THAT THE TOTALITY OF A HUGE PARADE COULD NOT BE SHOWN ON STAGE. (COLLECTION OF THE MCNAY ART MUSEUM, GIFT OF ROBERT L.B. TOBIN)

Express Yourself

1963–1965

"The idea of an open change today is so common; no one thinks anything of it. When we came into musical theatre, it was in the process of transforming; you had to sit and wait for the sets to change."

William Eckart

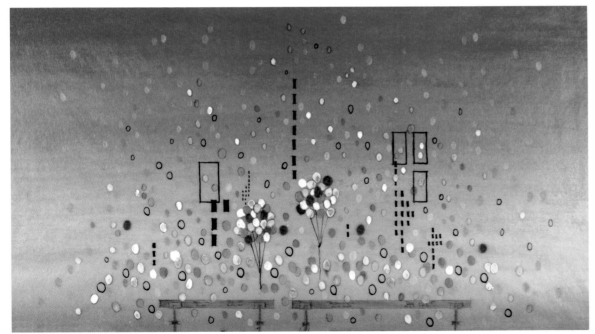

HERE'S LOVE. THE ECKARTS CREATED THE IMPRESSION OF A PARADE BY THE USE OF A SINGLE SCRIM BACKDROP BEHIND WHICH WERE LIT THREE-DIMENSIONAL SPHERES. THE ONES WITH HATS REPRESENTED SPECTATORS; THE OTHERS WERE BALLOONS IN BURSTS OF BRILLIANT COLOR. RECTANGLES WERE USED TO SUGGEST THE CITY SKY-LINE. BROWNSTONE STEPS AND LAMPPOSTS TRACKED ACROSS THE STAGE. IN THE FOREGROUND, THE CHORUS HAD TO RUN AROUND AND RE-ENTER STAGE LEFT AND THEN PARADE ACROSS TO STAGE RIGHT. (EC)

*H*ere's Love had all of the ingredients that *She Loves Me* lacked: a bunch of children, an on-stage marching band, a hint of fantasy, plenty of big, brassy dance numbers, and buckets of love for everyone. *Here's Love* was the musicalization of the 1947 film *Miracle on 34th Street,* whose plot concerns Kris Kringle descending on a disbelieving New York City and granting a little girl's Christmas wish. It starred Laurence Naismith as Kris Kringle, Janis Paige as the divorced mother, Valerie Lee as her daughter, and Craig Stevens as the bachelor attorney who defends Kringle, winning the court case and the love of Paige. The creative team was none other than the singular *Music Man* himself, Meredith Willson, handling book, lyrics, and music.

Stuart Ostrow, who is credited with the non-musical staging, also produced the show. Although Ostrow had been a protégé of Frank Loesser's (*Guys and Dolls* and *The Most Happy Fella*), he was untested as a producer and somewhat inexperienced to also take on the responsibility of directing. Three years earlier when the Eckarts were under consideration for Loesser's *Greenwillow,* Bill said, "We thought *Greenwillow* was a wonderful little book, but Loesser wanted us to work on spec and aside from being against union regulations, we didn't do that." *Greenwillow* flopped, but Bill and Jean had made such an impression on Ostrow, that when *Here's Love* came along, he brought them to meet Meredith Willson at his posh Central Park South apartment.

"We got there at around ten in the morning," Bill remembered "and Stu ushered us into the living room. We sat quietly and then Meredith made his appearance in a brocade dressing gown with a satin collar and ascot, just like a character in a Noel Coward play. He sat down at the piano, and his wife Rini appeared wearing a peignoir and sporting a Louise Brooks haircut. She sang all the female roles in a very high soprano. Jean and I sat and listened. At the time, we thought, 'Wow, this is quite an audition.'"

Since Willson was not a playwright, he stuck closely to the film, which meant that the set designers had to render all the recognizable locations of the movie. The list included: the Thanksgiving Day parade assembly area, along the parade route on Central Park West, Doris's apartment, Macy's Toy Department, a playground, an office, a stockroom, a judge's chambers, a courtroom, a corridor, etc. The Eckarts had faced challenges like this one before, namely in *Lil' Abner* in which they worked with Michael Kidd (musical staging) and Alvin Colt (costumes). To the Eckarts, this suggested creating an abstract background punctuated with representational architectural elements. Working together, they honed *Here's Love* into a masterpiece of precision.

Here's Love made use of the summer months to tour with extended engagements in Detroit, Washington, D.C., and Philadelphia. In Washington, Stu Ostrow remembered the show was a hit. "So much so that my wife got to go to the White House and sit in JFK's rocking chair because he wanted two tickets to the show. That was August 1963 and we had the chance to hear Martin Luther King's speech, 'I Have a Dream . . .' Sadly, after the show opened in New York, John F. Kennedy was assassinated."

Critical reaction in New York was mixed. There were four rave notices, but most of the focus, particularly in the notices that were less favorably disposed to the effort, concentrated on Meredith Willson. In typical Broadway fashion, Willson had been canonized for *Music Man* (1957). That show contained several popular songs, "76 Trombones," "The Wells Fargo Wagon," "Gary, Indiana," and "Good Night My Someone" which improvised off of "76 Trombones." Musically, *Here's Love* sounded like the poor relation of the earlier show decked out with hand-me-down tunes. The new show played to capacity over the holidays and ran long enough to require Ostrow to replace Janis Paige with Lisa Kirk of *Kiss Me Kate* fame. But in a pattern that was to become increasingly familiar in the 1960s, it never earned back its investment. Willson, whose career as a musician began with John Phillip Sousa, was no longer in step with New York audiences. "With Willson doing book, music, and lyrics," Bill said, "I think the show suffered from too much Meredith Willson."

PARADE CLIMAX—"AN AMAZING PIECE OF MECHANICS," OSTROW SAID. THE SLED CAME ON FROM THE RIGHT. AS IT GOT CENTER IT TURNED AROUND TO FACE THE AUDIENCE AND THE SCENERY STARTED MOVING UPSTAGE WHILE THE SLED MOVED DOWNSTAGE. THE CHORUS CAME IN FROM BOTH SIDES TO BE THERE AND GREET SANTA. "IT WAS LIKE A 3-D ZOOM CAMERA SHOT, ABSOLUTELY BREATHTAKING, AND THE AUDIENCE WAS OVERWHELMED BY IT." LIGHTING DESIGNER, THARON MUSSER, SAW IT DIFFERENTLY, "THE WORST THING ABOUT THAT SHOW WAS THEY HAD THE THANKSGIVING DAY PARADE IN THE FIRST FIFTEEN MINUTES. WELL, AFTER THAT, WHERE DO YOU GO?" (THEATRE BUFFS—ONE OF THE DANCERS IN THE CHORUS IS MICHAEL BENNETT WHO LATER WENT ON TO BE THE FAMOUS DIRECTOR AND CHOREOGRAPHER OF *A CHORUS LINE* AND *DREAM GIRLS*.) (EC)

Too Much Johnson

In January, at the behest of Burt Shevelove, the Eckarts returned to The Phoenix to design the scenery for William Gillette's 1894 farce *Too Much Johnson*. "We knew Burt socially. He was a good friend of Stephen Sondheim and Mary Rodgers," Bill said. Gillette is best remembered as the playwright of *Sherlock Holmes* (1899) and *Secret Service* (1896), but in his own time, he was probably better known as an actor. He wrote *Too Much Johnson* so he could perform the role of Augustus Billings, a chronic liar who becomes involved in a mistaken identity plot with a real individual named Johnson, a character he unwittingly made up to cover his marital infidelity. Shevelove, who was responsible with fellow author, Larry Gelbart, for *A Funny Thing Happened on the Way to the Forum*, thought the old Gillette vehicle might lead to a commercial project. John McMartin played the Gillette role, assisted by Nancy Berg, Dom De Luise, Dolph Sweet, Grover Dale, Pierre Epstein, and Gene Nye. The production stage manager was the then unknown Gordon Davidson, future head of the Mark Taper Forum in Los Angeles.

The critics were not impressed by the play, but they liked the scenery. "Finesse is not the special quality of the evening," Walter Kerr wrote in the *Herald Tribune*. "William and Jean Eckart's comfortable settings do have it." Howard Taubman in *The Times* thought the chief value of the production was that it caused you to feel superior to your forebears. *Too Much Johnson* ran for its regular subscription run of twenty-three performances and helped to pave the way for a future collaboration with Shevelove on *Halleluah, Baby!* three years later.

HERE'S LOVE, "LOVE, COME TAKE ME AGAIN." THE ECKARTS DESIGNED A TABLEAU PRESENTED CENTER STAGE AND FRAMED IN GOLD LIKE A CHRISTMAS CARD. SHOPPERS CLUSTER BEFORE THE WINDOW TO WATCH JANIS PAIGE AND ATTORNEY CRAIG STEVENS KISSING, REMINISCENT OF PATRONS PAINTED INTO AN EARLY RENAISSANCE DEVOTIONAL PAINTING. (EC)

TOO MUCH JOHNSON, ACT II. THE CHALLENGE FOR THE ECKARTS WAS GETTING TWO VERY DIFFERENT SETS, THE DECK OF A STEAMSHIP AND CUBAN SUGAR PLANTATION, TO WORK ON THE PHOENIX'S MOVIE HOUSE STAGE. BILL: "IN BACK OF THE STEAMSHIP WAS THE CUBA SET. WE USED A ROLL DOWN DROP FOR THE SKY. THIS MEANT THE SHIP WAS RATHER SHALLOW, AS IF THERE WERE STAIRS BETWEEN DECKS, WHICH WAS IMPORTANT FOR THE PLOT. WE BROKE THE BOAT INTO SMALL PIECES AND TOOK IT OFF DURING THE INTERMISSION REVEALING THE FULL STAGE PLANTATION SET." (EC)

A MILITANT MUSICAL

ANYONE CAN WHISTLE DROP FOR THE TOWN SQUARE, WHICH WAS VISIBLE THROUGHOUT THE SHOW, IS REGRETTABLY THE ONLY SURVIVING SKETCH FROM THIS PRODUCTION. THE MONDRIAN LOOK OF THIS DROP LEANED HEAVILY ON THE ECKARTS' EARLIER SUCCESSES. (EC)

Anyone Can Whistle

The Eckarts finally got their chance to work with Stephen Sondheim on their next show *Anyone Can Whistle,* which was billed as a "wild musical" and certainly lived up to its billing. "We met Steve at Mary Rodgers'," Bill recalled. "But it was Arthur Laurents who approached us about this project. He called us because they were in a jam. Ming Cho Lee had designed a set and done a model for *Anyone Can Whistle* which Herb Ross, who was choreographing the show, found unworkable. We liked the material very much, but we didn't think there was enough time to work on it, but we told Arthur the best we could do was to come up with our own clichés. He understood and accepted, and we agreed to do the show." What Bill and Jean meant by their own clichés was that they would make use of solutions that they had arrived at from working on other musicals.

Anyone Can Whistle starred Angela Lansbury, Lee Remick, and Harry Guardino—all actors, not singers whose musical talents at the time were unknown. *Anyone Can Whistle* was about a topsy-turvy world in which librettist Laurents maintained that madness and sanity were just a matter of perspective. The action takes place in a bankrupt town owned and run by corrupt Mayoress Angela Lansbury (making her Broadway musical début). To attract tourists the town leaders contrive a miracle fountain—water that flows out of a rock. Visitors to take the waters begin to gather until a nurse (Lee Remick) from the local sanitarium protests that her patients are not being given the opportunity to be cured. To Remick's rescue comes Harry Guardino, the new doctor at the sanitarium, whom we later find out is one of the inmates. The hoax unravels, the masks fall, and Remick and Guardino, now lovers, part leaving the stage in opposite directions. "There are some very exciting theatrical moments in it," Jean said. "Some people that you work with are so intense that the electricity crackles off of them and kind of buoys you up." Bill echoed these thoughts, "This was a musical with real content trying to take the form in a new direction."

The Eckarts' technique for this show was highly theatrical. The hotel set in the second act, which came out on stage and turned around resembling a little gazebo, was similar to the bedroom in *Happiest Girl in the World*. The Eckarts enlivened this scene by suggesting that Guardino call down to room service and have the bed sent up. "What we did," Bill recalled, "is to have panels open upstage and then have this enormous gaudy bed come down into the room. There was a big headboard and at one point when the seduction is not going well, the headboard lights up like a pinball machine and says, 'Tilt.' Tilt was certainly our contribution. The Fred and Ginger number which followed was further complicated by the fact that Arthur [Laurents] wanted to comment on foreign movies so Lee [Remick] did part of the scene in French. We came up with a way of making the set look more romantic. We lowered a big swag of drapes above the bed and draped the swag on giant roses. On a rectangular screen we projected English subtitles for the French part of the scene and then French subtitles for the English. I know if we had more time, we could have come up with a more consistent visual style for the show. As with many things with *Whistle,* there just wasn't enough time." Jean said, "I remember Steve and Arthur sitting around talking in the Variety Club in Philadelphia, saying 'We don't have time to do what we should do. We need to do now quickly what we know how to do.'"

An example of the stylistic inconsistency of *Anyone Can Whistle* appears when Guardino directly addresses the audience at the end of the first act saying, "You are all mad." Herbert Ross remembered, "It was written in the script where suddenly the stage became the audience looking at the audience . . . very much influenced by the theatre of the absurd of the period. The subtext of it was a gay subtext, I think, about exclusion. That layer became quite militant." Rather than quietly dropping the curtain, there was a burst of wild circus music, a row of lights resembling the balcony rail in the auditorium was flown in and aimed directly at the audience, while at the same time, two rows of theatre seats came in from either wing facing the audience occupied by actors dressed as theatre patrons, holding programs and applauding

Opinions rage about what went wrong and what could have been done to make it work. According to Jean, "It needed the Marx Brothers to pull it off. It needed to have been much more 'avant' than it was." And Bill said, "I think the mistake was casting for acting and not for singing." The recent performance of the score in the Live at Carneige Hall Series (April 8, 1995) by Madeline Kahn, Bernadette Peters, and Scott Bakula with the cut songs restored, gives a luminous idea of what *Anyone Can Whistle* could have been. *Anyone Can Whistle,* like many shows that do not make it the first time out, has become a cult musical.

louder and louder until the curtain finally fell. Entertainment had given way to confrontation.

"The audience didn't like being told they were mad," Bill stated. "Suddenly, they were looking in a mirror, and they didn't like it."

The critics in Philadelphia were tough and not terribly sympathetic. Henry Murdock writing for the *Inquirer* maintained that *Anyone Can Whistle* was an "anti-musical comedy." The New York corps was uncharacteristically split. There were two raves: one from Norman Nadel, *World Telegram and Sun*: "Sondheim's music and lyrics deserve an entire review in themselves." Taubman writing in *The Times* was not impressed either but admired the Eckarts' work: "There is more fun in the sets by William and Jean Eckart, which send beds, balconies, and rocks moving and pirouetting across the stage." Anne Sloper of the *Christian Science Monitor* shared his sentiments, "William and Jean Eckart surpassed Disney himself with their fantasia of mobile sets miraculously darting hither and yon, where needed." But sets don't put patrons in theatre seats and the show closed after only nine performances.

Fade Out-Fade In

The Eckarts' third musical of the season was *Fade Out-Fade In*, a zany satire of Hollywood in the 1930s, where a movie usher, Carol Burnett, accidentally becomes a star. There are a series of complications to add zest to the old boy meets girl formula but the show's raison d'être was Burnett. Originally slated for a November 1963 opening, *Fade Out-Fade In* arrived at the Mark Hellinger in late May due to Burnett's pregnancy.

During the hiatus, the Eckarts had designed Borden's "Elsie the Cow Show" and DuPont's "The Wonderful World of Chemistry Show" for the 1964 New York World's Fair in Flushing Meadows. The Fair was employing many members of the Broadway community including

FADE OUT-FADE IN. THE SHOW'S ACTION BEGAN AND ENDED WITH SCENES IN FRONT OF GRAUMAN'S CHINESE THEATRE WHERE HOLLYWOOD LEGENDS LEFT THEIR HAND AND FOOT PRINTS IN WET CEMENT. THE ECKARTS KNEW THAT BURNETT AS SHIRLEY TEMPLE WAS GOING TO BE THE SHOW'S BIG NUMBER, AND THEY MADE TEMPLE'S SIGNATURE LARGER AND MORE PROMINENT THAN ANYTHING ELSE ON THE DROP. IN THE SHOW'S PENULTIMATE SCENE BURNETT'S CHARACTER GOES TO GRAUMAN'S TO IMPRINT HER SMILE AND GET PERMANENTLY STUCK IN THE CONCRETE. (COLLECTION OF THE MCNAY ART MUSEUM, GIFT OF ROBERT L.B. TOBIN)

composer Jule Styne who also had what amounted to three musicals that season if one counted *Wonder World* at the World's Fair along with Broadway hit *Funny Girl* and *Fade Out-Fade In*.

The Eckarts took their cue for the sets from the show's title. Not only did they depict Tinsel Town's legendary sights—Los Angeles as seen from the Hollywood Hills, the gate at Paramount, and Sid Grauman's Chinese Theatre—but they employed film techniques such as the lap dissolve, the close-up, and the montage. Bill stated, "In *Fade Out* we used three donut turntables. Actually, it was one big turntable with three independently moveable parts. There was an outer ring, a middle ring, and a turning axle. They didn't all revolve together. In fact the rings and axle could revolve in opposite directions. What this allowed us to do was to merge different parts of a set together just like a dissolve works in film only what we superimposed was layers of scenery."

SPOOFING HOLLYWOOD 1930s ESCAPISM

FADE OUT-FADE IN. "YOU MUSTN'T BE DISCOURAGED." A DOWN-ON-HER-LUCK BURNETT IMPERSONATES SHIRLEY TEMPLE WHILE TIGER HAYNES RECREATES LUTHER "BOJANGLES" ROBINSON SATIRIZING THE READY OPTIMISM OF THE FILMIC THIRTIES AS REFLECTED IN *THE LITTLE COLONEL* (1935) AND THE MANY OTHER TEMPLE VEHICLES. (NEW YORK PUBLIC LIBRARY FOR THE PERFORMING ARTS)

FADE OUT-FADE IN. THE ECKARTS BASED THEIR STUDIO GATES ON PARAMOUNT'S. (EC)

BLUEPRINT FOR THE SIGN ON THE STUDIO GATES. LIKE MGM, FICTITIOUS "FFF PICTURES" HAD A MASCOT, THE SEAL OF APPROVAL; INSTEAD OF A LION'S ROAR THE SEAL BARKED THREE TIMES AND CLAPPED HIS FLIPPERS.(EC)

Fade Out-Fade In opened in New York to overwhelmingly favorable reviews with Walter Kerr the lone dissenter. John McClain of the *Journal-American* praised the Eckarts for giving the evening a "tinsel patina which delights and assaults the eye in the same moment" while *Variety* found the scenery "appropriately grandiose." Most of the attention, however, was on Carol Burnett. Even more than *Once Upon A Mattress*, this was her show, and the praise was lavish. The box office grosses reflected her appeal to audiences and *Fade Out* surpassed rivals *Dolly!* and *Funny Girl*. Seven weeks after the show opened, Burnett suffered a whiplash injury in a taxicab. Once the word was out that she was missing performances, the grosses fell to one-third of their previous highs. At the same time, Burnett's first TV series, *The Entertainers*, went on the air. The producers sued to get Burnett back into the show, and Burnett returned after her recovery to play out the two months left on her contract. Dick Shawn replaced Jack Cassidy and in time Burnett was replaced by Mitzi Welch. Bill said, "Mitzi was a decent performer, but nothing except Carol was going to keep the show open." Ironically, *Fade Out-Fade In,* which satirized the star system, was itself a victim of it. It closed after 271 performances, losing its entire investment.

A Sign of Affection

A Sign of Affection by Carolyn Green was a pre-Broadway tryout that played New Haven, Washington, and Philadelphia in the spring of 1965. The play was about a love triangle with a middle-aged couple (John Payne and Nan Martin, replaced by Lois Markle) and a young adventuress (Lesley Ann Warren). The setting was an elegant stable on a Long Island estate. "All I can remember," Bill stated, "besides the setting is that we never ran into any of those people again." One out of town critic quipped "*A Sign of Affection* is at its best when the curtain comes down."

THE MOST EFFECTIVE USE OF THE TURNTABLES WAS IN "THE FIDDLER AND THE FIGHTER," A TAKE OFF ON BUSBY BERKELEY NUMBERS. "WE BEGAN WITH DANCERS REHEARSING, AND THEN BROUGHT IN THE CAMERAS. AS THE PRODUCTION NUMBER BUILT, WE GRADUALLY FADED IN ALL THE ELEMENTS ASSEMBLING A GIANT JIG SAW PUZZLE FOR THE AUDIENCE. WE CREATED A BIG SPIRAL STAIRCASE, A PARODY OF THE ONE USED IN *THE GREAT ZIEGFELD* (1936). AT FIRST THE AUDIENCE SAW ONLY THE BACK OF THE CENTRAL SUPPORT COLUMN. AS IT REVOLVED, THE STAIRCASE CAME TOGETHER. WHEN COMPLETED THERE WERE GIRLS STANDING ON IT AND BIG VIOLINS CAME IN FROM THE SIDE ON TRAVELERS." (NYPL-PA)

Back to the Village

Unhappy as landlords, the Eckarts took time to move from the upper east side to the West Village where they bought a four-story, eleven-room townhouse on St. Luke's Place. Fourteen St. Luke's Place was in a row of houses that were all built in the middle of the nineteenth century and shared the same Anglo-Italian architectural style. They had chosen the West Village because they wanted to get away from the stuffiness of living uptown where they felt they had to get dressed to go grocery shopping. Ironically, the property they purchased belonged to Arthur Laurents, who had purchased it a few years earlier for investment purposes. As with many of the buildings in the area, the once-elegant single-family home had been converted into a warren of small apartments. The Eckarts reconverted the apartments back to a one-family dwelling. Bill said, "We had to redo the plumbing, wiring, and the roof. We added air conditioning and an intercom between the floors, quarters for a live-in babysitter, and in the backyard we built a two-story-high 'A' frame playhouse for Peter and Julie." Although they worked from the studio in St. Luke's Place, it was home first and foremost. There was no thought given to income from a rental apartment, and when they completed the project, the renovations had cost as much as the house. If it were a show, it would have closed out-of-town.

14 ST LUKE'S PLACE, GREENWICH VILLAGE, NY (EC)

CAROL BURNETT LITERALLY TOOK OFF IN *FADE OUT – FADE IN* AND INCIDENTALLY BROKE BOX OFFICE RECORDS. *FADE OUT* WAS THE ECKARTS' HOMAGE TO HOLLYWOOD DESIGNER VAN NEST POLGLASE. (NYPL-PA)

Flora, the Red Menace

The Eckarts' next project turned out to be their last collaboration with Hal Prince. With Senator Joseph McCarthy dead, a backlash feeling of nostalgia for the 1930s developed. It now seemed possible that a musical about a young girl's infatuation with a Communist Party worker might be appealing family entertainment.

Prince brought together John Kander and Fred Ebb to do their first book musical, *Flora, the Red Menace,* adapted from Lester Atwell's novel *Love Is Just Around the Corner.* Robert Russell, the librettist, selected the title, which Prince felt set the tone for the show, "affectionate, somehow rueful." Prince hadn't directed since *She Loves Me,* and he wanted to produce and direct *Flora* even though the Prince office had four productions that year including *Fiddler on the Roof.*

FLORA, THE RED MENACE BACKDROP. *FLORA* WAS A MUSICAL, A NOSTALGIC LOOK AT THE DEPRESSION PERIOD, SO THE ECKARTS CHOSE TO GO AGAINST EXPECTATION BY USING COLORS THAT WERE NOT DRAB. BECAUSE OF THE IMPORTANCE OF NEWSPAPERS DURING THIS TIME, THEY SUPERIMPOSED A NEW YORK CITY SKYLINE MADE OUT OF NEWSPAPER COLLAGE EMPHASIZ-ING THE PHRASES: "GOING OUT OF BUSINESS," "DISTRESS SALES," AND THE WORD "OPPORTUNITY." "OPPORTUNITY WAS A KEY WORD IN THE 1930s," BILL SAID, "AND IT WAS ALWAYS JUST AROUND THE CORNER." (EC)

LIZA MINNELLI AS FLORA IN HER TONY-WINNING BROADWAY DÉBUT. "LIZA HAD POTENTIAL, BUT SHE HADN'T FOUND HERSELF," BILL SAID. "YOU CAN SEE IT IN THE WAY SHE STYLED HER HAIR, MESSY HAIR, WHICH WOULDN'T STAY DOWN THROUGH ONE ACT. WE TRIED WIGS AND ALL SORTS OF THINGS. AFTER *FLORA*, SHE DEVELOPED THAT PERSONALITY THAT TODAY EVERYONE RECOGNIZES AS 'LIZA,'" (PHOTOFEST)

FLORA, THE RED MENACE COMPOSITE SKETCH OF UNION SQUARE. THIS SET SO IMPRESSED GEORGE ABBOTT THAT HE DECIDED TO REWRITE RATHER THAN CUT THE SET. (EC)

One day, while Prince was listening to the score in his office, George Abbott came in from next door and said, "What's going on here?" Then listened and said, "I've got to direct that." As Prince recalled, in a recent interview, "I didn't feel confident enough to say 'Oh no. I'm doing it.' After everything he'd done for me, if he felt that kind of enthusiasm then I thought well then it's his." With Abbott set to direct, he chose his favorite designers, Bill and Jean. The Eckarts were pleased to be working with Prince again and were willing to set aside their feelings of disappointment over not getting *Fiddler on the Roof*. At the time, *Flora* looked like it would be a star vehicle for Barbra Streisand, but it soon developed that Abbott wanted Eydie Gorme. As it turned out, neither was available, and instead, the role went to a virtual unknown, Liza Minnelli.

Lyricist Fred Ebb was responsible for hiring Minnelli. "We taught her a song from the show so she could audition, and it would be clear she was our choice," Ebb stated. At the audition, "Mr. Abbott said loudly, as she walked across the stage, 'Well, *this* is a waste of time.' It carried so loudly in the theatre that Liza heard it. She auditioned under those circumstances, and he did not take her." At seventy-seven, Abbott was spending his winters in Florida. "We called Mr. Abbott with Hal Prince on the phone, and then Mr. Abbott relented and said, 'All right, take her. If you all like her, take her.'"

While Minnelli hadn't quite matured, George Abbott certainly had. "George was not wanting to work as hard," Bill said. "He didn't want to be in New York during the winter. He wanted to be in Miami. Hal [Prince] felt the book needed work, but George wouldn't come north. So Hal decided to send Kander, Ebb, and Jean to Florida, but Jean didn't want to go because she thought they would be spending sev-

eral weeks in Miami. As it turned out, Kander and Ebb went. "They arrived in Florida one day," Prince stated, "they were back in New York twenty-four hours later . . . They returned empty-handed but ecstatic, buoyed up by the assurance of the man."

The Eckarts also noticed a change in Abbott. "George was thinking of cutting the Union Square set," Bill said. "But after he saw the sketches, he said, 'Well, the set's good so we'll keep it.' In earlier years, he wouldn't have done that." It wasn't just the physical distance between Miami and New York that was inhibiting the creative process. Abbott was directing a show about a subject for which he had no particular feeling. Prince has written in *Contradictions, Notes on Twenty-six Years in the Theatre:*

"Abbott felt the affection, but the quality of the emotion eluded him. He was born in 1886. He has lived through three wars, two police actions, the Crash, and Joe McCarthy. Just as he was about to be drafted in 1918, armistice was declared. He predicted the Crash and was out of the market six months before it happened. He has been secure financially for over sixty years . . . " He brought to *Flora* no clear attitude about the Party. His Communists were cartoon characters, some of them farcical, others evil.

Flora, the Red Menace opened in New Haven to surprisingly good reviews even though the show ended on a downer; Minnelli's Communist boyfriend, Bob Dishy, dumps her for a comrade played by Cathryn Damon who seduces him with a number that might have been

DUPONT'S "THE WONDERFUL WORLD OF CHEMISTRY SHOW." (EC)

BORDENS "ELSIE THE COW SHOW." (EC)

written about the 1960s, "Express Yourself." To reconcile Flora to her loss, Kander and Ebb had written, "You Are You." It was a strange way to end a musical, which had more or less abandoned the Party line for a love story. Critics were already taking "You Are You" out of context as a song to purposely proclaim Minnelli's own individuality. No ersatz copy she, not the daughter of Judy Garland, but a star in her own right. Still, ending with the heroine at her lowest point did not suit this musical. In New Haven, Kander and Ebb decided to write "Sing Happy." It was the first, but certainly not the last, song they would write for Minnelli. The new song was added in Boston where the reviews expressed enthusiasm about the actors but not the show. Elinor Hughes in the *Boston Globe* was the most succinct: "Strangely enough for a George Abbott show, slow-paced and not too well organized."

It was also in Boston that Hal Prince and the Eckarts parted ways. "Hal called one night from Boston," Bill recalled. "They had gotten a new running crew and a lot of mistakes were made. Hal called us, hysterical and told us to take the next plane from New York immediately.

We laughed at him, and he was angry."

When the show opened in New York, it hadn't pulled together. Howard Taubman in *The New York Times*, "[*Flora*] has the appearance of being pasted together . . . A promising idea has not been enlivened by a creative spark." Walter Kerr in the *Herald Tribune*, "Having decided to look at an era fairly, the show hedges, can't quite cut loose. In spite of competence everywhere, some heart is hesitant." The big news in New York was Liza Minnelli. Norman Nadel in the *World Telegram and Sun* wrote, "Liza is this year's Liza—individual, unduplicated and electrifying—and she will be a star on her own terms for as many years as she can and will give so generously of her talent, spirit and love." The headline in the *Journal-American* was simply "Liza Minnelli, Big, New Star." There was absolutely no mention of the show. At Tony time, Liza Minnelli won the distinction of Best Actress in a Musical. In another era, this might have been enough to light up the box office, but sadly, in 1965, there was simply too much competition, and *Flora, the Red Menace* closed after only eighty-seven performances.

ATTACKING APARTHEID

The Zulu and the Zayda

By midsummer, the Eckarts were back at work on two new shows: *The Zulu and the Zayda* and *Mame*. *The Zulu and the Zayda* was a play with music directed and co-produced by Dore Schary, Hollywood executive with more than 350 films to his credit. Bill recalled, "What I remember about Dore was that he was still behaving as if he were still the head of MGM. He flew us out to the Coast and put us up in the Hotel Bel-Aire where he was staying. It was very luxurious. . .*The Zulu and Zayda* was like a film script, it went all over the place. There were fast scene changes between a house, a general store, a dining room, a garden, a hospital, a jail, and a court."

A play with music set in South Africa about two friends, an old Jewish grandfather (zayda) and a young Black man (Zulu), living under the conditions of apartheid. The Zulu of the title was Louis Gossett and the zayda (the Yiddish word for grandfather) was Menasha Skulnik. The diminutive Skulnik, who when standing was more than a foot shorter than Gossett, was well known in the Yiddish theatre. Gossett had played George Murchison in *Raisin in the Sun* on stage and in the film and, in 1982, would win an Oscar for *An Officer and a Gentleman*. Ossie Davis played the narrator.

In *The Zulu and the Zayda*, Skulnik refuses to recognize that with the racial policies of South Africa, any friendship means trouble with the authorities. After a couple of run-ins, the son, who is jealous of the Zulu's closeness, intervenes and the two are separated. When the old man suddenly takes ill, the family decides to reunite them, much to Skulnik's satisfaction, and his health recovers.

Harold Rome, who had first distinguished himself with his socially significant score to *Pins and Needles* (1937), was hired to compose the words and music. Rome set songs for the three leading actors that utilized the distinctive rhythms and accents of Jewish and African folk music, and as a result the score was radically inconsistent. Unfortunately, there were no dance numbers, which might have added a bit of authenticity and color to the African element in the play.

The Zulu and the Zayda was scheduled to open the night of November 9, at the Cort Theatre, but the opening had to be postponed due to the first East Coast blackout. "Everything went off," Bill said. "Arthur Laurents lived just down the street. When the lights went out, we went over to his place and drank the champagne before it warmed up." On the following night, *The Zulu and the Zayda* opened. Press reaction was favorable toward the acting of Skulnik, Gossett, and Davis, but unfavorable to the play. The basic problem with the show was that apartheid could not be circumscribed within the narrow confines of a sentimental story. Howard Taubman in *The Times* wrote, "When it uses music for its purpose, it can be disarming. When it seeks to be dramatic, it makes one wish one knew the Zulu word to go with the Yiddish descriptive, schmaltz." The reaction to the Eckarts' scenery and lighting was positive. Walter Kerr in the *Herald Tribune*: "Behind and around these two buddies [Skulnik and Gossett], slips a rhododendron-leaved landscape, comfortably arranged by designers William and Jean Eckart to accommodate the straying during any part of their journey."

"We solved the scene problems well enough," Bill said. "The play just wasn't good enough for a long run." *The Zulu and the Zayda* ran for 179 performances and closed in April, the month before *Mame* opened.

IN *THE ZULU AND THE ZAYDA,* THE JAIL AND COURTROOM WERE COMBINED. THE ECKARTS' SET BECAME A STATEMENT ABOUT THE LEGAL SYSTEM UNDER THE UNNATURAL CONDITIONS OF APARTHEID. THE OUTLINED CITYSCAPE BACKGROUND WAS RIGID AND COLD AND THE OPPRESSIVE BUILDINGS CROWD OUT THE NATURAL WORLD, PERFECTLY CAPTURING THE ALIENATION OF THE BLACK MAN FROM HIS OWN COUNTRY. (EC)

"OPEN A NEW WINDOW." COMPOSITE RENDERING SHOWING THE STAIRCASE IN ITS TURNED POSITION, THE FLYING WINDOW, AND THE BACKDROP AS SEEN THROUGH SCRIM. (COLLECTION OF THE MCNAY ART MUSEUM, GIFT OF ROBERT L.B. TOBIN)

Mame

1966 Open a New Window

THE MUSICAL OF AUNTIE MAME ABOUT A YOUNG ORPHAN BOY BROUGHT UP BY HIS ECCENTRIC AUNT WHOSE PHILOSOPHY IS TO LIVE LIFE TO THE FULLEST.

"We were working one day with Gene Saks when Gene said 'I'd like Mame's first entrance to be center stage.' And that's what started it going for us. A staircase was sort of an identifying piece of Mame's apartment and linked to the staircase was the idea that Mame was constantly redecorating."

William Eckart

With *Mame* the Eckarts demonstrated that in the hands of artists, the set is more than a visual element of a show; it's a performer as well. In *Mame*, the no-nonsense title character never takes the time to say the simple things she feels in her heart. What better way to convey her feelings than to have her house become a land of enchantment, magically expressing her every wish? Although that idea is already present in the title character's passion for decorating and redecorating her Beekman Place apartment, it took the Eckarts to push it to another level so that the entire city becomes Mame's canvas. In the first act Mame, while looking out her penthouse window, nonchalantly discharges her credo—"Live, live, LIVE! Life is a banquet and most poor sons-of-bitches are starving to death!" Jerry Herman, composer/lyricist, encapsulated this moment into the song "Open a New Window," and then the Eckarts transformed this song into theatrical magic.

"*Mame* is back with a splash," wrote Stanley Kauffman in *The New York Times*, May 25, 1966, while

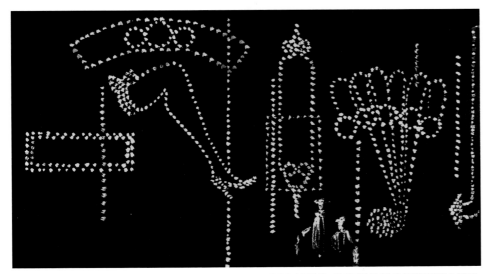

THE PROLOGUE—THERE WAS NO SHOW CURTAIN FOR *MAME*. INSTEAD THE ECKARTS USED FREE HANGING ELECTRIC SIGNS WITH KINETIC MOVEMENT TO INDICATE MANHATTAN. (EC)

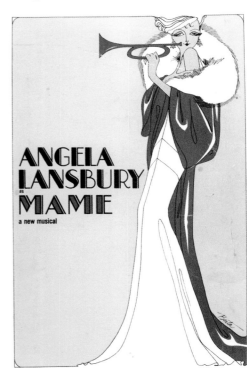

ANGELA LANSBURY as MAME a new musical

BREAK AWAY STAIRCASES THAT TURN

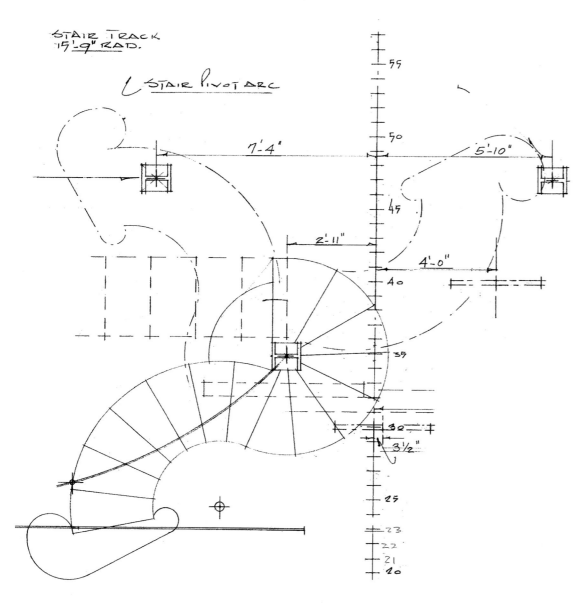

STAIR TRACK
15'-9" RAD.

STAIR PIVOT ARC

7'-4"

5'-10"

2'-11"

4'-0"

3½"

55

50

45

40

35

30

25

23

22

21

20

"OPEN A NEW WINDOW." FLOOR PLANS FOR THE ROTATING STAIRCASE SHOWING THE STAIRS IN THREE DIFFERENT POSITIONS, 180 DEGREE TURN UPSTAGE AS BRIDGE FLIES UP AND OUT. (EC)

his counterpart on the *Herald Tribune*, Walter Kerr, began his review with an extraordinary encomium to the Eckarts:

Just when I thought I'd given up breakaway scenery forever—I mean the sort of scenery that pulls itself apart before your eyes and drifts piecemeal to the heavens or the wings while new splinters and patches are coming together to take its place—along came *Mame*. For *Mame*, designers William and Jean Eckart have turned the process into music, letting their isolated uprights glide away like forever-held whole notes and scooping their black silk opera-draping upwards like an arpeggio aimed at the moon. Disintegration itself becomes a matter of style, and in at least one instance the Eckarts' detached and firmly musical mobiles provide an image that is as up to date as Saul Steinberg and as enchanting as you used to think musical comedies were going to be.

The instance comes early. Angela Lansbury, who looks as though Augustus John were being kept backstage to paint her in fresh oils for each entrance, has taken charge of her young nephew, as Auntie Mames are always required to do in each of their various reincarnations. Singing a pleasant song called "Open a New Window," she clasps the boy firmly by the hand and begins to lead him up the Eckarts' centerpiece, a curving staircase that toils not but does spin. Everything else in the room now softly steals away, leaving our two adventurers coiling vertically into space, rather as though life could be concentrated into a mountaintop with the least bit of determination and a sufficient amount of cheer. Arriving at the top, with nowhere to go, the new companions are unperturbed. An obliging window slips down behind them and they settle themselves onto its sill, scarcely bothering to notice that transportation has been made available. Then the window rides off into open air, secure, serene, and blithe mistress of all it surveys. The moment conveys its meaning simply and blissfully, and I wish all musicals could be taught to behave as effortlessly.

WINDOWS THAT FLY . . .

TO KEEP THE ACTION FLOWING, THE STAIRCASE BROKE AWAY FROM THE ESCAPE PLATFORM. THE WINDOW FRAME FLEW IN LIKE A BIG SWING. "WHEN WE STARTED TO PLAN THE NUMBER," BILL SAID, "THE FLYING WINDOW WAS GOING TO BE POSITIONED IN FRONT OF MAME AND PATRICK. THEY WERE GOING TO STEP OFF THE STAIRCASE ONTO A BIG TRAPEZE, BUT AFTER WE WORKED ON IT AWHILE WE DECIDED THAT ANGIE AND THE KID COULDN'T STEP ONTO IT WITHOUT LOOKING INSECURE. SO WE BROUGHT THE WINDOW IN BEHIND THEM. THEY SAT ON THE SILL AS THE WINDOW TRAVELED AND DESCENDED." THE CHANGE ALLOWED MISS LANSBURY TO CONTINUE SINGING WITHOUT INTERRUPTION WHILE THE WINDOW FLEW ACROSS THE STAGE AND THE STAIRS TRACKED OFF MAGICALLY.

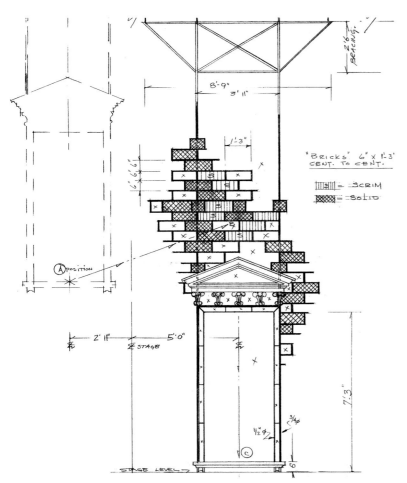

"OPEN A NEW WINDOW" ARCHITECTURAL DRAWING FOR FLYING WINDOW RIGGING. TOP OF DRAWING: THE WINDOW IS HUNG FROM A TRAVELER TRACK TO ENABLE ITS MOVEMENT ACROSS THE STAGE. (EC)

"OPEN A NEW WINDOW." ANGELA LANSBURY (MAME) AND FRANKIE MICHAELS (PATRICK) FLY ACROSS THE STAGE IN THE TRAVELING WINDOW. (BILL RAY, GETTY IMAGES)

"AIRY DESIGNS WHICH CHANGE AS EASILY AS MISS LANSBURY CHANGES HATS"

(ERNEST SCHIER, *THE EVENING BULLETIN*, PHILADELPHIA, APRIL 5, 1966)

THE STAIRCASE BECAME THE SHOW'S KEY DESIGN ELEMENT AND THE ECKARTS MANAGED TO DESIGN THE SHOW WITHOUT THE USE OF CONVENTIONAL FLATS, THE BASIC BUILDING BLOCKS OF STAGE SCENERY. "WE BASED THE DÉCOR," BILL SAID, "ON WHAT ART SHE WOULD COLLECT.

"IN THE 1920s, WE STARTED WITH A BARCELONA CHAIR, AND A PIECE OF SCULPTURE BASED ON MARCEL DUCHAMP'S 'NUDE DESCENDING A STAIRCASE.' SINCE THE CHAIR WAS CHROME AND BLACK LEATHER, THIS BECAME THE BLACK CHIFFON AND SILVER PERIOD, AND WE HUNG THE APARTMENT WITH LONG FLOWING DRAPES IN THOSE COLORS."

THE NEXT PERIOD COMES AFTER MAME HAS ACCEPTED HER POSITION AS PATRICK'S GUARDIAN. "WE CALLED THAT THE 'MADONNA PERIOD,'" BILL SAID. THE LINES WERE VERY DIFFERENT, MORE CONTROLLED AND RECTANGULAR. THE ECKARTS DID A PAINTING IN THE STYLE OF MODIGLIANI, CALLED 'MADONNA AND CHILD' AND A BRANCUSI STATUE OF THE SAME SUBJECT. FOR THIS PERIOD, THE COLOR SCHEME WAS SOFT PASTEL, SHADES OF PALE BLUE, PINK, AND WHITE, AND THE FURNITURE WAS LOUIS XVI."

THE DEPRESSION ERA FOLLOWED AND EVERYTHING OF VALUE HAD TO BE SOLD AND WHAT WAS LEFT WAS COVERED WITH FADED CHINTZ SLIP COVERS. EVEN THOUGH MAME'S BROADTAIL GAVE WAY TO CORDUROY, SHE WAS ALWAYS STYLISH. (NOT SHOWN)

LATER IN THE PLAY AFTER BEAU BURNSIDE IS ACCIDENTALLY KILLED IN SWITZERLAND, MAME RETURNS TO THE APARTMENT. "WE CALLED THIS THE 'PACKING CRATE PERIOD'," BILL SAID. "SHE'S BEEN ALL AROUND THE WORLD COLLECTING THINGS. AMIDST THE PACKING CRATES IS AN OUTLANDISH CARVED WOODEN PEACOCK CHAIR, NOT THE WICKER FAN BACK VARIETY YOU SEE TODAY. ALL THE FURNITURE WAS UNDER DUST COVERS, AND WHEN BEA ARTHUR [WHO PLAYED MAME'S BOSOM BUDDY, VERA CHARLES] LOOKED AT THE CHAIR, IT ALWAYS GOT A LAUGH."

ACT I, SCENE 2 AND 5: BLACK CHIFFON AND SILVER PERIOD (EC)

ACT I, SCENE 6: MADONNA PERIOD (EC)

PAINTINGS FOR MADONNA PERIOD FEATURED BOTH REPRESENTATIONAL AND ABSTRACT VERSIONS. (EC)

THE LITERARY PERIOD FOLLOWED, MARKED BY MAME BEGINNING HER MEMOIRS. THE DÉCOR IS ENGLISH, MID-19TH CENTURY WITH A LOT OF BOOKS IN THE BOOKCASES BECAUSE THE ECKARTS FELT MAME THINKS SHE'S ONE OF THE BRONTE SISTERS.

ACT II, SCENE 3: LITERARY PERIOD (EC)

ACT II, SCENE 2: PACKING CRATE PERIOD (EC)

THIS IS FOLLOWED BY A 1950s PERIOD. IN THE ORIGINAL SCRIPT, MAME HIRED A DECORATOR AND EVERYTHING BECAME DANISH MODERN. BUT THE ECKARTS DIDN'T THINK THAT WAS AMUSING. "SO WE CAME UP WITH JAPANESE MODERN," BILL SAID. "THIS MEANT THAT THE FURNITURE WOULD BE VERY LOW TO THE GROUND. WE GOT A CERTAIN AMOUNT OF HUMOR OUT OF GOOCH [PLAYED BY JANE CONNELL], WHO IS VERY PREGNANT, TRYING TO SIT DOWN."

THE FINAL PERIOD IS CONTEMPORARY, THE 1960s. MAME IS WITH HER GRAND NEPHEW, PATRICK'S SON, WHO SHE IS ABOUT TO TAKE TO INDIA. "WE BROUGHT BACK THE BARCELONA CHAIR," JEAN SAID, "FROM THE 1920s. IT WAS JUST AS SMART IN THE 1960s AND COULD BE REUSED. IT WAS A KIND OF IN-JOKE THAT WE LIKED." BUT THE ARTWORK IN THE APARTMENT CHANGED. THE 1960s PAINTINGS ARE ABSTRACT EXPRESSIONIST. BY BRINGING BACK THE BARCELONA CHAIR, THE ECKARTS MADE A STATEMENT ABOUT MAME'S CHARACTER. LIKE THE BARCELONA CHAIR, MAME HADN'T CHANGED. IT WAS A VISUAL WAY OF STATING THAT THE PLAY HAD COME FULL-CIRCLE AND THAT PERFECTLY COMPLEMENTED THE ACTION. (NOT SHOWN)

ACT II, SCENE 5: JAPANESE MODERN PERIOD (EC)

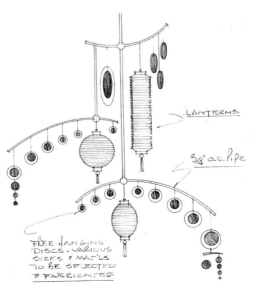

MOBILE SKETCH FROM JAPANESE MODERN PERIOD (EC)

THE ABSTRACT "OPEN A NEW WINDOW" BACKDROP WAS CREATED TO APPEAR BEHIND THE SCRIM. (COLLECTION OF THE MCNAY ART MUSEUM, GIFT OF ROBERT L.B. TOBIN)

Mame started slowly. The Eckarts recalled the first director, Joshua Logan, didn't want Angela Lansbury for the lead, and he was subjecting the material to a psychological/Actor's Studio approach. As Jean said, "It was all very intense and (*Mame*) wasn't really that sort of thing at all." Logan was fired and, according to Jean, "After that, it all just began to flow." Bill also questioned the new project, "Why would they want to make a musical out of *Auntie Mame*? It's practically a musical already." Years earlier, they had been approached by producer Frederick Brisson to do the clothes for his wife, Rosalind Russell, for the Broadway show of *Auntie Mame*. (They'd become friendly with Russell and her husband, whom they nicknamed the Lizard of Roz, when he was a producer on *Damn Yankees*.) Bill and Jean considered Brisson's offer but turned it down because they were working on *Li'l Abner* at the time, and they didn't want to get into doing just costumes. Later, when they were in Hollywood filming *Damn Yankees*, Bill and Jean spent time on the adjoining sound stage watching Rosalind Russell do the film version of *Auntie Mame*. "Roz had been marvelous as Mame, Peggy Cass was outstanding as Gooch. We just had our doubts [about a musical]," Bill said.

"But then," Jean said, "we heard the music and got into working on it." Gene Saks replaced Josh Logan and brought with him his wife, Bea Arthur, to play Vera Charles. At that point, there were songs but the script hadn't been fully conceptualized. Richard Grayson, the company manager, read the preliminary script and said, "I didn't think we'd have much of a chance. All the characters seemed like good people but none of the scenes had endings." Instead, the scenes ended with tableaux followed by blackouts. It was choppy. Stop-and-go stories are the bane of musicals, which ought to sweep the audience along through expressive music and dance. The *Auntie Mame* play had always been a "big lady" show just as the novel was a "most-unforgettable-characters-I've-ever-met" story. But, for the musical to work, the audience needed more than wit; they needed to feel just how much Mame loved her nephew. This meant going beneath the brittle banter and finding a way to make the heroine vulnerable.

The breakthrough for the design concept occurred when director Saks stated that he wanted Mame's first entrance center stage. The central character's penthouse duplex was a given. Both the play and the film of *Auntie Mame* utilized staircases, but in both instances the staircases had not been center stage. The reason was simple. On stage, staircases must have an

"OPEN A NEW WINDOW"—THE ENSEMBLE, ANGELA LANSBURY (MAME) AND FRANKIE MICHAELS (PATRICK) ARRIVE AT A SPEAKEASY AND DANCE. (FRIEDMAN–ABELES, BILLY ROSE THEATRE COLLECTION, NYPL)

MAME'S BEDROOM, ACT I, SCENE 4—FRANKIE MICHAELS (PATRICK, AGE 10), ANGELA LANSBURY (MAME). (FRIEDMAN–ABELES, BILLY ROSE THEATRE COLLECTION, NYPL)

THE SHOW WITHIN A SHOW: "THE MAN IN THE MOON IS A LADY"

THE DROP FOR THE BEGINNING OF THE MOON SEQUENCE (EC)

OPERETTA STYLE SETTING WITH THE FLYING MOON AND MOON GAZERS (EC)

escape exit at the top for actors to leave. Therefore, stage stairs begin center but the steps go off right or left to one wing or the other. But a center entrance meant something different. "We thought of our old house on Washington Mews," Bill said. "We had designed an 'S' shaped staircase in the middle of the balcony where we had our bedroom and work room because we didn't want a long hallway. So, we decided that the staircase for *Mame* needed to be a variation of that idea." The whole set for *Mame* was a paraphrase of the Eckarts' Washington Mews house, from its exposed "I-beams" and rafters to its structural staircase.

As designers, the Eckarts were thinking like playwrights. "We felt we were there to help tell the story of the play," Bill said. "You have Mame, a strong spirit, and you do things around her. Her spirit goes through the years, and it doesn't wear, it doesn't date, it doesn't age. Mame is very vital and has great class. Perhaps, the word ought to be elegance. That's the essence of the character, and the actress who plays the role has got to naturally have that quality. What you put around her expresses that idea."

"The sets for *Mame*," Angela Lansbury said, "were the first of the really magnificently choreographed sets. The furniture and the set pieces moved on and off without breaking the flow of the action. We never needed the curtain to come down for a change of scenery. It never stopped. Everything was just so fluid and marvelous."

"In a musical, the music, song, and dance is all there to convey emotions, so we knew we weren't representing rooms and places but expressing a state of mind," Bill said. "It wasn't a question of mechanics, we were thinking about how to make the character's emotions flow. We worked with Roger Adams [dance arranger] and Onna White [choreographer]. We'd say we need four more bars here and two more there."

Terry Little (stage manager) remembered, "The scenery was choreographed to flow with the music and the lyrics. It was absolutely integral to the show." Even though there were no computers and only limited mechanization, the movement of every winch and every piece of stage rigging was timed to the music.

"GET YOUR ASS BACK UP ON THAT MOON!" BEA ARTHUR

FOLLOWING THE GREAT DEPRESSION, MAME IS DESTITUTE. HER FRIEND, VERA CHARLES (BEA ARTHUR), GETS MAME A JOB AS A FEATURED PLAYER IN A "TERRIBLY MODERN OPERETTA" IN WHICH VERA STARS. MAME STEALS THE SHOW FROM HER FRIEND BY FALLING OFF A RISING MOON. THE NUMBER WAS STAGED AS A SPOOF OF A 1920s GLITTERING TIN-SEL SHOW. THE SCENERY FOR THE NUMBER WAS PICTURESQUE. THE SHOW CURTAIN DROP ROSE, REVEALING AN OPERETTA SETTING. THE ECKARTS HAD PROVEN EARLY IN *MAME* HOW EFFORTLESSLY THEY COULD CONTROL MACHINERY, AND ALL OF THEIR SCENERY WAS SEAMLESSLY INTEGRATED INTO THE SHOW. "THE MAN IN THE MOON" NUMBER WAS THE OPPOSITE OF THE ECKARTS' MINIMALIST STYLE. IT WAS HEAVY HANDED, UNNECESSARILY COMPLICATED, AND OVER-PRODUCED. ITS ARTIFICIALITY WAS DEMONSTRATED WHEN MAME, WHO WAS SUPPOSED TO RIDE THE MOON UP FROM THE STAGE FLOOR, DOESN'T GET INTO POSITION BEFORE THE MOON STARTS RISING. SHE ALMOST FALLS OFF, PROMPT-ING BEA ARTHUR TO YELL, "GET YOUR ASS BACK UP ON THAT MOON!" MAME'S CALAMI-TOUS ENTRANCE IS THE MOST AMUSING ASPECT OF THIS PLAY WITHIN A PLAY.

AMONG THE STAR GAZERS, BEA ARTHUR (VERA CHARLES) CENTER (FRIEDMAN–ABELES, BILLY ROSE THEATRE COLLECTION, NYPL)

ANGELA LANSBURY (MAME) HANGING ON THE MOON (BILL RAY, GETTY IMAGES)

"WHY DO YOU WANT TO CUT THAT CLASSIC?"

EARLY ON, WHEN PRODUCER ROBERT FRYER REAL-
IZED THE SCENERY BUDGET WAS $110,000, THE
ECKARTS HAD ELIMINATED THE LAST SCENE OF THE
PLAY TO BRING IT IN AT JUST UNDER $100,000.
"LAURENCE AND LEE HAD WRITTEN THE LAST SCENE
OF *MAME* TO TAKE PLACE AT THE AIRPORT," BILL SAID.
"TOGETHER WITH GENE SAKS, WE WORKED OUT A
WAY TO DO THAT SCENE BACK AT MAME'S APART-
MENT. JERRY LAWRENCE CALLED US AND SAID 'WHAT
ARE YOU DOING TO ME? WHY DO YOU WANT TO
CUT THAT CLASSIC?' BUT THE PLANE WENT, AND IT
ELIMINATED A SCENE CHANGE RIGHT AT THE END OF
THE SHOW. ALL THEY HAD TO DO WAS TO REWRITE
A COUPLE OF LINES, AND IT MADE THE SHOW FLOW
BETTER."

PRELIMINARY SKETCH FOR PLANE ENDING WHICH WAS CUT FROM THE SHOW (EC)

During rehearsals, there were problems with the second number, "It's Today." "I don't know if the lyrics were the same," Bill said, "but the song was something that Jerry [Herman] had written for a revue Off-Broadway or maybe it was written when they were think- ing that Ethel Merman would play the role. It was a razzle-dazzle musical number that required a big sound and Angie just couldn't produce what the number needed vocally. So, we were asked to come one day to see that number. They were trying to make a deci- sion. I don't know whether they were thinking of replacing Angie, but they wanted everyone to see the number and see what everyone thought. Onna re-staged the number so that the chorus came in to create the big sound under Angie and top the orchestra. That meant that it no longer depended solely on Angie, and I think that was a turning point. As time went on, Angie became surer of herself. At the end of that scene, Gene Saks did a little bit of staging that made a tremendous difference. It was a crucial moment when Mame has to accept the child as her responsibility. Mame's line is, 'It's Patrick's Day. Not *St.* Patrick's Day. *My* Patrick's Day!' and then she goes on to reprise 'It's Today' to the boy. Gene had Patrick stand downstage and face Angie so that she acted that moment directly to the audience. Angie did it with such sincerity that it made the rest of the play work. Those kind of things are subtle, but they are what makes the difference between something connecting and not con- necting."

Fate of the Show

Mame opened at the Shubert Theatre in Philadelphia on April 4, 1966. "No matter how good a show was," stage manager Terry Little said, "if it was running too long in Philly, the commuting half of the audience had to leave to catch the 11:45 train. Opening night—and I'll always remember this—the audience stayed there until the end of the show. That's when we knew we had a hit." The next morning the critics agreed, and Jerry Gaghan of the *Philadelphia Daily News* praised the Eckarts for their "shifting scenic wonders."

In the following month-and-a-half of tryouts, there were a great many small cuts as well as several numbers that had to be eliminated. *Life* magazine caught up to the show in Boston. And although it was rare in the 1960s for that magazine to pay attention to Broadway, the editors broke with tradition and did a cover story on *Mame*. By the time *Mame* opened in New York, it was a well-paced show. Two single releases on the charts were added insurance: Bobby Darin's jazzy rendition of the title tune and Eydie Gorme's Grammy-winning "If You Walked Into My Life."

Mame opened to rave notices, and even though Jerry Herman had another musical playing down the street (*Hello, Dolly!*), the critics restrained themselves from making too many comparisons. Even critics like Martin Gottfried (*Women's Wear Daily*), who disliked the show, praised the Eckarts, dubbing them "the most original and modern designers for the Broadway theatre."

Less than three weeks after *Mame* opened, the Tony Awards were given out. *Mame* was nominated for eight awards including scenic design. But the fact that the show opened so close to the voting date was disadvantageous. Still, Angela Lansbury and Bea Arthur were both awarded Tonys in their respective categories of Musical Star and Musical Supporting Actress.

The show went on to a five-year history racking up 1,508 performances on Broadway. A host of Mames followed Lansbury into the role: Celeste Holm, Janis Paige, Ann Miller, Jane Morgan, Susan Hayward, Juliet Prouse, Elaine Stritch, Janet Blair, Joan Brickhill, Patrice Munsel, Gretchen Wyler, Jan Clayton, Sheila Smith, and Giselle MacKenzie.

Still, Bill and Jean lamented, "*Mame* was old-fashioned." They had always been on the cutting edge. But old-fashioned though it may have been, *Mame* proved to be the Eckarts' most successful show. The magical kingdom the Eckarts created for the great lady of Beekman Place went on to London and traveled with a variety of road show companies, sometimes showing up in altered states. Jean remembered that at Caesar's Palace in Las Vegas the sets were too high for their stage house. "They cut down one of the travelers from the wrong end so that the fence we designed became croquet hoops." In spite of this alteration, *The Hollywood Reporter* raved, "The sets by William and Jean Eckart were the best that have ever been seen in Las Vegas with absolutely no exceptions."

"With *Mame*," Bill said, "we weren't doing anything new. It was just a distillation of all the things we'd done before. Only this time, we were doing them with more authority."

The emotional impact of *Mame* continues. Recently, its comforting message was poignantly reprised when New York's Thanksgiving Day Parade following 9/11 concluded with a touching rendition of "We Need a Little Christmas."

THE ECKARTS CREATED A "JACKSON POLLACK" FOR MAME'S MODERN PERIOD (1965). (EC)

"MISS BACALL IN SOME STUNNING CLOTHES"

CYNTHIA LOWRY, ASSOCIATED PRESS

BACALL IN A BLACK AND WHITE SILK
PANTS SUIT, NEXT TO JOHN FORSYTHE
IN ABC STAGE 67 "THE LIGHT
FANTASTIC" (PHOTOFEST)

Disenchantment: Age of Aquarius

"We were experimenting with some ideas about palette, and again encapsulated scenery—mini scenery."

Jean Eckart

"FEET DO YO' STUFF," A 1920s CHARLESTON. THE CONGO CUTIES WITH TIP AND TAP AT THE COTTON CLUB. (LEFT TO RIGHT) HOPE CLARKE, WINSTON DEWITT HEMSLEY, SANDRA LEIN, SAUNDRA MCPHERSON, ALLAN WEEKS, AND LESLIE UGGAMS (FRIEDMAN-ABLES, BILLY ROSE THEATRE COLLECTION, NYPL-PA)

"**W**e were surprised that *Mame* was such a big hit," Bill said. "It came very late in what was the era of the Rodgers and Hammerstein show combining an old-fashioned musical comedy and a sentimental book." Their success with *Mame* brought a raft of new projects. In 1967–68, there were no fewer than five major musicals, six, if one considers a touring production of *Where's Charley*, as well as a Broadway comedy, a film, a television special, a ballet, and an American Shakespeare Festival production of *A Midsummer Night's Dream*.

Before the 1966 season ended, they did sets and lights for a touring production of *The Circle* for Helen Hayes. "We did a really minimal set," Bill said, "because they didn't have much money." At about the same time, they became involved with Judith Abbott's production of her father and Frank Loesser's 1948 hit *Where's Charley*, which toured the Midwest. Bill and Jean enjoyed working with Cyril Ritchard, and the show was their first collaboration with Agnes de Mille.

Back in New York, the Eckarts were again teamed with the Abbotts for a new comedy, *Agatha Sue, I Love You*, starring Ray Walston. Abbott thought he had another *Never Too Late*, but the script was weak, and the show closed after a short run.

The Light Fantastic

The season brightened when Arthur Laurents, a neighbor and friend, involved the Eckarts in two unusual productions: one a television special called "The Light Fantastic–OR–How To Tell Your Past, Present and Maybe Your Future Through Social Dancing" (*ABC Stage 67*) and the other a stage musical entitled *Hallelujah, Baby!* The shows shared a similar concept. Each gave a sociological perspective to changes in the field of popular entertainment. In "The Light Fantastic," Laurents utilized a skeptical television viewer, Lauren Bacall, to argue with an avuncular television commentator, John Forsythe. Forsythe maintained that there is a direct correlation between the style of social dancing and stock market fluctuations. Because the Frug was so similar to the Charleston, Forsythe fears another stock market crash like the one in 1929. Through a series of dances, Bacall charms him out of his doomsday demeanor, and the two agree that if the waltz survives, all will be right with the world.

"We did the scenery and clothes, and there were a lot of them," Bill noted. "There were 116 costume changes in fifty minutes. We rented what we could, but we designed all the clothes for Bacall. The opening consisted of the Charleston shot through a Dow Jones graph of the stock market painted on glass. The first panel shattered when the graph hit 1929. The second glass panel showing the 1960s was also supposed to shatter as the graph reached 1967, but it didn't. The Rolling Stones' song, 'Satisfaction' came up, but the point was lost. The cameras just kept rolling. Today, there would have been editing and post-production, but then the technology for splicing videotape did not exist. Costume changes were accomplished by stopping the cameras, changing, and then continuing to shoot. It was just like live broadcasting."

Minimalism typified the sets, but the costumes were witty and clever. The Eckarts got mileage out of the unisex craze by showing a dancer dressed in a red pants suit exactly like Lauren Bacall's. The viewer is caught off guard when Bacall enters. As the unknown dancer turns towards the camera, the viewer recognizes a stylishly dressed young man with long blond hair. But the ultimate send-up of 1960s, long haired-fashion was a Frug outfit made entirely out of hair. Actually, the outfit was a wig that hung from the top of the head down to mini-skirt length. The attack on long hair as a style issue trivialized the violent confrontations taking place on college campuses across the country over the war in Vietnam, and it was consistent with the generational pandering of the Broadway theatre of the time. After all, "The Light Fantastic" was lighthearted family entertainment. Only in the Bossa Nova segment, with its interracial dancing, did Laurents attempt anything risky. As he noted in an article for *The Sunday Times* (February 5, 1967), "Partners are exchanged with no comment but a point is made."

Hallelujah, Baby!

If Laurents and the Eckarts appeared to be soft peddling their response to racism in "The Light Fantastic," it was only because they were planning a direct attack on the issue in *Hallelujah, Baby!* Like so many shows of that era, the leading lady was the *raison d'être* for the project. "Arthur had written *Hallelujah, Baby!* for Lena Horne," Bill said. "At that time, David Merrick was the producer. Lena was going to do it, and

HALLELUJAH, BABY!, TITLE TUNE, A BIT OF 1960s GOSPEL, UGGAMS (CENTER) SANG, "I BELIEVE IN ME!" (LEFT) ALLAN WEEKS AND (RIGHT) WINSTON DEWITT HEMSLEY. BEFORE A CHORUS LINE THE ECKARTS USED MIRRORS TO MERGE THE STAR WITH THE AUDIENCE. (PHOTOFEST)

then she changed her mind. That's when Merrick dropped it." New producers were found, and they hired Leslie Uggams, whose fame rested on the years she had spent as a lead singer on the popular TV program "Sing Along With Mitch." At age twenty-three when many performers' careers were taking off, Miss Uggams' career seemed to be stalled. Like Carol Burnett and Barbra Streisand before her, she needed a Broadway hit to put her into the limelight. With the time-tested team of Jule Styne and Comden and Green to help package her singing talent, Uggams had every reason to be optimistic. In an era when fewer and fewer Broadway songs were becoming hit tunes, Styne had more than managed to buck the trend. Perhaps, Uggams would strike gold as Streisand had with "People" from *Funny Girl*.

What was problematic about the project was Laurents' book, a series of vignettes designed to take the temperature of American race relations from 1900 to 1967. To give the book a feeling of universality, the librettist decided to freeze the lead character at the age of twenty-five. He hoped that the audience could be made to feel about race relations the way they usually felt about character development as the book leapfrogged decade by decade through the century. The trajectory of the story was straightforward. At the top of the show (1900), Uggams sings longingly for a bed she can call her own in "My Own Morning," and as the show ends, Uggams sings "Now Is the Time." What Laurents was attempting was a concept-driven musical. As Richard Cooke, the critic for the *Wall Street Journal* (April 28, 1967) noted, *Hallelujah, Baby!* was "sociology set to music."

The Eckarts took their cue from the book which introduces Uggams as Georgina, the kitchen maid battling to escape her mother's life. "In each era, there is a kitchen," Bill said. "It was our conceit to use the same basic elements in the same relationship for each of these scenes. There would always be a stove and a refrigerator in the kitchen. Since the first scene is set in the nineteenth century, the show began with a wood burning stove. Behind Uggams, there's a piece of latticework with morning glories growing through it. As the play progressed, we updated the stove and the other elements so that by the time we reached the 1960s, she had a radar range and behind her were big daisies printed in the wallpaper that corresponded to the earlier morning glories." It was a promising idea, but as in "The Light Fantastic," it had more to do with style than substance, just as the plot had more to do with show biz than with race relations.

Hallelujah, Baby! opened at Boston's Colonial Theatre on March 20, 1967. The critics had nothing but praise for Uggams, the music, the dances, and the visual elements of the show. But critics felt the book did not develop, instead repeated the same issue without progression through to the end. Samuel Hirsch

THE KITCHEN CHRONOMETER

TELLING TIME BY THE KITCHEN: IN *HALLELUJAH, BABY!* THE ECKARTS CREATED A KITCHEN FOR EACH DECADE USING THE SAME ELEMENTS: STOVE, FLOWERS, AND REFRIGERATOR.

"MY OWN MORNING" THE TURN-OF-THE-CENTURY KITCHEN (EC)

"SMILE, SMILE" 1920s KITCHEN (EC)

"THE BRIGHTEST NEW STAR SINCE BARBRA STREISAND"

JOE FRANKLIN,
WOR TV AND RADIO

LESLIE UGGAMS AS GEORGINA SINGING "MY OWN MORNING" (BILLY ROSE THEATRE COLLECTION, NYPL-PA)

(*Boston Herald*, March 21, 1967) took issue with what the Eckarts called mini-scenery. Even though the wagons were three-dimensional, he felt they seemed "two-dimensional as old-fashioned vaudeville olios" and only helped to emphasize "the segmented flatness of the story." He liked "their curved many faceted glass wall for Leslie's title tune, *Hallelujah, Baby!* [because it] makes you see lots of Leslies in her red and silver gown and that's a big red and silver plus."

A month later, *Hallelujah, Baby!* opened on Broadway. John Chapman (*Daily News*, April 27, 1967) raved, but Walter Kerr (*The New York Times*, April 27, 1967) represented the majority, "The musical that Mr. Styne, Arthur Laurents, Betty Comden and Adolph Green have put together with the best intentions in the world is a course in Civics One when everyone in the world has already got to Civics Six." What Kerr was alluding to was the change in the climate of race relations. As Betty Comden, lyricist, said, "It was the high tide of integration, the mid-1960s, a good feeling between the races … We never thought of ourselves as white people writing about black people… But then the militant movement started … Suddenly it was not a happy time between the races. We were looked on as quite suspect, and it was sort of uncomfortable."

On the basis of its strong entertainment values, *Hallelujah, Baby!* received several Tony Awards including Best Musical. Leslie Uggams won Leading Actress in a Musical. Lillian Hayman, who played her mother, won Best Featured Actress, and Styne, Comden, and Green won as Best Composer and Lyricists. But, *Hallelujah, Baby!* never returned its investment, and closed after 293 performances. Uggams' career, however, did advance, but not as Striesand's had because none of Styne's tunes turned golden. Ironically, Styne won his only Tony for *Hallelujah, Baby!* and evidently critics didn't care that he had recycled a tune from *Fade Out-Fade In* to do it. According to Bill, Laurents became hysterical when he learned of the ruse, and he blamed the Eckarts for not telling him about it in rehearsal. But as Bill said, "It wasn't our job to police the composer." And maybe it was inevitable. Broadway tunes were becoming increasingly generic along with the Street's plots, sets, and costumes. Catering as they did to an audience that didn't change, creative teams were beginning to hit a wall. What was turning the lights off on the Great White Way was not its courageous failures but the pallid imitations of its successes.

The Night They Raided Minsky's (United Artists)

The Night They Raided Minsky's was an historically based film, actually, an affectionate tribute to burlesque. It came a full decade after the Eckarts' Hollywood work, and was an independent feature. *Minsky's* was going to be shot in New York and that made it appealing. "When we decided to do the film, we started scouting locations," Bill said. "One day we were traveling south on Second Avenue and I noticed 'X's' on the windows of a whole section of buildings in the lower Twenties. We stopped and discovered that two streets were going to be demolished. We had just enough time to do the filming. Within these two blocks, there was an alleyway cutting between the two streets that we were able to dress so that it looked like the lower east side. We filled it with pushcarts. The shots inside the burlesque house were done at the old Phoenix Theatre on Second Avenue and Twelfth Street. We also found that the Minsky's had a collection of old vaudeville and burlesque drops in storage. We got them out, unfolded them, and used them."

The Eckarts had learned that a film was seldom if ever re-shot for production values. "In the theater, you do something and you see it. Then you can adjust it and make changes. With film you don't have much control. The designer is low man on the totem pole. If you look through the camera and you think something could be improved, you have to really fight for it. Even if you see something you think is awful, they're not going to re-shoot it unless it's crucial to the film. You can be more effective if you are there when the shot is being set up. Once it's shot and in the can, that's it."

Minsky's was not a box-office smash. Bert Lahr, one of the leads, died during production and the script had to be pieced together to hide his absence. However, the Eckarts' production design won praise. Kevin Thomas (*Los Angeles Times,* December 15, 1968) described the film as "so perfect in its re-creation of a vanished era that it draws 'oohs' and 'ahs' from the audience…If this isn't the way it was, it's the way it should have been."

Their next assignment, *A Midsummer Night's Dream* at the American Shakespeare Festival, Stratford, Connecticut, was their first professional production of the bard. They created a large, magical tree from which Cyril Ritchard's pixie persona delighted and astonished audiences. Not only did Ritchard play multiple roles, he also directed. Conceptually, this *Dream* was at the opposite end of the spectrum from Peter Brook's hauntingly stark production a few years later. Ritchard's *Dream* was a merry romp, and the Eckarts caught just the right note of lush enchantment. Unfortunately, their next collaboration, working with Agnes de Mille on the ballet *Golden Age*, made it necessary for them to decline an invitation from Joseph Papp to remodel the Delacorte Theatre in Central Park for the New York Shakespeare Festival. As a result, they did not design another Shakespeare production until they moved to Dallas.

"Agnes summered in upstate New York in the same private community where George Abbott had his summer home," Bill said. They had attempted to work with de Mille on several occasions on dance pieces but without success. *Golden Age* was commissioned by the Harkness Ballet and de Mille set her story at the Paris Ballet circa 1860. There were a lot of different settings: scenes at rehearsals, during a performance, and in the wings backstage as well as in the *Bois de Boulonge.* "Agnes *agonized* over everything," Bill said. "Nothing was going right, and she worried constantly. We referred to her as *Agon*ness. She didn't get much help from Rebekah Harkness or Brian MacDonald, the Artistic Director of the company. It was every man for himself."

Unfortunately for de Mille, newly arrived British critic Clive Barnes (*The New York Times,* November 9, 1967) found the piece derivative and mediocre. One of the few aspects of the evening's performance he cared for was the set. He commended the Eckarts, and concluded his review with, "It's pleasant to praise something in an otherwise murky ballet."

"We resented being singled out in that way," Bill said, "and we expressed how we felt to a lot of people. We were certain it got back to him. At any rate, the next few shows we did, he gave us terrible reviews."

STAGE LEGENDS JASON ROBARDS, JR. AND BERT LAHR IN FRONT OF MINSKY'S BURLESQUE HOUSE. LAHR DIED DURING FILMING. (PHOTOFEST)

The Education of H*Y*M*A*N K*A*P*L*A*N

The Eckarts' notices from Barnes for *The Education of H*Y*M*A*N K*A*P*L*A*N* were not terrible. They were consistent with his response to the entire production, tepid praise; and although this might have been appropriate for the show, it was grossly inadequate for the Eckarts' work, which was enthusiastically received by the other critics. John Chapman (*Daily News*, April 5, 1968) gave the Eckarts the second paragraph of his review stating, "the lower east side—a neighborhood most beautifully evoked by the imaginative sets of William and Jean Eckart" and echoed in *Variety*, etc. Perhaps Barnes, a foreigner, did not appreciate what the Eckarts had done to transform the lower east side, a series of grim and forbidding tenements. The Eckarts' version with its pastel tinted palette and ghostlike traceries seemed more like Utrillo's Paris than the area south of Delancey Street.

*K*A*P*L*A*N* was based on Leo Rosten's stories in *The New Yorker* centered around the abrasive but amusing title character, played on stage by Tom Bosley. "Jean's family loved the stories," Bill said, "and her aunt knew the real Mr. Parkhill, [one of the characters in the play and stories]." In the wake of *Fiddler on the Roof*, *K*A*P*L*A*N* appeared to be just another show appealing to Jewish ethnicity, but with none of the former's strength or vitality. But *K*A*P*L*A*N* had a charm of its own, something lost on the critics. Abbott, who was directing his 110th Broadway show, wasn't working with people who knew how to respond to him. The result was that there were problems with the book. The first act was slow, uncharacteristic of Abbott whose fame rested on pace.

A. CIGAR SHOP

B. P.S. 102 SCHOOL

C. GROCERY

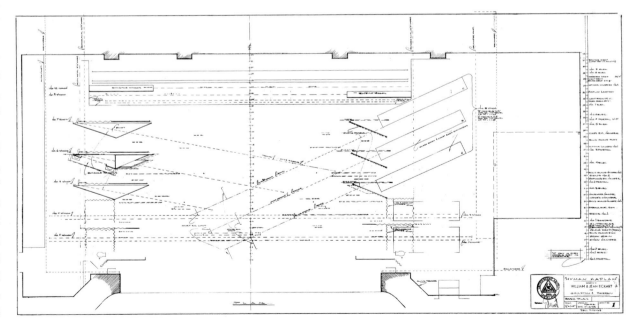

INDIVIDUAL RENDERINGS OF THE THREE TRIANGULAR UNITS WHICH TOGETHER COMPRISED THE OPENING STREET SCENE FOR H*Y*M*A*N K*A*P*L*A*N (EC)

CITYSCAPE KALEIDOSCOPE

THE ECKARTS' LOWER EAST SIDE FOR *H*Y*M*A*N K*A*P*L*A*N* WAS COMPRISED OF THREE PERIAKTOI OF PIERCED BUILDINGS. EACH UNIT REVOLVED AND COULD BE TRACKED OFF OR ON STAGE TO CREATE VARYING PATTERNS AND LOCATIONS. AT THE REAR OF THE STAGE, A SLIDING GROUND ROW OF BUILDINGS PROVIDED FOR ADDITIONAL POSSIBILITIES. THERE WAS NO SPECIFIC VANISHING POINT IN THE ECKARTS' COMPOSITION. RATHER, THEY EXCHANGED THAT NOTION FOR A DANCING KALEIDOSCOPE OF VIEWS. (EC).

CUTOUT BEHIND A TRANSLUCENT DROP

"I don't think that Bosley was the right actor to play Kaplan," Bill said. "There was an actor named Oscar Karlweis who had played the lead in *Jacobowsky and the Colonel*. We always thought that he would have been a wonderful Hyman Kaplan. Bosley was too 'white bread.' At one point the producers wanted to get Red Buttons to play the role, but Abbott refused to work with Buttons." Even so, there were strong performances throughout the show, particularly from Hal Linden, Dick Latessa, Barbara Minkus, and Donna McKechnie.

Choreographer Jaime Rogers created a role for McKechnie, who was at a low point in her career. Six years later, Michael Bennett used this situation to craft the character of Cassie in *A Chorus Line,* played in the original Broadway production by McKechnie. But *K*A*P*L*A*N* was too weak to be much help. It closed after twenty-eight performances. For Abbott, it was his seventh flop in a row, the last hit having come six years earlier in 1962.

Maggie Flynn

The Eckarts were pleased with their work on *H*Y*M*A*N K*A*P*L*A*N*, and disappointed the show didn't run. "It wasn't good enough," Bill said, and by the mid-1960s, Broadway had become a business of superlatives. Nothing ran without rave reviews. They were engaged to design three new musicals all set to open in the fall season of 1968, and that left them little time to "obsess." *Maggie Flynn* went out of town for tryouts in September, *A Mother's Kisses* in October, and *Fig Leaves Are Falling* in November. "This was quite an endeavor for any designer," Ken

THE ECKARTS ACCOMPLISHED SWIFT SCENE CHANGES THROUGH AN INNOVATIVE USE OF LIGHTING TO THE COURTROOM SCENE BY BRINGING IN A HUGE WINDOW. MARTIN ARONSTEIN, LIGHTING DESIGNER, DESCRIBED THE PROCESS IN A RECENT INTERVIEW: "FOR THE COURTROOM SCENE IN THE SECOND ACT, THE CUTOUT OF THE WINDOW WAS LIT AND APPEARED AS AN IMAGE. IN FRONT OF THE DROP WAS A JUDGE'S BENCH. I DON'T REMEMBER ANY CHAIRS. WHEN I LIT THE WINDOW THE STAGE BECAME THE COURTROOM. THE ELLIS ISLAND SET (ALSO IN THE SECOND ACT) WAS SIMPLY A BACKDROP AND THEN BEAMS BUT IT CAME ACROSS WHEN LIT AS BEING A HUGE HALL. THROUGHOUT *K*A*P*L*A*N*, THE ECKARTS RELIED ON CHANGING THE LIGHTING OF CUT-OUT PIECES BEHIND A TRANSLUCENT DROP. IT'S A VERY NICE TECHNIQUE." (COLLECTION OF THE MCNAY MUSEUM, GIFT OF ROBERT L. B. TOBIN)

Billington, assistant lighting designer said, "and I don't know if anyone has done this either before or since."

Maggie Flynn, a vehicle for husband and wife team Shirley Jones and Jack Cassidy, had book, music, and lyrics by Hugo Peretti, Luigi Creatore (Elvis Presley's "Can't Help Falling in Love"), and George David Weiss (Louis Armstrong's "What a Wonderful World"). Morton "Tek" Da Costa, whom the Eckarts had met in Hollywood on the *Auntie Mame* sound stage, was set to direct. "We'd worked with 'Tek,'" Bill said, "trying to get a project on stage called *Beat the Drum*, based on *The Drunkard*, so we knew him well. *Maggie Flynn* was a promising idea. John [Bowab] and 'Tek' asked us to do the costumes, but we didn't want to. There were just too many of them." Robert LaVine, an aide to Cecil Beaton, designed the costumes.

Flynn opened soon after *Hair* moved to Broadway. *Hair* was billed as an example of a "new" style musical. The "tribal rock musical" was a style-dominated show in which the director Tom O'Horgan, who restaged the show for Broadway with a number of nude men and women at the front of the stage, emerged as the show's true star. Without any fanfare, a new era was being ushered in, one in which the style of a show would be increasingly dictated by the director and the choreographer. Bill resented the sensationalism, pyrotechnics, and the weak book. He quipped that he longed for a sequel which would reveal the barrenness of the evening and would be called "Bald." Like many in his generation, he attributed the show's success to the vicarious experience of participation that audiences felt as waves of anti-establishment protest swept the country. Although he had supported Adler and Ross when they tried to convince Abbott to put a rock and roll number into *Damn Yankees*, he was unable to appreciate *Hair's* thoroughly contemporary musical sound, which through the popularity of one of its songs lent its name to the entire era as the "Age of Aquarius."

In contrast, *Flynn* was old with the look and feel of "Tek" Da Costa's last big hit, *The Music Man*. The bouncy score felt like a John Phillip Sousa concert, certainly not tribal, but rather militaristic, a feeling totally at odds with the plot, which was based on the draft riots of the Civil War. In fact, *Maggie Flynn* sought to

A FIERY ESCAPE

"WE GAVE THE SHOW A CINEMATIC TWIST," BILL SAID, "BY SHOWING ACTORS AS THEY MOVED FROM THE PARLOR FLOOR DOWN TO THE BASEMENT." THE ECKARTS' RENDERING SHOWS THE STAIRCASE ABLAZE AND CHILDREN HIDING BEHIND THE CRATES STAGE LEFT. (EC)

CHRISTOPHER STREET, A ROMANTIC VIEW OF NEW YORK CITY DURING THE CIVIL WAR. THE SIGN AT STAGE RIGHT IS A RECRUITING POSTER FOR THE UNION ARMY. THE CLOUD BACK DROP SUGGESTS AN OMINOUS NOTE OF WAR AND THE SMOKE INDICATES THE RIOTS. THE ECKARTS WANTED THE RIGGING VISIBLE TO MAKE THE CLOUDS MORE METAPHORIC THAN LITERAL. (EC)

draw a provocative, if somewhat obvious, comparison between those riots, when Irish protesters lynched Negroes on city streets, and the current protests over the war in Vietnam. The subject matter didn't lend itself to a nostalgic treatment and nostalgia was the sole business of *Maggie Flynn*.

Producer Bowab, with the backing of his Tin Pan Alley associates, wanted a spectacular production. Like *Hair's* O'Horgan, Bowab wanted to overwhelm the audience. Although spectacle had never been the Eckarts' strong suit they tried to oblige. There were two aspects of the show that did appeal to Bill and Jean. One was the opportunity to present Christopher Street in New York City as it might have appeared at the time of the Civil War. The Eckarts were now living in an antebellum townhouse on St. Luke's Place and had become interested in the history of their West Village neighborhood. The other was a spectacular scene that called for the slave children hiding in the basement of Maggie Flynn's orphanage to flee the burning building. The Eckarts had rotated a staircase in *Mame*. In *Flynn*, they decided to hydraulically lift a staircase from the stage level into the scene loft revealing multiple floors as the children ran to escape the advancing flames.

In September, the show opened at the Fisher Theatre in Detroit. For Jerry Herman, Detroit had been the scene of many miracles during the tryouts of *Hello, Dolly!* and miracles were what *Maggie Flynn* needed. Unfortunately, there were problems in places where people least expected them. "If we had had performers who were more generous toward one another than Jack (Cassidy) and Shirley (Jones) were, we might have had a show," Jean said. "But instead of turning out to be the Lunts of the musical theatre, they were busy upstaging each other." When the show opened in New York, the critics were mixed, and it was difficult to get audiences, but according to Jean, "There were so many producers on it, and a lot of them came from the Brill Building [Tin Pan Alley]. I never saw so much white on white—neckties and shirts and shiny suits. They kept that show running long after they should have closed it, because it was a kind of ego thing, vanity, not to have their show close."

A Mother's Kisses

A Mother's Kisses followed hard upon *Maggie Flynn*. With a book by Bruce Jay Friedman based upon his semi-autobiographical novel, *Kisses* featured music and lyrics by Richard Adler. Gene Saks, who had turned his wife Bea Arthur down for the lead in *Mame*, was set to direct her in the starring role of Meg, a monstrous version of the overly possessive Jewish mother she later played in television's *Maude*.

"We made an enormous mistake," Bea Arthur said in a recent interview. "We assumed that everyone had read Friedman's novel. We had read it and thought the novel was in the play. It wasn't."

Like many other novels, *Kisses* was heavily episodic and, according to Bill, "went all over the place. It started in Bensonhurst [Brooklyn] with scenes in Meg's apartment, on the street and in offices. Then it shifted to a summer camp with scenes outside, in a rec hall and a bunk house. Next there was a sequence in Kansas on campus, in temporary classrooms, hotel, Methodist church, a railroad station, etc." To mark the larger shifts in location, the Eckarts created generic backdrops. For the Kansas scenes, they created rows of receding telephone poles, a design element they developed for rural America as far back as *Li'l Abner*, reduced for *Kisses* to its absolute essence. Specific scenes within Kansas were created by placing the skeletal outlines of buildings in

SUMMER CAMP, UPSTATE NEW YORK. "THE PINE FOREST BACKDROP GAVE US THE BASIC LOCATION," BILL SAID, "WHILE ESTABLISHING ELEMENTS FOR INDIVIDUAL LOCALES WERE EITHER FLOWN IN OR WINCHED IN ON WAGONS." THE "WELCOME PARENTS" BANNER WAS A VARIATION OF THE BANNER FROM *THE GOLDEN APPLE*. (EC)

BORSCHT AND "AMERICAN GOTHIC"

KANSAS BACKDROP, THE ECKARTS' MOST ESSENTIAL RENDERING OF RURAL AMERICA. (EC)

COMPOSITE SKETCH, METHODIST CHURCH AND SOCIAL HALL. THE SKELETAL SET IN FRONT OF THE KANSAS BACKDROP WITTILY QUOTES GRANT WOOD'S "AMERICAN GOTHIC." (EC)

front of the drop. The result was minimalist with planes overlaying planes, creating a strong graphic composition in the modernist tradition, a technique which had become an Eckart signature.

What was so appealing about the Eckarts' work for this show was the understated turn they gave to Friedman's satiric thrust. In one scene, for instance, Bea Arthur accompanies her son to a church social in Kansas. To poke fun at the bigotry and small mindedness of the church-going crowd, Bill and Jean set up a visual reference to America's best-known regional artist, Grant Wood. The skeletal framework of the church was a quotation from his "American Gothic," an image used by the counter culture to comment on the "squareness" of mid-America. The Eckarts' approach was subtle and unobtrusive. They created "Grant Wood lenses" to frame the stage picture. Like the Barcelona chair in *Mame*, it was something totally right for the scene. The quotation from Wood was subtle enough not to draw attention to itself, and yet it was unmistakably there.

"This show had problems from the beginning," said Ken Billington, assistant lighting designer. "During rehearsals in New York, Bernadette Peters found that her role was deleted, leaving her free to take a part in the Off-Broadway *Dames at Sea*, which launched her to stardom. And during the tryout in New Haven, the show was rewritten everyday, changing the order of scenes at each performance. A credit to the Eckarts was that no matter what happened, the scenery flowed from one scene to the next even when Scene Five came up right after Scene One, and this would be decided at 1:00 in the afternoon the day of the performance."

"Bea did a good job of portraying the character of Meg, but the audience wasn't having it," Bill said, "they hated her. The character was like Mama Rose in *Gypsy* but without the charm."

"We were having dinner in Baltimore," Billington remembered, "when Jean said to the director Gene Saks, 'Why are we doing this show?' We all gasped. There was this huge silence."

Jean was weary of being on the road and concerned about her children at home with a nanny. She was also ahead of the pack. Composer/lyricist Adler came to the same realization a few days later: "It really didn't make any sense to go on. So at the end of the week, we just closed in Baltimore."

FIG LEAVES ARE FALLING. "LIGHT ONE CANDLE." THARON MUSSER, WHO DESIGNED THE LIGHTS, DESCRIBED THE LOOK AS EARLY PSYCHEDELIC, "I HAD COLOR WHEELS UNDER THE FIBER-GLASS ROCKS. I WAS TRYING TO DO ALL THE EFFECTS I COULD. EVERYTHING WAS IN ITS INFANCY, AND THERE WEREN'T ANY SPECIAL EFFECTS PEOPLE FOR ME TO CALL." "MY PARENTS RESEARCHED THIS SCENE BY TAKING ME TO THE FILMORE EAST TO SEE 'SLY AND THE FAMILY STONE,'" PETER ECKART RECALLED. (COLLECTION OF THE MCNAY ART MUSEUM, GIFT OF ROBERT L. B. TOBIN)

Fig Leaves Are Falling

Fig Leaves Are Falling was an old-fashioned musical comedy with book and lyrics by Allan Sherman and music by Albert Hague (*Plain and Fancy* and *Redhead*). New to Broadway, Sherman was known for his million-seller comedy albums, *Hello Muddah, Hello Fadduh* and *My Son, the Folk Singer.* Jack Klugman (TV's *The Odd Couple* and *Quincy*) was originally slated to direct but was unable to pull the show together. At the Eckarts' suggestion, George Abbott took over. As it turned out, he was absolutely the wrong man for the job. What the show cried out for was a director with the sensibilities of *Hair's* Tom O'Horgan and a rock score to match. Bill defended his choice, "We thought George could do it very well," Bill said. "Sherman had written a very lively and funny script. Even at the gypsy run-through in New York, it seemed quite good. Everyone was very enthusiastic about it. Then we got to Philadelphia and found out that it didn't work in front of an audience. Apparently, it was a show that got worse as it went along."

Sherman's script was semi-autobiographical and it concerned his current mid-life crisis. "Allan was having an affair with a hippie [girl]," company manager Richard Grayson said, "while he was still married to the woman with whom he had children. When the girl came to Philadelphia to see the play, it ended with Allan's character going off with the hippie. When the girl went back to New York and his wife came, he'd revise the script so that the show ended with his going back to his wife." Sherman, in a drug-besotted stupor, came up with the idea of polling the audience each night and telling them that his fate was in their hands. Barry Nelson, who played Sherman's role in the play, as a goof would then go out into the house and give chickens away as prizes to members of the audience.

Taking their cue from the use of this vaudeville shtick, the Eckarts decided on a style that exposed lighting instruments and placed them amongst large daisies. The "square," middle-class world was represented by finishing out Nelson's Madison Avenue office in gray flannel.

"The wall, the furniture, everything in his office was gray flannel," Bill said. "The house in the suburbs was black and white as if it were in a black and white film. The point was that his hippie friend [Pookie played by Jenny O'Hara] brought color to his life." A crucial scene took place at a "love-in" in Central Park. Bill and Jean turned an outcropping of rock into a kind of psychedelic jukebox. The rocks were lit from inside. After the "love-in," Nelson returns to his suburban house and finds everything in vivid colors. "Actually, we used the same fabrics and patterns," Bill said, "only we had them specially dyed. Maybe, it was a little too cute."

Through their use of color, the Eckarts found a way of making audiences empathize with Sherman's drugged state of consciousness while Abbott, always the total showman, sought ways to make the show more entertaining. Three days before the opening in New York, Abbott made the decision to take the song "All My Laughter," which Pookie performed on the LOVE car, and give it to the wife played by Dorothy Loudon. "No one had any idea where Dorothy was or how she was

FIG LEAVES ARE FALLING. THE LOVE CAR. THE ECKARTS CONSTRUCTED A WAGON BASED ON ROBERT INDIANA'S POP ART LOVE LITHOGRAPH. IN ONE SCENE, BARRY NELSON, THE TWO-TIMING HUSBAND, AND POOKIE, PLAYED BY JENNY O'HARA, SIT ON THE "E" AND ARE SWEPT INTO THE WINGS SINGING AND YELLING, ECSTATICALLY HAPPY. (EC)

FIG LEAVES ARE FALLING. THE HOUSE IN THE SUBURBS IN COLOR. BEFORE THE AFFAIR WITH THE HIPPIE, EVERY-THING APPEARED AS IF IT WERE IN A BLACK AND WHITE FILM. THE ECKARTS MADE USE OF THEIR SIGNATURE LINEAR STYLE, A BACKDROP ETCHED BY ELEMENTS OF A SKELETAL HOUSE HUNG IN A SEPARATE PLANE. IN KEEPING WITH THE LIGHT-HEARTED FUN OF THE EVENING, THE ECKARTS PAID HOMAGE TO NEW YORKER CARTOONS. (EC)

playing the Devil, hitch his trousers and reveal his red socks. But he was unaware that in switching the song he had upset whatever balance existed in the script between the girlfriend and the wife.

"On opening night," Ken Billington said, "after Loudon had finished singing, the audience would not let the show continue until she did an encore. It was one of the few real show-stopping moments I have ever seen." Loudon made such a strong impression, she earned a Tony nomination, a rarity for a performer appearing in a show that ran for only four performances.

The reviews were dismal. Clive Barnes of *The New York Times* was particularly negative. He panned everything about the show (except for Loudon) and that included the scenery. "I remember," Bill said, "one of the kids in the chorus asking, 'How can the scenery be *nasty*?' That was the word Barnes used, but he was trashing the show."

Doing *Fig Leaves*, Jean noticed a big change in octogenarian George Abbott. "He kept a performer that he would have let go in a minute, without thinking about it, years before. Abbott said, 'Oh, well, he's doing wall-papering to earn a living.' And his answer before would have been, 'He can go back to wallpapering.'"

The truth was Abbott was not even in the same universe as Sherman. He was as unlikely to "tune in, turn on, and drop out" as he was to fly to the moon. The kind of chaos he saw in the streets surrounding the theatre revolted him. This was a man who ten years earlier had told the Eckarts he wouldn't venture below 12th Street to direct *Mattress* unless they agreed to be his escort. What sense could he possibly make of hippies, panhandlers, and "love-ins" in Central Park? Every drop of his old Yankee blood boiled at the waste and self-indulgence of the "Age of Aquarius," and the last thing he should ever have been asked to do was serve as its spokesman. "Slime Square," as it was now called by *Show Business* publisher Leo Schull, was not the elegant theatrical world Mister Broadway had conquered in the 1920s, and he couldn't wait to catch the next plane back to Florida.

going to do that number," John Bowab recalled. "The stage was completely bare. Abbott was thinking she would just come downstage and deliver the number in one. But Bill and Jean thought otherwise. They came up with a big, twelve-foot-high broken heart that was tied together with a rope. After the LOVE wagon disappeared, the heart came gliding in from the wings. When it reached center stage, you noticed Dorothy [the wife] for the first time. She had been walking behind the heart. The Eckarts had designed it so you saw the broken heart before you saw its owner. As she emerged, Dorothy said, 'I guess you wonder what I've been doing.' The audience just cracked up. It was just another example of the kind of contribution the Eckarts made to the shows they designed."

Abbott liked the change. It was similar to the kind of witty contribution the Eckarts made to *Damn Yankees* when they had Walston,

1969–70 Season

The 1969–70 season has to rank as one of Broadway's grimmest. Half of the new musicals, seven out of fourteen, ran less than a week. Three of those closed on their opening nights. Of the remaining seven, none was a runaway success. Two owed their longer runs to star drawing power, which meant in one instance that Katherine Hepburn would be compensated while the show's investors went without. Revivals and imports were put forth to swell the meager fare. But with a war in Southeast Asia, skyrocketing inflation, and almost daily riots and protest marches, the health of Broadway was not of much concern to most Americans.

During the summer of 1969, Hilly Elkins met with the Eckarts at the newly christened Eden Theatre on East 12th Street, the site of previous triumphs, *The Golden Apple* and *Once Upon a Mattress*. The producer proposed that Bill and Jean design his new show, *Oh! Calcutta*. They assumed he was joking. What kind of sets and costumes were they to devise for a nude cast on a bare stage? Years later, Bill said, "We probably should have accepted Hilly's offer. Certainly, it was a show that we wouldn't do out of town." Instead the Eckarts signed to design Murray Schisgal's *A Way of Life*, an offbeat contemporary comedy with a satiric thrust. The plot followed the escapades of a ne'er-do-well, older brother who comes for a visit and then takes over his younger brother's life, wife, mistress, and job. Unlike Schisgal's *Luv*, the new play had a Pinteresque quality. Director Alan Schneider assembled a strong cast: Estelle Parsons, Elliott Gould, John McGiver, Melinda Dillon, and Lou Jacobi. After a week of rehearsals, Gould was fired and Bob Dishy, co-star of *Flora, the Red Menace*, was brought in as his replacement. After the first week of previews, Jacobi and Schneider had a disagreement and Schneider was let go. Harold Stone was brought to direct. "He was not very good and not very pleasant to work with," Bill said. "The show had been playing in front of audiences. Everything was set. He wanted to change silly things, like the way the doors opened. We would have been willing to make changes, but the producer didn't want to spend any more money. So, the show closed before it opened."

A WAY OF LIFE. THE MOST INTRIGUING OF THE INTERIORS WAS AN OLD DOWNTOWN OFFICE INSPIRED BY THE PAINTINGS OF EDWARD HOPPER. THERE WAS AN OUTER AND AN INNER OFFICE THAT MOVED AS IF IT WERE ON A TURNTABLE SO THAT THE AUDIENCE COULD FOLLOW THE ACTION AS IT MOVED FROM ONE PLACE TO ANOTHER. "WE DID BIG UNITS THAT CAME IN AND MATCHED A FLOOR," BILL SAID. "THE OFFICES MOVED IN AN ARC, WHILE THE OTHER SETS SLID UP OR DOWNSTAGE AS NEEDED." (EC)

Ironically Bill got his wish; at least he didn't have to go out-of-town.

The Eckarts' set for *Way of Life* was more dimensional than that for *Fig Leaves Are Falling*. They made use of a platform that swung like a pendulum from one side of the stage to the other, which made it possible for the audience to see different sides of the set but not at the same time. The idea was not new, and it has been used countless times since by shows such as *Noises Off*. But what it did show was that the Eckarts were moving away from their signature style of skeletal traceries backed by painted drops. There was a harder edge to this style, less fanciful and more realistic.

By February 1, the frenzied pace of a year of non-stop work came to an end. Since mid-August, the Eckarts had been in rehearsal or on the road or hurrying off to attend previews. Four shows, three of them big musicals, had opened. Two of these shows had closed before their official New York openings. The most successful, *Maggie Flynn*, ran a total of eighty-one performances, thanks to the popularity of Shirley Jones. But by mid-January 1969, it too was history. The Eckarts were thankful that *Mame* was continuing to run and that meant royalty payments would continue. An entire year passed without one viable job offer, and then on January 3, 1970, *Mame* closed on Broadway. The Eckarts' income was reduced to royalties from *Mame's* national and London companies.

When at last the Eckarts did get a show to design, it was a script that they both abhorred. *Norman, Is That You?* was essentially a one-joke show. "It was sitcom," Bill said, "and not a very good one. A father and mother come to visit their son in New York and find out that their son is a homosexual. The father thinks he's not really gay so he gets a hooker for him, and that's where the show's title is introduced. The mother sees the hooker from across the room and says, 'Norman, is that you?' That's the level of the humor." Even so, the production starred Lou Jacobi and Maureen Stapleton. It was George Abbott's 113th show. "George got Maureen to do it," Bill said. "She was only in one scene, but she and George

REACHING FOR THE THIRD DIMENSION

SENSATIONS, AN OFF-BROADWAY ROCK MUSICAL, FOUND THE ECKARTS EXPERIMENTING WITH PIPE-SCAFFOLDING AND RAMPS, A STYLE MADE POPULAR BY MING CHO LEE. WORKING IN A CONVERTED CHURCH, THE EMPHASIS WAS ON ENVIRONMENT NOT ILLUSION. (EC)

were having an affair at the time, so she couldn't say no." *Norman, Is That You?* ran for twelve performances. It became popular in summer stock, and was eventually made into a film starring Redd Foxx and Pearl Bailey. Evidently, a black family dealing with a gay son was more amusing.

Another eight months passed before Charles Bowab offered the Eckarts an Off-Broadway musical. During the interim, Bill found employment painting drops for the circus and other designers. Although the fee for the Off-Broadway musical would be nominal and the production budget minuscule, the Eckarts eagerly accepted the assignment. Suggested by *Romeo and Juliet*, *Sensations*, with music by Wally Harper and lyrics by Paul Zakrewski, was to be staged at Theatre

Four, a converted church. "It was a time of 'found art' and happenings," Bill said. "We were aiming at a contemporary aesthetic, mixing visual media and musical sounds. Romeo and Juliet are a biracial couple. We worked out the design with the musical director: A rock band performed in the tiny pit while the lateral balconies held a string quartet and a harpist. The sound was wonderful. The strings floated over the top of the rock band."

"The Eckarts did things they probably hadn't done in years," Bowab said. "They used egg cartons, ripped burlap, old tires, just junk. They created platforms on either side of the stage—something I hadn't seen before. The Eckarts' scenery wasn't literal, just the two platforms."

At Theatre Four, Bill and Jean were essentially designing an environment. Actors were working deep within the set, which was fully three-dimensional. Bill worked directly with a model of the space and abandoned the idea of using planes upon planes. It was a far cry from the kind of proscenium mounted musicals they had designed on Broadway. It was closer to the work they had done two decades earlier at the Theatre de Lys, a converted movie house. There they constructed their sets in the alley. With *Sensations*, they were returning to Off-Broadway. Their careers had come full circle, and it was as if they were starting over again. But this time there were four Eckarts at work. "I don't remember ever seeing two grown-ups have such fun," Bowab said. "The kids were helping them paint and put the show together, and they were all having a wonderful time. I have a fond memory of that experience."

Sensations needed rave reviews to extend beyond the initially planned sixteen performances. It didn't receive them.

More than a year and a half of their lives had been spent waiting for another Broadway musical, but the telephone didn't ring. They did not question their talents but they felt they were in danger of losing the freshness and enthusiasm they had felt for commercial theatre.

"We had gained a certain kind of experience and assurance of knowing how to go about things and what's going to happen," Bill said. "Sometimes you repeat yourself. You can't help that. Often you will fall back on your own old clichés because you don't have a new idea. But it wasn't that that bothered us. We knew that the theatre has always been rather cruel to some of its senior citizens—to most of them. It's very 'faddy' and you are a fad, a part of a fashion, and when you go out of fashion, you don't work much anymore. We had watched that happen to others—to Don Oenslager to Jo Mielziner, and by the time we came along, Robert Edmond Jones wasn't working in New York. And that's what should happen, new people have to come along, and the people you've worked with retire or die, and there isn't enough theatre to go around for everyone. Abbott kept working until he was eighty and then some, but people like Tek Da Costa, who was also a great director, discovered that he was no longer popular . . . It happens, and you have to move on. We had a certain point of view, not so much a look or a style, but a way of solving the problems of musicals, for instance, the way we dealt with scene changes. Some of the mechani-

cal things we developed, like decks and winches, have become the dominant way of shifting scenery. When we did *Mister Johnson*, we had only crude little drive wagons that attached to things. Today, our drive wagons are called 'dogs' and there is a whole range of technical apparatus for winching sets on and off stage far beyond our wildest dreams."

A couple of years earlier, the Eckarts had done a presentation at the American Theatre Association's national convention. The students and faculty who attended were extremely responsive and the question and answer session really took off. After the session, they were approached by one of the officers of the Association. "You know," he said, "if you should ever want to work in academia, I'm certain that there would be a place for you at one of the universities." He pressed his business card into Bill's hand and added, "Call me if you should ever want to do that." Although it was the furthest thing from their minds at the time, the Eckarts had kept the business card. They were now facing the prospect of a third season without a major show, and so they played that card.

JAMES EARL JONES (LENNIE) AND KEVIN CONWAY (GEORGE) IN JOHN STEINBECK'S STAGE ADAPTATION *OF MICE AND MEN* (1974) (EC)

Epilogue

Another Opening . . .

"William and Jean Eckart designed impressionist sets and costumes evoking the Salinas River country of California, the isolation of the ranch, even the bleak aura of Depression. Critics conjectured that our revival surpassed the original production."

James Earl Jones

JEAN'S COSTUME SKETCH FOR LENNIE IN *OF MICE AND MEN* AIMS AT SUGGESTING CHARACTER. (EC)

In April 1971, the Eckarts traveled to Dallas where they worked out the details of their contracts with the Meadows School of the Arts, Southern Methodist University. Bill's arrangement was flexible so that he could accept professional work whenever it was available, and Jean accepted a part-time position teaching costume design. For SMU's Theatre Department, started just six years earlier with twelve students, the Eckarts were a major coup. Upon their return to New York, there was a letter waiting for them from Stanley Marcus of Neiman-Marcus expressing his delight and welcoming them to Dallas.

By mid-July, they had made the move. Of course, they would miss New York. Nothing could replace it. Not only was it the theatre center and so the source of their livelihood, but for years it had been the main source of their artistic inspiration. Yet their love for the City was severely strained, not only by the difficulties they were having in finding employment, but by the concerns they had as parents for the safety of their two pre-teen children. Ironically, while Bill and Jean were out-of-town with *A Mother's Kisses*, their son Peter had been terrorized by a gang of neighborhood ruffians. Although he escaped any physical harm, the experience of returning home and not being able to see his parents left its toll. Bill and Jean recounted how as a youngster Peter had packed himself into a valise to accompany them to New Haven, and a wan smile betrayed their genuine sense of guilt. They hadn't waited seventeen years into their marriage to become parents merely to be absentees. Dallas, they hoped, would be different, and the children, not the theatre, would come first. Their idea about what university teaching would be like was based on their own youthful admiration for "Doc" Lippman and his wife Ruth at Tulane. Bill and Jean's decision to attend graduate school was based on the advice of the Lippmans. The Eckarts had no way of knowing they would become commercially successful and so their careers in academia had had to wait for more than two decades while they did post-graduate work on Broadway. They were now ready to return to what they had thought was going to be their life's work, college teaching.

Even so, the transition wasn't an easy one, and it was far harder on Jean than on Bill. "When we arrived," Jean said, "I thought I would take six months to get us settled, and then I would figure out what I was going to do. Well, by the end of three weeks, I was climbing the walls. 'I've got to do something. I can't go to people's houses for coffee and get into what color crepe paper we're going to use for the PTA meeting.'

"I had been interested in psychotherapy for a long time, and there was an organization in Dallas called Suicide Prevention that wanted volunteers. I spent a year doing that. The following year I went to the Dallas Mental Health Clinic and became a full-time volunteer. With supervision, they allowed me to do a lot of casework. When I left there to go to the School of Social Work, I had a full caseload; and I was co-therapist in five groups. I loved it. And so I thought, 'I better get my union card so I can get paid for this.' I graduated from the University of Texas at Arlington, School of Social Work, with an MSSW (1976). It was a really exciting and exhilarating two years. People would say to me 'Jean, how can you leave the theatre?' What I used to say, sort of glibly was, 'What's the difference between design for the theatre and design for living? They're both problem solving.'"

While Bill taught and designed shows, Jean co-founded the Community Psychotherapy Center, a not-for-profit facility serving Dallas, and became its director. Yet on another level, she never really stopped designing for the theatre. It was too much a part of her and Bill's lives. Their dynamic collaboration continued. Bill brought Jean

into every decision, a fact he willingly acknowledged when he talked about his work, preferring to use the first person plural "we" when he talked about process. And, of course, Jean continued to teach costume design, attend faculty meetings and tech rehearsals, and give notes.

Designing under vastly different circumstances, the Eckarts' approach to design changed. The graphic, plane-upon-plane style they originated with *The Golden Apple* became increasingly more sculptural. Scaffold sets with ramps and poles replaced the use of drops and skeletal structures. For Sophocles' *Oedipus* (1971), Bill employed his first raked platform and nothing flew. It was a breakthrough. In time, the Eckarts would reintroduce various elements from their Broadway days, creating an amalgam of styles idiosyncratic and unique.

Not long after the Eckarts settled in Dallas, Broadway producer Elliot Martin, whom Bill and Jean had known since the Westport Country Playhouse back in the early 1950s, approached them to design

AT THE BEGINNING AND THE END OF THE PLAY, LENNIE AND GEORGE DAYDREAM ALONGSIDE THE SALINAS RIVER. THE RIVER BANK INCLUDED ONLY THE CENTRAL RAMP OF THE UNIT SET AND RELIED HEAVILY ON PROJECTIONS OF LEAVES AND BUSHES TO CREATE MOOD. (EC)

THE BARN WAS CREATED BY HAVING HIGH INTENSITY LIGHTING POUR THROUGH SLIT DROPS AND DEFUSED BY TRANSLUCENT SCRIM. (EC)

sets, lights, and costumes for a revival of John Steinbeck's *Of Mice and Men* (1974), directed by Ed Sherin and starring James Earl Jones. What Martin had in mind was a two-week out-of-town tryout at SMU's Bob Hope Theatre, which had a Broadway-caliber stage. This engagement would involve students in apprentice positions backstage before New York and its subsequent booking at the Kennedy Center in Washington, D.C. The Eckarts were enthusiastic about combining their new roles as teachers with their professional careers. And there was even something in it for the University. For its $35,000 contribution to the physical production, it stood to benefit as limited partners sharing in the show's net profits.

Martin, who remembered how the Eckarts had re-crafted old sets for *Glad Tidings* (1951), was banking on Bill and Jean to create something artistically effective out of forced minimalism. He was not disappointed. Bill designed a ramped platform with two portable wings that rolled in with the barn, the lean-to, and later, the bunkhouse. The

design called for the use of slit drops and high intensity light to simulate rustic walls. The Eckarts departed from the literalism of the original production designed by former Yale professor and mentor Donald Oenslager. In 1937, Oenslager's set featured a representational tree and a transparent plastic river along with sedges and grasses in the riverbed. For their riverbank scene, Bill and Jean used only the central ramp and projections of leaves and bushes. The settings were highly romantic and impressionistic, owing their inspiration to the abstract landscape paintings of Milton Avery. The unusual unit set was placed on an open stage and the scene-shifting, what little there was of it, was accomplished in darkness without curtains. By utilizing open set changes, they helped to sustain the mood of the drama, which was a blend of fantasy and grinding realism.

After receiving generally excellent notices, *Of Mice and Men* settled in for a run at the Brooks Atkinson Theatre on Broadway. With Christmas approaching, Bill and Jean rented an apartment and arranged for Peter, age thirteen, and Julie, age twelve, to spend the holidays in the City. Although their home was more the 1,200 miles from the "Main Stem," they were still first class talent.

The Eckarts continued to teach and design not only at SMU but at regional and summer theatres. As time passed, the phone calls from New York became less and less frequent. Yet their interest in Broadway continued, and they designed several shows that were Broadway-bound but never made it to the Big Apple.

At their zenith as designers, the Eckarts' work was as important to the shows they designed as the work of the director and the choreographer. With wit and style, they had helped to shape the musicals that they had worked on and to give them a lightness and fluidity that allowed them to flow from one scene to another with a dreamlike rapidity. They had found a way to substitute imagination for literalism and to translate naturalism into representational language that both stimulated and challenged audiences.

The Eckarts remained active as designers and educators until the time of their deaths. On September 6, 1993, Jean died at age seventy-two. Bill passed on January 24, 2000, in his eightieth year, having just finished the final drawings for a production of *Macbeth*.

OF MICE AND MEN. JAMES EARL JONES (LENNIE) AND KEVIN CONWAY (GEORGE) WALKING ON THE ECKARTS' RENDITION OF THE BANKS OF THE SALINAS RIVER (EC)

Chronology

NYPL-PA

The Little Screwball
Author: Walt Anderson
Theatre: Westport Country Playhouse, Westport, CT, July 16, 1951
Producer: Theatre Guild (Nancy Stern)
Director: Walter Abel
Stars: Walter Abel, Edward Gargan, Sal Mineo, Jr.
Sets, Lighting and Costumes: W and J

NYPL-PA

Glad Tidings
Author: Edward Mabley
Theatre: Lyceum Theatre, October 11, 1951
Producer: Harald Bromley
Director: Melvyn Douglas
Costumes: John Derro
Stars: Melvyn Douglas, Signe Hasso, Haila Stoddard
Sets and Lighting: W and J

To Dorothy, A Son
Author: Roger MacDougal
Theatre: John Golden Theatre, November 19, 1951
Producer: Herman Shumlin
Director: Herman Shumlin
Costumes: Hazel Roy
Stars: Ronald Howard, Hildy Parks, Stella Andrew, Martin Rudy
Sets and Lighting: W and J

1952

Gertie
Author: Enid Bagnold
Theatre: Plymouth Theatre, January 30, 1952
Producer: Herman Shumlin
Director: Herman Shumlin
Costumes: Hazel Roy
Stars: Glynis Johns, Albert Dekker, Alan Napier, Polly Rowles
Sets and Lighting: W and J

1953

Maya
Author: Simon Gantillon
Theatre: Theatre De Lys, June 9, 1953
Producer: Terese Hayden
Director: Roger Kay, Sanford Meisner
Stars: Kay Medford, Susan Strasberg, Helen Craig, Martin Ritt
Sets, Costumes. and Lighting: W and J

The Scarecrow
Author: Percy MacKaye
Theatre: Theatre De Lys, June 16, 1953
Producer: Terese Hayden (Liska March)
Director: Frank Corsaro

Costumes: Ruth Morley
Stars: Patricia Neal, Douglass Watson, Eli Wallach, Anne Jackson
Sets and Lighting: W and J

School for Scandal
Author: Richard Brinsley Sheridan
Theatre: Theatre De Lys, June 23, 1953
Producer: Terese Hayden
Director: Terese Hayden
Costumes: Frances Malek
Stars: Patricia Neal, John Heldabrand, David Stewart, Leo Penn, Orson Bean, Vivian Matalon
Sets and Lighting: W and J

The Little Clay Cart
Author: Shudraka, translated by Arthur William Ryder
Theatre: Theatre De Lys, June 30, 1953
Producer: Terese Hayden (Liska March)
Director: Edward Greer
Costumes: Ruth Morley, Dale Clement
Stars: Sono Osato, Richard Waring
Sets and Lighting: W and J

Oh Men! Oh Women!
Author: Edward Chodorov
Theatre: Henry Miller's Theatre, December 13, 1953
Producer: Cheryl Crawford (Anderson Lawler)
Director: Edward Chodorov
Costumes: Paul du Pont
Stars: Franchot Tone, Betsy von Furstenberg, Anne Jackson, Larry Blyden, Henry Sharp, Gig Young
Sets and Lighting: W and J

Dead Pigeon
Author: Leonard Kantor
Theatre: Vanderbilt Theatre, December 23, 1953
Producer: Harald Bromley
Director: Harald Bromley, Haila Stoddard
Stars: Lloyd Bridges, Joan Lorring, James Gregory
Sets and Lighting: W and J

1954

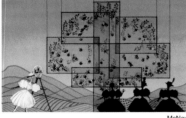

McNay

The Golden Apple
Author: John Latouche, book and lyrics; Jerome Moross, music
Theatre: Phoenix Theatre, March 11, 1954
Producer: Phoenix Theatre, T. Edward Hambleton, Norris Houghton
Director: Norman Lloyd
Choreographer: Hanya Holm
Costumes: Alvin Colt
Lighting: Klaus Holm
Stars: Priscilla Gillette, Stephen Douglass, Kaye Ballard, Jack Whiting, Bibi Osterwald, Jonathan Lucas, Portia Nelson
Sets: W and J

Wedding Breakfast
Author: Theodore Reeves
Theatre: Forty-Eighth Street Theatre, November 20, 1954
Producer: Kermit Bloomgarden
Director: Herman Shumlin
Costumes: Edith Lutyens
Stars: Lee Grant, Harvey Lembeck, Anthony Franciosa, Virginia Vincent
Sets and Lighting: W and J

Portrait of A Lady
Authors: William Archibald, play; adapted from Henry James
Theatre: ANTA Theatre, December 20, 1954
Producer: Lyn Austin, Thomas Noyes
Direcor: Jose Quintero
Costumes: Cecil Beaton
Stars: Jennifer Jones, Robert Flemyng, Cathleen Nesbitt, Douglass Watson
Sets and Lighting: W and J

1955

Damn Yankees
Authors: George Abbott, Douglass Wallop, play; Jerry Ross, music; Richard Adler, lyrics
Theatre: Forty-Sixth Street Theatre, May 23, 1955
Producers: Frederick Brisson, Robert E. Griffith, Harold S. Prince, Albert B. Taylor
Director: George Abbott
Choreographer: Bob Fosse
Lighting: Klaus Holm (supervised by the Eckarts)
Stars: Gwen Verdon, Stephen Douglass, Ray Walston
Sets and Costumes: W and J

Reuben Reuben
Author: Marc Blitzstein, play and music
Theatre: Shubert Theatre, Boston, October 10, 1955 (Closed in Boston)
Producer: Cheryl Crawford
Director: Robert Lewis
Choreographer: Hanya Holm
Stars: Eddie Albert, Evelyn Lear, Kaye Ballard, George Gaynes, Enzio Stuarti
Sets, Costumes, and Lighting: W and J

1956

Mister Johnson
Author: Norman Rosten, play; adapted from Joyce Cary
Theatre: Martin Beck Theatre, March 29, 1956
Producers: Cheryl Crawford, Robert Lewis
Director: Robert Lewis
Choreographer: Pearl Primus
Stars: Earle Hyman, William Sylvester, Gaby Rodgers, Josephine Premice
Sets, Costumes and Lighting: W and J

The Marriage of Figaro
Authors: Edward Eager, translator; Leonard Kastle, translator; Mozart, music
Theatre: National Tour, October 11, 1956
Producers: Samuel Chotzinoff, Chandler Cowles, Schuyler Chapin
Director: Peter Hermann Adler
Choreographer: NBC Touring Opera
Costumes: Alvin Colt
Stars: Ralph Herbert, Adelaide Bishop, Walter Cassel, Phyllis Curtin, Frances Bible
Sets and Lighting: W and J

Madam Butterfly
Authors: Ruth and Thomas Martin, translators; Puccini, music
Theatre: National Tour, November 13, 1956
Producers: Samuel Chotzinoff, Chandler Cowles, Schyuler Chapin
Director: Bill Butler
Choreographer: NBC Touring Opera
Costumes: Alvin Colt
Stars: Phyllis Curtin, Edith Evans, Thomas Hayward, John Tyers
Sets and Lighting: W and J

Li'l Abner
Author: Norman Panama, play; Melvin Frank, play; Johnny Mercer, lyrics; Gene de Paul, music
Theatre: St. James Theatre, November 15, 1956
Producer: Norman Panama, Melvin Frank, Michael Kidd
Director: Michael Kidd
Costumes: Alvin Colt
Stars: Edith Adams, Peter Palmer, Howard St. John, Stubby Kaye, Charlotte Rae
Sets and Lighting: W and J

1957

The Pajama Game
Warner Brothers, 1957
Directors: George Abbott and Stanley Donen
Associate producers: Frederick Brisson, Robert E. Griffith, Harold S. Prince
Screenplay: George Abbott and Richard Bissell, from their 1954 musical play of the same name, based on the 1953 novel *Seven-and-a-Half Cents*, by Richard Bissell
Music and lyrics: Richard Adler and Jerry Ross
Director of photography: Harry Stradling
Editor: William Ziegler
Art director: Malcolm Bert
Assistant art director: Frank Thompson
Set decorator: William Kuehl
Choreography: Bob Fosse
Musical director: Ray Heindorf
Orchestrations: Nelson Riddle, Buddy Bregman
Cast: John Raitt, Doris Day, Carol Haney, Eddie Foy, Jr., Reta Shaw
Costumes, Color Consultants: W and J

Cinderella
Authors: Richard Rodgers, music; Oscar Hammerstein, II, play and lyrics
Theatre: CBS Studio 81, March 31, 1957
Producer: CBS (Richard Lewine)
Director: Ralph Nelson
Choreographer: Jonathan Lucas
Lighting: Bob Barry
Stars: Julie Andrews, Howard Lindsay, Dorothy Stickney, Ilka Chase, Kaye Ballard, Alice Ghostley, Jon Cypher, Edith Adams
Sets and Costumes: W and J

Livin' The Life
Authors: Dale Wasserman, play; Bruce Geller, play and lyrics; Jack Urbont, music
Theatre: Phoenix Theatre, April 28, 1957
Producers: Phoenix Theatre, T. Edward Hambleton, Norris Houghton
Director: David Alexander
Choreographer: John Butler
Costumes: Alvin Colt
Lighting: Klaus Holm
Stars: Stephen Elliot, Alice Ghostley, James Mitchell, Lee Becker, Patsy Bruder, Lee Charles, Timmy Everett, Loren Hightower, Richard Ide, Ronald Rogers, Jack DeLon
Sets: W and J

A Soft Touch
Authors: Claude Binyon and Mac Edwards
Theatre: Music Box (Closed in Rehearsal), October 1957
Producers: George Abbott, Robert E. Griffith, Harold S. Prince
Director: George Abbott
Stars: Elsa Lanchaster, George S. Irving, Loring Smith, Russell Nype
Sets and Lighting: W and J

Copper and Brass
Author: Ellen Violett, play; David Craig, play and lyrics; David Baker, music
Theatre: Martin Beck Theatre, October 17, 1957
Producer: Lyn Austin, Thomas Noyes, Anderson Lawler
Director: Marc Daniels (replaced); Burt Shevelove
Choreographer: Anna Sokolow (replaced); Bob Fosse
Costumes: Alvin Colt
Stars: Nancy Walker, Benay Venuta, Dick Williams, Alice Pearce, Alan Bunce
Sets and Lighting: W and J

1958

The Body Beautiful
Authors: Joseph Stein, play; Will Glickman, play; Sheldon Harnick, lyrics; Jerry Bock, music
Theatre: The Broadway Theatre, January 28, 1958
Producers: Richard Kollmar, Albert Selden
Director: George Schaefer
Choreographer: Herbert Ross
Costumes: Noel Taylor
Stars: Mindy Carson, Jack Warden, Lonnie Sattin, Mara Lynn, Barbara McNair, Steve Forrest
Sets and Lighting: W and J

Damn Yankees
(British title: Whatever Lola Wants)
Warner Brothers, 1958
Directors: George Abbott and Stanley Donen
Producers: George Abbott and Stanley Donen
Associate producers: Frederick Brisson,
Photofest
Richard Griffith, Harold S. Prince
Screenplay: George Abbott, from his and Douglass Wallop's 1955 musical play, based on the 1954 novel by Wallop, *The Year the Yankees Lost the Pennant*
Music and lyrics: Richard Adler and Jerry Ross
Director of photography: Harold Lipstein
Editor: Frank Bracht
Art director: Stanley Fleischer
Set decorator: Maurice Binder
Choreographer: Bob Fosse
Musical direction: Ray Heindorf
Sound recordists: Stanley Jones, Dolph Thomas
Cast: Tab Hunter, Gwen Verdon, Ray Walston, Russ Brown, Shannon Bolin, Nathaniel Frey, Rae Allen, Jimmy Komack, Robert Shafer, Jean Stapleton, Albert Linville, Elizabeth Howell, Bob Fosse
Production and Costumes: W and J

Far Away, the Trainbirds Cry
October 1958
Author: Edward Davis and Lionel Kranitz
Producer: Louis D'Almeida and Milton Greene
Director: John Frankenheimer
Stars: James MacArthur, Patricia Neal
(Preliminary sketch. This show failed to capitalize.)
Sets and Lighting: W and J

1959

Once Upon a Mattress
Authors: Jay Thompson, play; Marshall Barer, play and lyrics, Dean Fuller, play; Mary Rodgers, music
Theatre: The Phoenix Theatre, May 18, 1959
Producers: Phoenix Theatre, T. Edward Hambleton, Norris Houghton, William and Jean Eckart
Director: George Abbott
Choreographer: Joe Layton
Lighting: Tharon Musser
Stars: Joe Bova, Carol Burnett, Allen Case, Jack Gilford, Anne Jones, Matt Mattox, Harry Snow, Robert Weil, Jane White
Sets, Costumes, Lighting, and Co-producers: W and J

Fiorello!
Authors: Jerome Weidman, play; George Abbott, play; Sheldon Harnick, lyrics; Jerry Bock, music
Theatre: Broadhurst Theatre, November 23, 1959
Producers: Robert E. Griffith, Harold S. Prince
Director: George Abbott
Choreographer: Peter Gennaro
Stars: Tom Bosley, Patricia Wilson, Ellen Hanley, Howard Da Silva, Mark Dawson, Nathaniel Frey
Sets, Costumes, and Lighting: W and J

1960

Viva Madison Avenue
Author: George Panetta
Theatre: Longacre Theatre, April 6, 1960
Producers: Selma Tamber, Martin H. Poll
Director: Ira Cirker (replaced); Aaron Frankel
Costumes: Frank Thompson
Stars: Buddy Hackett, Fred Clark, Paul E. Richards, Frances Sternhagen, Jed Allan
Sets and Lighting: W and J

1961

The Happiest Girl in the World
Authors: Fred Saidy, play; Henry Myers, play; E.Y. Harburg, lyrics; Jacques Offenbach, music
Theatre: Martin Beck Theatre, April 3, 1961
Producer: Lee Guber
Director: Cyril Ritchard
Choreographer: Dania Krupska
Costumes: Robert Fletcher
Stars: Cyril Ritchard, Janice Rule, Dran Seitz, Bruce Yarnell
Sets and Lighting: W and J

Let It Ride
Authors: Abram S. Ginnes, play; Jay Livingston, music; Jay Livingston and Ray Evans, lyrics; adapted from John Cecil Holm and George Abbott
Theatre: Eugene O'Neill Theatre, October 12, 1961
Producer: Joel Spector
Director: Stanley Prager
Choreographer: Onna White
Costumes: Guy Kent
Stars: George Gobel, Sam Levene, Barbara Nichols, Paula Stewart
Sets and Lighting: W and J

Take Her, She's Mine
Authors: Phoebe and Henry Ephron
Theatre: Biltmore Theatre, December 21, 1961
Producer: Harold S. Prince
Director: George Abbott
Costumes: Florence Klotz
Stars: Art Carney, Phyllis Thaxter, Richard Jordan, June Harding, Elizabeth Ashley
Sets and Lighting: W and J

1962

Oh Dad, Poor Dad, Mamma's Hung You in the Closet and I'm Feelin' So Sad
Author: Arthur L. Kopit
Theatre: Phoenix Theatre, February 26, 1962
Producers: Phoenix Theatre, T. Edward Hambleton, Norris Houghton
Director: Jerome Robbins
Costumes: Patricia Zipprodt
Lighting: Thomas Skelton
Stars: Jo Van Fleet, Sandor Szabo, Barbara Harris, Austin Pendleton
Sets: W and J

Never Too Late
Author: Sumner Arthur Long
Theatre: Playhouse Theatre, November 27, 1962
Producers: Elliot Martin, Daniel Hollywood
Director: George Abbott
Costumes: Florence Klotz
Stars: Paul Ford, Maureen O'Sullivan, Orson Bean
Sets and Lighting: W and J

1963

She Loves Me
Authors: Joe Masteroff, play; Sheldon Harnick, lyrics; Jerry Bock, music; adapted from Mikos Laszlo
Theatre: Eugene O'Neill Theatre, April 23, 1963
Producers: Harold Prince, Lawrence N. Kasha, Philip C. McKenna
Director: Harold Prince
Choreographer: Carol Haney
Costumes: Patricia Zipprodt
Stars: Barbara Cook, Daniel Massey, Barbara Baxley, Jack Cassidy, Nathaniel Frey, Ralph Williams
Sets and Lighting: W and J

Here's Love
Author: Meredith Willson, play, lyrics, and music
Theatre: Shubert Theatre, October 3, 1963
Producer: Stuart Ostrow
Director: Stuart Ostrow
Choreographer: Michael Kidd
Costumes: Alvin Colt
Lighting: Tharon Musser
Stars: Lawrence Naismith, Craig Stevens, Valerie Lee, Fred Gwynne, Janis Paige
Sets: W and J

1964

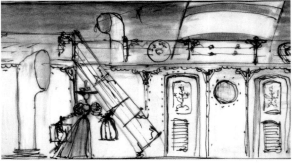

Too Much Johnson
Author: William Gillette
Theatre: Phoenix Theatre, January 15, 1964
Producers: Phoenix Theatre, T. Edward Hableton, Norris Houghton
Director: Burt Shevelove
Costumes: Patricia Zipprodt
Lighting: Klaus Holm
Stars: John McMartin, Nancy Berg, Grover Dale, Dom De Luise, Josip Elic
Sets: W and J

Anyone Can Whistle
Authors: Arthur Laurents, play; Stephen Sondheim, lyrics and music
Theatre: Majestic Theatre, April 4, 1964
Producers: Kermit Bloomgarden, Diana Krasny
Director: Arthur Laurents
Choreographer: Herbert Ross
Costumes: Theoni V. Aldredge
Lighting: Jules Fisher
Stars: Lee Remick, Angela Lansbury, Harry Guardino, Gabriel Dell
Sets: W and J

Fade Out-Fade In
Authors: Betty Comden and Adolph Green, play and lyrics;
Jule Styne, music
Theatre: Mark Helinger Theatre, May 26, 1964
Producers: Lester Osterman, Jule Styne
Director: George Abbott
Choreographer: Ernest Flatt
Costumes: Donald Brooks
Stars: Carol Burnett, Jack Cassidy, Lou Jacobi, Dick
Patterson, Tina Louise
Sets and Lighting: W and J

The Sign in Sidney Brustein's Window
October 15, 1964
Author: Lorraine Hansberry
(The production that opened at the Longacre Theater, October
15, 1964, was not designed by the Eckarts.)
Sets: W and J (preliminary sketches only)

1965

A Sign of Affection
Author: Carolyn Green
Theatre: Shubert Theater, New Haven, March 10, 1965,
(Closed April 10, 1965, Walnut Theatre, Philadelphia)
Producer: Gayle Stine
Director: Ron Winston
Costumes: Patricia Zipprodt
Stars: John Payne, Lesley Ann Warren, Nan Martin (succeeded by Lois Markle)
Sets and Lighting: W and J

Flora, The Red Menace
Authors: George Abbott, play; Robert Russell, play; Fred Ebb, lyrics; John Kander, music
Theatre: Alvin Theater, May 11, 1965
Producer: Harold Prince
Director: George Abbott
Choreographer: Lee Theodore
Costumes: Donald Brooks
Lighting: Tharon Musser
Stars: Liza Minnelli, Bob Dishy, Anne C. Russell, Louis Guss, Clark Morgan, Cathryn Damon
Sets: W and J

The Zulu and the Zayda
Authors: Howard De Silva, play; Felix Leon, play; Harold Rome, music and lyrics; adapted from Dan Jacobson
Theatre: Cort Theatre, November 10, 1965
Producers: Theodore Mann, Dore Schary
Director: Dore Schary
Costumes: Frank Thompson
Stars: Menasha Skulnik, Ossie Davis, Louis Gossett, Jr., Joe Silver
Sets and Lighting: W and J

1966

The Circle
Author: Somerset Maugham
Theatre: Brown Theatre, Louisville, KY, April 8, 1966 (Tour closed Hartford, CT, May 15, 1966)
Producer: Helen Hayes Repertory Company
Director: Jack Manning
Costumes: Patton Campbell
Star: Helen Hayes
Sets and Lighting: W and J

McNay

Mame
Authors: Jerome Lawrence, play; Robert E. Lee, play; Jerry Herman, music and lyrics; adapted from Patrick Dennis
Theatre: Wintergarden Theatre, May 24,1966
Producers: Robert Fryer, Lawrence Carr, Joseph P. Harris
Director: Gene Saks
Choreographer: Onna White
Costumes: Robert Mackintosh
Lighting: Tharon Musser
Stars: Angela Lansbury, Beatrice Arthur, Jane Connell, Willard Waterman, Jerry Lanning, Frankie Michaels
Sets and Lighting: W and J

Where's Charley?
Authors: George Abbott, play; Frank Loesser, music and lyrics; based on Brandon Thomas
Theatre: National Tour: Shubert Theater, Cincinnati, OH,
October 3, 1966
Producer: Martin Tahse
Director: Cyril Ritchard
Choreographer: Agnes de Mille
Costumes: Winn Morton
Lighting: Martin Aronstein
Stars: Tony Tanner, Fred Clark, Marion Marlowe, Virginia Sandifur
Sets: W and J

Agatha Sue, I Love You
Author: Abe Einhorn
Theatre: Henry Miller's Theater, December 14, 1966
Producers: Judith Abbott, Edwin Wilson, Tommy Valando, John Pransky
Director: George Abbott
Costumes: Patton Campbell
Stars: Ray Walston, Corbett Monica, Reneé Taylor, Betty Garde, Lee Lawson
Sets and Lighting: W and J

1967

Light Fantastic–OR–How to Tell Your Past, Present and Maybe Your Future Through Social Dancing.
February 9, 1967. ABC Stage 67.
Teleplay: Arthur Laurents
Director: Marc Breaux
Choreography: Marc Breaux and Deedee Wood
Musical director: Peter Matz
Cast: Lauren Bacall and John Forsythe
Production design: W and J

NYPL-PA

Hallelujah, Baby!
Authors: Arthur Laurents, play; Betty Comden, lyrics; Adolph Green, lyrics; Jule Styne, music
Theatre: Martin Beck Theater, April 26, 1967
Producers: Albert W. Selden, Hall James, Jane C. Nusbaum, Harry Rigby
Director: Burt Shevelove
Choreographer: Kevin Carlisle
Costumes: Irene Sharaff
Lighting: Tharon Musser
Stars: Leslie Uggams, Robert Hooks, Allen Case, Lillian Hayman, Barbara Sharma
Sets: W and J

A Midsummer Night's Dream
Author: William Shakespeare
Theatre: Festival Theatre, Stratford, CT, June 17, 1967
Producer: American Shakespeare Festival
Director: Cyril Ritchard
Costumes: Robert Fletcher
Lighting: Tharon Musser
Stars: Cyril Ritchard, Diana Davila, Tom Aldredge, Ted Graeber, John Cunningham, Dorothy Tristan
Sets: W and J

The Golden Age (ballet)
Authors: Genevieve Pilot, music; adapted from Rossini, Agnes de Mille, play

Theatre: Broadway Theater, November 8, 1967
Producers: Rebekah Harkness, Harkness Foundation
Choreographer: Agnes de Mille
Costumes: Stanley Simmons
Lighting: Jennifer Tipton
Stars: Elisabeth Carroll, Claudia Corday, Susan Whelan, Richard Wagner, Dale Muchmore, Roderick Drew, Hester FitzGerald
Sets: W and J

1968

The Education of H*Y*M*A*N K*A*P*L*A*N
Authors: Benjamin Bernard Zavin, play; Paul Nassau and Oscar Brand, music and lyrics; based on Leo Rosten
Theatre: Alvin Theatre, April 4, 1968
Producers: André Goulston, Jack Farren, Stephen Mellow
Director: George Abbott
Choreographer: Jaime Rogers
Costumes: Winn Morton
Lighting: Martin Aronstein
Stars: Tom Bosley, Barbara Minkus, Nathaniel Frey, Hal Linden, Gary Krawford
Sets: W and J

A Mother's Kisses
Authors: Bruce Jay Friedman, play; Richard Adler, music and lyrics
Theatre: Shubert, New Haven,

September 23, 1968 (Closed out-of-town in Baltimore, MD)
Producers: Lester Osterman, Richard Horner, Lawrence Kasha, Frederic S. and Barbara Mates
Director: Gene Saks
Choreographer: Onna White
Costumes: Alvin Colt
Lighting: Tharon Musser
Stars: Beatrice Arthur, Bill Callaway, Rene Roy, Carl Ballantine, Ned Wetimer
Sets: W and J

Maggie Flynn
Authors: Hugo Peretti, play, lyrics, and music; Luigi Creatore, play, lyrics, and music; George David Weiss, play, lyrics, and music
Theatre: ANTA Theater, October 23, 1968
Producer: John Bowab
Director: Morton Da Costa
Choreographer, Brian MacDonald
Costumes: Robert LaVine
Lighting: Tharon Musser
Stars: Shirley Jones, Jack Cassidy, Robert Kaye, William James, Sibyl Bowan
Sets: W and J

Photofest

The Night They Raided Minsky's
United Artists release of a Bud Yorkin-Norman Lear production
Director: William Friedkin
Associate producer: George Justin
Screenplay: Arnold Schulman, Sidney Michaels, Nornan Lear; based on the Rowland Barber book
Cinematography: Andrew Laszlo
Music: Charles Strouse; songs, Strouse, Lee Adams
Dances, musical numbers, and sketches astaged by Danny Daniels
Art design: John Robert Lloyd
Set designer: John Godfrey
Costumes: Anna Hill Johnstone
Sound: Jack Fitzstephens
Visual consultant and 2nd unit director: Pablo Ferro
Film editor: Ralph Rosenblum
Assistant director: Burt Harris
Cast: Jason Robards, Britt Eckland, Bert Lahr, Harry Andrews, Joseph Wiseman, Denholm Elliot, Elliott Gould, Forrest Tucker, Jack Burns, Norman Wisdom, Gloria LeRoy, Dick Libertini, Judith Lowery, William B. Able, Mike Elias, Frank Shaw, Chanin Hale
Narration and title song: Rudy Vallee
Production design: W and J

1969

The Fig Leaves Are Falling
Authors: Allan Sherman, play and lyrics; Albert Hague, music
Theatre: Broadhurst Theatre, January 2, 1969
Producers: Joseph Harris, Lawrence Carr, John Bowab
Director: George Abbott
Choreographer: Eddie Gasper
Costumes: Robert Mackintosh
Lighting: Tharon Musser
Stars: Barry Nelson, Dorothy Loudon, Jenny O'Hara, Kenneth Kimmins, Jay Barney, Louise Quick, David Cassidy
Sets: W and J

A Way of Life
Author: Murray Schisgal
Theatre: ANTA Theatre, January 18, 1969 (Closed in previews)
Producers: Edgar Lansbury, Marc Merson

Director: Alan Schneider (replaced); Harold Stone
Costumes: Theoni V. Aldredge
Lighting: Tharon Musser
Stars: Estelle Parsons, Bob Dishy, John McGiver, Melinda Dillon, Lou Jacobi
Sets: W and J

1970

Norman, Is That You?
Authors: Ron Clark, Sam Bobrick
Theatre: Lyceum Theater, February 19, 1970
Producer: Harold D. Cohen
Director: George Abbott
Costumes: Florence Klotz
Lighting: Fred Allison
Stars: Martin Huston, Walter Willison, Lou Jacobi, Dorothy Emmerson, Maureen Stapleton
Sets: W and J

Sensations
Authors: Paul Zakrewski, play and lyrics; Wally Harper, music; adapted from Shakespeare's *Romeo and Juliet*
Theatre: Theatre Four, October 25, 1970
Producers: John Bowab, Charles Celian
Director: Jerry Dodge
Costumes: Jeanne Button
Lighting: Beverly Emmons
Stars: John Savage, Judy Gibson, Ron Martin, Bruce Scott, Arthur Bartow
Sets: W and J

Match Girl (ballet)
Theatre: Curtis Hixon Convention Center, Tampa, FL, December 1970
Producer: Tampa Ballet Theatre
Choreographer: Frank Rey
Costumes: Betty Lee Rey
Lighting: Sydne Morris
Sets: W and J

1971

Oedipus the King
Author: Sophocles
Theatre: Bob Hope Theatre, Dallas, TX, November 1971
Producer: Southern Methodist University (SMU) Theatre Department
Director: Burnett M. Hobgood
Costumes: Joe I. Tompkins
Lights: Allen Heaton
Sets: W

1972

Love For Love
Author: William Congreve
Theatre: Bob Hope Theatre, SMU, Spring 1972
Producer: SMU Theatre Department
Director: Jack Clay
Costumes: Joe I. Tompkins
Lighting: Allen Heaton
Sets: W

Twelfth Night
Author: William Shakespeare
Theatre: Bob Hope Theatre, SMU, Fall 1972
Producer: SMU Theatre Department
Director: Burnett M. Hobgood
Costumes: Lee Austin
Lighting: Allen Heaton
Sets: W

1973

Liberty Ranch
Authors: Dick Vosburgh, play; John Cameron, music; Caryl Brahms and Ned Stravin, lyrics
Theatre: Bob Hope Theatre, SMU, October 1973
Producer: SMU Theatre Department
Director: Jack Clay
Choreographer: Betty Ferguson
Costumes: Giva R. McBride
Lighting: Ronald A. Castleman
Sets: W

Dance '73
Theatre: Bob Hope Theatre, SMU, 1973
Producer: SMU Dance Department
Choreographers: Toni Beck, Robert Beard, Nikita Talin, David Kirby
Costumes: Jean Eckart and Costume Design Class
Lighting: Allen Heaton
Sets: W

1974

The President's Gang
Producer: Bill Graham
Lighting: Martin Aronstein
1974 (Did not open, scheduled for Los Angeles.)
Star: William Sargent
Sets: W

Of Mice and Men
Author: John Steinbeck
Theatre: Brooks Atkinson Theatre, December 18, 1974
Producer: Elliott Martin
Director: Ed Sherin
Stars: James Earl Jones, Kevin Conway
Sets, Costumes, and Lighting: W and J

1975

Comedy of Errors
Author: William Shakespeare
Theatre: Margot Jones Theatre, SMU, November 1975
Producer: SMU Theatre Department
Director: Jim Hancock
Costumes: Giva R. McBride
Lighting: Amaranti L. Lucero
Sets: W

1976

Mass: A Theatre Piece for Singers, Players and Dancers
Author: Leonard Bernstein
Theatre: Tarrant County Convention Center, Fort Worth, TX, April 1976
Producer: Fort Worth Symphony Orchestra Association
Musical Director: John Girodano
Director: Carolyn Dyer
Choreographer: Carolyn Dyer
Sets and Costumes: W

The Winter's Tale
Author: William Shakespeare
Theatre: Bob Hope Theatre, SMU, November 1976
Producer: SMU Theatre Department
Director: Jack Clay
Choreography: Robert Beard
Music: Dean Crocker
Costumes: Giva R. McBride
Lighting: D. Edmund Thomas
Sets: W

1977

Ring Around the Moon
Author: Jean Anouilh/ Christopher Fry
Theatre: Bob Hope Theatre, SMU, 1977
Producer: SMU Theatre Department
Director: Jack Clay
Lighting: Robert J. Pierson
Sets: W, Costumes: J

Guys and Dolls
Authors: Abe Burrows and Jo Swerling, play; Frank Loesser, music and lyrics
Theatre: Bob Hope Theatre, SMU, March, 1977
Producer: SMU Theatre Department
Director: Jim Hancock
Choreographer: J. David Kirby
Costumes: Giva R. McBride
Lighting: D. Edmund Thomas
Sets: W

A Christmas Carol
Author: Charles Dickens; adapted by Nagle Jackson
Theatre: McFarlin Auditorium, SMU, December 1977
Producer: Shakespeare Festival of Dallas
Director: Charles Grey
Costumes: Giva R. McBride
Lighting: C. Dall Brown
Sets: W

1978

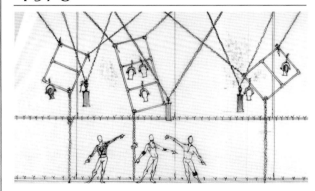

Rite of Spring (ballet)
Theatre: McFarlin Auditorium, SMU, March 1978
Producer: Dallas Ballet
Choreographer: Brian McDonald
Costumes: Debra L. Amonette, Michael James Skeene, and Doris Schiffer
Lighting: Charles C. Suggs, II
Sets: W

Scream
Author: Arthur Laurents
Theatre: The Alley Theatre, Houston, TX, October 19, 1978
Producer: The Alley Theatre
Director: Arthur Laurents
Costumes: Ellen Rybs
Lighting: Jonathan Duff
Sets: W and J

1979

Much Ado About Nothing
Author: William Shakespeare
Theatre: B. Iden Payne Theatre, Austin, TX, February 1979
Producer: University of Texas, Department of Theatre and Dance
Director: Michael Finlayson
Costumes: Paul D. Reinhardt
Lighting: David Nancarro
Sets: W

Measure for Measure
Author: William Shakespeare
Theatre: Margot Jones Theatre, SMU, 1979
Producer: SMU Theatre Department
Director: Jack Clay
Costumes: Susan Cox
Lighting: David Jacques
Sets: W

Triptych
Author: Oliver Hailey
Theatre: Tower Theatre, Houston, TX, 1979
Producers: Nell Nugent, Clyde Kuermmele
Director: Arthur Sherman
(This production did not open.)
Sets: W

1980

On A Clear Day You Can See Forever
Authors: Alan Jay Lerner, play and lyrics; Burton Lane, music
Theatre: Dorothy Chandler Pavillion, Los Angeles, June 1980
Producers: Cy Ferrer and Earnest Martin
Director: Alfred Drake
Choreographer: Danny Daniels
Costumes: Alvin Colt
Lighting: Marilyn Rennagel
Stars: Robert Goulet, Joanna Gleason
Sets: W and J

Cyrano de Bergerac
Author: Edmond Rostard
Theatre: Pabst Theatre, Milwaukee, WI, September 12, 1980
Producer: Milwaukee Repertory Theatre
Director: Richard Cottrell
Costumes: Susan Tsu
Lighting: Spencer Mosse
Sets: W

A Funny Thing Happened on the Way to the Forum
Author: Burt Shevelove and Larry Gelbart, play; Stephen Sondheim, music and lyrics
Theatre: Southwest Texas State University Theatre, October 1980
Producer: Southwest Texas State Theatre Department
Director: Dennis Maganza
Costumes: Sheila Hargett
Sets, Lighting: W

1981

The Time of Your Life
Author: William Saroyan
Theatre: Margot Jones Theatre, SMU, 1981
Producer: SMU Theatre Department
Director: Mesrop Kesdekian
Costumes: Mark E. Jensen
Lighting: James Paccone
Sets: W

1982

As You Like It
Author: William Shakespeare
Theatre: Playhouse Theatre, University Park, PA, 1982
Producer: Douglas N. Cook, Penn State University
Director: Robert E. Leonard
Costumes: Patricia Dohert
Lighting: Stephen Petrilli
Sets: W

Walls
Author: Jonna Gault, play, music and lyrics
Theatre: Burt Reynolds Dinner Theatre, Jupiter, FL, September 1982
Producer: Burt Reynolds Jupiter Theatre
Director: Al Rossi
Choreographer: Stan Mazin
Costumes: Sylvia Moss
Lighting: Martin Aronstein
Stars: Dick Patterson and Patti Karr
Sets: W and J

1983

Charley's Aunt
Author: Brandon Thomas
Theatre: Bob Hope Theatre, SMU, November 1983
Producer: SMU Theatre Department
Director: Mesrop Kesdekian
Costumes: Rondi Hillstrom Davis
Lighting: Marilyn Rennagel
Sets: W

1984

The Dining Room
Author: A. R. Gurney, Jr.
Theatre: Plaza Theatre, Dallas, TX, January 1984
Producer: Kjehl Rasmussen
Director: Mesrop Kesdekian
Costumes: Patty Greer McGarity
Lighting: C. Dall Brown
Sets: W

1985

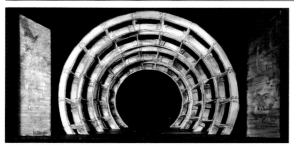

Guys and Dolls
Authors: Abe Burrows and Jo Swerling, play; Frank Loesser, music and lyrics
Theatre: Burt Reynolds Dinner Theatre, Jupiter, FL, Winter/Spring 1985
Producer: Karen Poindexter
Director: Charles Nelson Reilly
Choreographer: Tony Stevens
Costumes: Lori Robinson
Lighting: Pat Simmons
Stars: Jed Allan, Christine Ebersole
Sets: W and J

1986

The Glass Menagerie
Author: Tennessee Williams
Theatre: Kalita Humphrey's Theatre, Dallas Theatre Center, March 1986
Producer: Dallas Theatre Center
Director: Thomas Hill
Costumes: Donna M. Kress
Lighting: Susan Takis
Sets: W

The Mother of Us All (opera)
Authors: Gertrude Stein, libretto; scenario by Maurice Grosser; Virgil Thomson, music
Theatre: Majestic Theatre, Dallas, TX, April 1, 1986
Producer: Dallas Opera
Director: Charles Nelson Reilly
Lighting: Larry French
Sets and Costumes: W and J

1987

Lucky Guy
Author: Willard Beckham, play, lyrics, and music
Theatre: Plaza Theatre, Dallas, TX, May 1987
Producers: Bailey and Schwartz Productions; Victor I. Rosenbert
Director: Gerald Gutierrez
Choreographer: Peter Gennaro
Costumes: Ann Hould-Ward
Lighting: Marilyn Rennagel
Sets: W and J

1989

A Funny Thing Happened on the Way to the Forum
Author: Burt Shevelove and Larry Gelbart, play; Stephen Sondheim, music and lyrics
Theatre: Bob Hope Theatre, SMU, November 1989
Producer: SMU Theatre Department
Director: Andre De Shields
Choreographer: Andre De Shields
Lighting: John Santiago
Sets and Costumes: W

1990

As You Like It
Author: William Shakespeare
Theatre: Mary Rippon Theatre, Boulder, CO, July 1990
Producer: Colorado Shakespeare Festival
Director: Jack Clay
Lighting: Richard Devin
Sets and Costumes: W

Confucius, Jesus Christ, and John Lennon of the Beatles
Author: Sha Yexin
Theatre: Hong Kong Cultural Center Grand Theatre, Hong Kong, October 1990
Producer: Hong Kong Repertory Theatre
Director: Daniel S.P. Yang
Choreographer: Law Wing-Fan
Lighting: Richard Devin
Sets and Costumes: W

1991

Bonjour, La Bonjour
Author: Michel Tremblay
Theatre: Margot Jones Theatre, SMU, 1991
Producer: SMU Theatre Department
Director: Cecil O'Neal
Costumes: Pat Turton
Lighting: David Goodman
Sets: W

Die Fledermaus
Author: Johann Strauss
Theatre: Bob Hope Theatre, SMU, 1991
Producer: SMU Opera Theatre
Director: Dejan Miladinovic
Choreographer: Nathan Montoya
Costumes: Giva Taylor
Lighting: David Jacques
Sets: W

1992

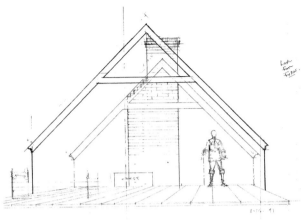

The Crucible
Author: Arthur Miller
Theatre: Bob Hope Theatre, SMU, February 1991
Producer: SMU Theatre Department
Director: Cecil O'Neal
Costumes: Karen Pascho
Lighting: David Jacques
Sets: W

Wonderful Town
Authors: Joseph Fields and Jerome Chodorov, play; Leonard Bernstein, music; Betty Comden and Adolph Green, lyrics
Theatre: Bob Hope Theatre, SMU, November 1992
Producer: SMU Theatre Department
Director: Richard Sibellico
Choreographer: Richard Sibellico and Joe Orlando
Costumes: Giva Taylor
Lighting: David Jacques
Sets: W

1994

The Importance of Being Earnest
Author: Oscar Wilde
Theatre: Caravan of Dreams, Fort Worth, TX, November 1994
Producer: Texas Stage
Director: Charles Marowitz
Costumes: Giva Taylor
Lighting: David Jacques
Sets: W

1995

Julius Caesar
Author: William Shakespeare
Theatre: Bob Hope Theatre, SMU, February 1995
Producer: SMU Theatre Department
Director: Wayne Ballantyne
Sets: Carolyn Adams
Lighting: Chris Reay
Costumes: W

The Golden Apple
Authors: John LaTouche, play and lyrics; Jerome Moross
Theatre: Illinois Music Theatre, Evanston, IL, August 1995
Producer: Light Opera Works, Pegasus Players
Director: Dominic Missimi
Costumes: Shifra Werch
Lighting: Kenneth Moore
Sets: W and J

Better Half Dead
Author: Joan Torres
Theatre: Circle Theatre, Fort Worth, TX, August 1995
Producers: Andrew Harris and Ann L. Rhodes
Director: Andrew B. Harris
Costumes: Giva Taylor
Lighting: Bill Newberry
Sets: W

1996

Big River: The Adventures of Huckleberry Finn
Author: William Hauptman; adapted from novel by Mark Twain
Theatre: Northeast Louisiana State University Theatre, March 1996
Producer: NLU Theatre and NLU School of Music, Monroe, LA
Director: Paul Siemers
Choreographer: Samuel Stiles
Costumes: Donna Meester
Lighting: Tom Heiman
Sets: W

Better Half Dead
Author: Joan Torres
Theatre: Victory Gardens Theatre, Chicago, IL, September 1996
Producers: Andrew B. Harris and Ann L. Rhodes
Director: Dennis Zacek
Costumes: Alexander A. Sargent and William Eckart
Lighting: Andrew Meyers
Sets and Costumes: W

Cowardy Custard
Authors: Noel Coward, words and music; devised by Gerald Frow, Allen Strachan, Wendy Toye
Theatre: Bob Hope Theatre, SMU, October 1996
Producer: SMU Theatre Department
Director: Candace Evans
Choreographer: Candace Evans
Costumes: Rondi Hillstrom Davis
Lighting: David Jacques
Sets: W

1997

The Greeks
Author: Aeschylus, Euripides; adapted and translated: John Barton, Kenneth Cavander
Theatre: Bob Hope Theatre, SMU, October 1997
Producer: SMU Theatre Department
Director: Michael Connolly
Costumes: Rondi Hillstrom Davis
Lighting: Suzanne Lavender
Sets: W

Stronghold
Author: Jim Tyler Anderson
Theatre: Arts District Theatre, Dallas Theatre Center, February 1997
Producer: Playwright's Project
Director: Andrew B. Harris
Costumes: Karrie Anderson
Lighting: Suzanne Lavender
Sets: W

Funny Girl
Author: Isobel Lennart, play; Jule Styne, music; Bob Merrill, lyrics
Theatre: MUNY, St. Louis, MO, June 1997
Producer: Paul Blake
Director: Barry Dennen
Choreographer: Tony Parise
Costumes: Robert Fletcher
Lighting: Martin Aronstein
Sets: W

Three Coins in a Fountain
Author: Jule Styne, music;
Theatre: MUNY, St. Louis, MO, July 1997
Producer: Paul Blake
Director: Paul Blake
Costumes: Robert Fletcher
Lighting: Martin Aronstein
Sets: W

South Pacific
Author: Joshua Logan, play; Oscar Hammerstein, II, play and lyrics; Richard Rodgers, music
Theatre: MUNY, St. Louis, MO, August 1997
Producer: Paul Blake
Director: Charles Repole
Choreographer: Tony Parise
Costumes: Robert Fletcher
Lighting: Martin Aronstein
Sets: W

1998

The Rover
Author: Aphra Behn
Theatre: Greer Garson Theatre, SMU, April 1998
Producer: SMU Theatre Department
Director: Gretchen Elizabeth Smith
Costumes: Claudia Stephens
Lighting: Suzanne Lavender
Sets: W

The Robber Bridegroom
Author: Alfred Uhry, play and lyrics; adapted from Eudora
Welty; Robert Waldman, music
Theatre: Bob Hope Theatre, SMU, October 1998
Producer: SMU Theatre Department
Director: Carole Brandt
Choreographer: Sara J. Romersberger
Costumes: Claudia Stephens
Lighting: Steve Woods
Sets: W

What the Butler Saw
Author: Joe Orton
Theatre: Studio Theatre, Denton, TX, November 1998
Producer: University of North Texas
Director: Marjorie Hayes
Costumes: Barbara Cox
Lighting: Russell Reed
Sets: W

1999

The Illusion
Author: Pierre Corneille; adapted by Tony Kushner
Theatre: Margot Jones Theatre, SMU, October 1999
Producer: SMU Theatre Department
Director: René Moreno
Costumes: Susan Mayes
Sets and Lighting: W

2000

Macbeth
Author: William Shakespeare
Theatre: The Quad C Theatre, Plano, TX, February 2000
Producer: Collin County Community College, TX
Director: Gail Cronauer
Costumes: Sandra Snyder
Lighting: Craig Erickson
Sets: W

Notes

Several citations below refer to unpublished materials (letters, family documents, office files, etc.) and interviews in the Eckart Collection (hereafter EC), Billy Rose Theatre Collection, New York Public Library for the Performing Arts, unless otherwise noted. The number next to each note refers to the relevant text page.

Getting Together

2 William Eckart, in discussions with the author from 1995–2000. The author met with Eckart at least once a week during this period. Interviews were recorded and transcribed and are a part of the Eckart Collection. During this period, I made use of interviews conducted by Ronald L. Davis, May 12, 1986, Interview #351, transcript SMU Oral History Collection, Dallas, Texas, as well as the notes made by Jerome Weeks columnist, *Dallas Morning News*. For ease in reading, I have made no attempt to annotate William Eckart's remarks except in those rare instances where I am quoting a publication.

Onna White (choreographer), in discussion with the author, March 13, 1999.

3 Stuart Ostrow (producer and director), in discussion with the author, May 6, 1999. Others besides Ostrow have also referred to the Eckarts as storytellers.

Elliott Martin, to author letter, May 18, 1999.

Jerome Robbins had the Eckarts fly to Boston in early May 1954. He wanted them to design *Peter Pan*, but confusion over the appointment resulted in them missing each other and the Eckarts returned to New York and did not get *Peter Pan*. Jerome Robbins to Mr. and Mrs. William Eckart, May 19, 1954 (EC).

4 Arthur Laurents, in discussion with the author, June 15, 1999.

5 Jean Eckart, interview by Ronald L. Davis, May 14, 1986, interview #352, transcript SMU Oral History Collection, Dallas, Texas. Much of what is attributed to Jean in this book is quoted from the Davis' interview. In some instances, William Eckart attributed certain statements to Jean. For ease in reading, I have made no attempt to distinguish the source used to create Jean's voice except in those rare instances where Jean was interviewed for publication. Although I had many conversations with Jean during the years 1985 to 1993, I did not interview her for this book.

Jean Eckart, interview by Phyllis Lee Levin, "No Campaign Is Won Without Support," unpublished MS for The *New York Times*, February 14, 1960 (EC).

Ming Cho Lee, in discussion with the author, May 23, 2001.

Genealogies concerning the Eckart and Levy families came from a variety of sources. Jean Eckart's genealogical tables and notes, discussion and correspondence with Rosemary Bernard (William's older sister), Dorothy Monohan (Jean's cousin), Ed Levy (Jean's brother), and Herta Kahn (Jean's stepmother).

8 Jean Eckart note to William Eckart (EC).

10 Donald Oenslager, *Theatre of Donald Oenslager*, Middletown, CT: Wesleyan University Press, 1978, p. 7. The full quote is, "Good scene design is good thinking, with freedom of imagination supplemented by reasonable performance in execution."

11 Donald Oenslager, interview by Levin, Phyllis Lee, "No Campaign Is Won Without Support," unpublished MS for the *New York Times*, February 14, 1960.

13 Lynn Riggs' 1931 play was entitled *Green Grow the Lilacs*.

Richard Grayson (company manager), in discussion with the author, January 27, 1998.

14 Jac Venza, in discussion with the author, April 6, 1999.

15 Venza interview.

16 Elliott Martin (assistant producer), in discussion with the author, October 12, 1999.

Vern., *Variety*, July 18, 1951, p. 56.

17 Elliott Martin letter, May 18, 1999.

Haila Stoddard (producer), in discussion with the author, August 14, 1999.

All New York newspaper reviews quoted are from newspapers published the day following an opening, (here October 12, 1951), unless otherwise noted.

19 Enid Bagnold, "The Flop," *The Atlantic Monthly*, Boston: October 1952, Vol. 190, # 4, p. 55.

George Jean Nathan, "Theatre Week: It's Now *Gertie* That Gets Shumlin's Garter," *New York Journal-American*, February 12, 1952.

The term "industrials" is generally used to describe a corporate theatrical event aimed at promoting products or services to members of the industry.

Teresa Hayden (producer), in discussion with the author, April 20, 1999.

21 Walter Kerr, review, *Herald Tribune*, June 17, 1953.

22 John Keating, "Downtown Data," *Cue*, July 11, 1953.

24 Grayson interview.

John LeTouche, "*The Golden Apple*: American Musical on Greek Legend," *Herald Tribune*, March 7, 1954, p. 22.

Enchantment: The Golden Apple

27 Susanna Moross Tarjan (composer's daughter), in discussion with the author, November 30, 1996. Tao Strong, a dancer, and Julian Stein, Assistant Musical Director for *The Golden Apple*, also contributed to the discussion.

31 T. Edward Hambleton (producer), in discussion with the author, August 2, 1999.

John Latouche, *Herald Tribune*.

35 Norman Lloyd, *Stages of Life in Theatre, Film, and Television*, New York: Limelight Edition, 1993.

Hope Abelson (assistant producer), in discussion with the author, October 3, 1996.

36 Kaye Ballard, in discussion with the author, June 19, 1997.

Harold Clurman, "Theatre," *The Nation*, New York, March 27, 1954.

Walter Kerr, "New Musical Made of Old Mythology," *Herald Tribune*, March 28, 1954.

38 Jo Mielziner to William Eckart, New York, March 12, 1954, (EC).

Split Screen and A "Style" Show

41 Levin, Phyllis Lee (EC) .

"The Hate Song" appeared in a Julius Monk revue *Dressed to Kill*, lyrics by Dion McGregor and Michael Barr. *Newsweek*, "The Madness Upstairs," October 10, 1960, p. 93.

Irving Paul Lazar (Hollywood Agent), to Mr. and Mrs. Eckart, June 7, 1954 (EC). Correspondence between Lazar and the Eckarts ended September 13, 1954, when the Eckarts signed with Audrey Wood, MCA.

Meryle Secrest, *Stephen Sondheim a life*, New York: Alfred A. Knopf, 1998, pp. 106-107.

42 Jay Carmody, "The Passing Show: *Portrait of a Lady* Brings Jennifer Jones to National," *The Evening Star*, Washington, D.C., November 24, 1954.

Damn Yankees

45 Gwen Verdon, in discussion with the author, April 1999.

49 The red socks have continued to appear in such films as *Bedazzled*, another twist on the Faust legend.

51 Richard Adler, with Lee Davis, *You Gotta Have Heart*, New York: Donald I. Fine, 1990.

53 Verdon interview.

David Halberstam, *The Fifties*, New York: Villard Books, 1993, pp. 132-142.

54 Jerome Weeks, in discussions with the author, 1998-2005.

55 Hal Prince (producer), in discussion with the author, May 7, 1999.

56 Verdon interview.

57 Ethan Mordden, *Coming Up Roses, The Broadway Musical in the 1950s*, New York: Oxford University Press, 1998.

Sets That Move, Shows That Don't

59 Robert Lewis, *Slings and Arrows, Theatre in My Life*, New York: Stein and Day, 1984.

60 Eric A. Gordon, *Marc the Music, The Life and Work of Marc Blitzstein*, New York: St. Martin's Press, 1989.

62 Kaye Ballard interview.

Cheryl Crawford, *One Naked Individual, My Fifty Years in the Theatre*, Indianapolis: Bobbs-Merrill Co., 1977.

Gordon, *Marc the Music*.

64 Kaye Ballard interview.

Earle Hyman in discussions with the author, May 4, 2001.

Actual song title is "Somewhere".

66 Hyman interview. Earle Hyman letter to the author, May 22, 2001. Hyman supplied an excerpt from Himes's letter dated April 13, 1956.

67 Adler, *You Gotta Have Heart*.

NBC Opera Company, press release, July 3, 1956. The presenter Community Concerts Inc. was affiliated with Columbia Artists Management. Judson, O'Neill and Judd handled the tour.

Li'l Abner

69 Hobe, *Variety*, November 16, 1956, Vol. 93, # 52.

Deedee Wood, in discussion with the author, August 9, 1999. Ms. Wood was assistant choreographer to Michael Kidd.

70 Terry Little (stage manager) and Maureen Hopkins (dancer), in discussion with the author, August 2, 1999.

Alvin Colt (designer), in discussion with the author, May 4, 1999.

71 Maureen Hopkins interview. Al Capp, as quoted "Lil Abner - Broadway," *Life*, January 14, 1957, p. 83.

Edie Adams, *Sing a Pretty Song, the "Offbeat" Life of Edie Adams*, New York: William Morrow, 1990.

Charlotte Rae (actress playing Mammy Yokum), in discussion with the author, May 19, 1999.

72 William and Jean Eckart, "How We Got to Dogpatch," *Dixie, Times Picayune States Roto Magazine*, New Orleans: April 21, 1957.

73 Tharon Musser (lighting designer), in discussion with the author, July 1999.

Deedee Wood interview.

74 Harry MacArthur, "The Passing Show: *Li'l Abner* Is a Hit But It Needs Surgery," *Evening Star*, Washington, D.C.: September 18, 1956. MacArthur was one of the few critics who mentioned the political satire. Actually, Charles E. Wilson, Secretary of Defense in the Eisenhower Administration, 1953-57, said, "What was good for the country was good for General Motors and vice versa," but the former G. M. President's statement was misquoted as, "What's good for G. M. is good for the country."

Lynn Pecktal, *Costume Design, Techniques of Modern Masters*, New York: Watson Guptill, 1993.

77 Sensenderfer, R. E. P., "*Li'l Abner* Dogpatchers Win Plaudits at Erlanger," *Bulletin*, Philadelphia: October 24, 1956.

Norton, Elliot, "The Theatre, First New Musical at Shubert Theatre," *Post*, Boston: October 13, 1956.

Al Capp letter to William and Jean Eckart, November 15, 1956, (EC). Capp loved the look of the show. He wrote, "You've made it the prettiest show in town. Thanks."

Robin Wagner (designer), in discussion with the author, May 2001.

Cinderella

79 Adams, *Sing A Pretty Song*. Information also from Windeler, Robert, *Julie Andrews, A Life on Stage and Screen*, Secaucus, New Jersey: Birch Lane Press, 1997, p. 61-63.

Hugh Fordin, *Getting to Know Him, A Biography of Oscar Hammerstein II*, New York: Random House, 1977, p. 333.

Richard Rodgers, *Musical Stages, An Autobiography, New York*: Random House, 1975, p. 290. Rodgers' affection for Andrews included recommending her to Alan Jay Lerner for the role of Eliza in *My Fair Lady* two years earlier.

80 William Eckart attributed Rodgers' emphasis on humor to Rodgers' state of depression, a subject covered extensively in Meryle Secrest's biography of Rodgers, *Somewhere for Me*.

82 Information has been gathered from several newspaper sources including: Chase, Ilka, "As I was Saying: How Television brings an Ancient Fairy Tale to Glowing Life Tonight," *Sunday Tribune*, Chicago, March 31, 1957, pt. 7, p. 4; and Pogrebin, Robin, "Magical Find Excites TV Historians," *The New York Times*, June 20, 2002, Sec. B, pp. 1, 5.

Don Langer, "Tips on Photography, Assignment *Cinderella*," *Sunday New York Times*, March 31, 1957, Sec. 4, p. 6.

Harold Messing, "The CBS Television Production of *Cinderella*," MA thesis, Stanford University, Stanford, California: 1957.

84 Julie Andrews, in discussion with the author, April 1999.

Women's Wear Daily, March 25, 1957.

87 Tao Strong (dancer) interview (see *The Golden Apple*). Strong remembers sliding out of her dress on a lift.

90 Messing.

Larry Wolters, "*Cinderella* TV Show of the Year," *Tribune*, Chicago, April 1, 1957.

Ethan Mordden, *Rodgers and Hammerstein*, New York: Henry N. Abrams, 1999.

Tony Walton (designer), in discussion with the author, May 2001.

Ted Chapin (Executive Director, Rodgers and Hammerstein), in discussion with the author, April 2004.

Hollywood

94 Stephen M. Silverman, *Dancing on the Ceiling, Stanley Donen and His Movies*, New York: Alfred A. Knopf, 1996, pp. 244-248.

95 William K. Zinsser, "Screen, *The Pajama Game*," *Herald Tribune*, New York, August 30, 1957, p.6.

96 Silverman, pp. 257-259.

Quoted in Silverman, p. 254.

Verdon interview.

99 Silverman gives an account of the tension on the set, pp. 254-255.

Ironically, *Bye Bye Birdie* didn't open until April 7, 1960.

Gerald Mast, *Can't Help Singin,' The American Musical on Stage and Screen*, Woodstock, New York: Overlook Press, 1987, p. 316.

Riding the Broadway Roller Coaster

103 Walter Kerr, "Theater, *Livin' the Life*," *Herald Tribune*, New York, April 29, 1957.

Brooks Atkinson, "Theatre: *Livin' the Life*," *The New York Times*, April 29. 1957.

104 Ellen Violett (playwright), in discussion with the author, August 14, 1999.

Chapman, John, "Nancy Walker Carries Big Show, *Copper and Brass*, as Easy as Pie," *Daily News*, New York, October 19, 1957, p. 22.

Murdock, Henry T., "Dull Comedy at Erlanger, *Copper and Brass* Needs Polish," *Philadelphia Inquirer*, September 26, 1957, p. 16.

Cue, New York, October 12, 1957, p. 8.

105 The Eckarts received a letter form James Simpson, Public Relations Director for Ellington Advertising dated March 11, 1958, (EC), requesting them to plug Martex as their client. The Eckarts continued to do industrials including "Les Towels" for Martex. They did not honor his request.

106 Walter Kerr, "Theater: Scenic Gimmicks, The Ground Moves and The Air Speaks," *Sunday Herald Tribune*, New York, February 16, 1958, Sec. 4, p. 1.

Walter Winchell, "*Mein Kampf* Best Seller in Egypt," *Times Picayune*, New Orleans, February 8, 1958. The column was syndicated appearing in New York in *The Journal-American*.)

Martha Schmoyer LoMonaco, "Broadway in the Poconos, The Tamiment Playhouse," PhD diss. New York University, 1988. The camp served as a training ground to wide range of talent over its thirty-five year history including: Danny Kaye, Imogene Coca, Carol Burnett, Dick Shawn, Woody Allen, Jerome Robbins, and Jerry Bock; but *Once Upon a Mattress* was one of only two shows to originate there, the other was *The Straw Hat Revue* (1939).

Once Upon a Mattress

109 Tharon Musser (lighting designer), in discussion with the author, May 1999.

110 Mary Rodgers (composer), in discussion with the author, April 23, 1999.

111 Mary Rodgers interview.

116 Jay Thompson (playwright), in discussion with the author, May 13, 1999.

118 Troy, *Variety*, New York, May 13, 1959, p. 72.

Jack Kroll, *Newsweek*, May 25, 1959, p.78.

Emory Lewis, "The Theatre," *Cue*, New York, May 23, 1959.

Thomas R. Nash, "Theatres, New Fairy Tale Musical Whimsical and Entrancing," *Women's Wear Daily*, New York, May 12, 1959, p. 64.

Mary Rodgers interview.

Prince interview.

119 Walton interview.

Thompson interview.

Fiorello!

121 William and Jean Eckart, as told to John S. Wilson, "Scenic Design and Lighting," *Theatre Arts Magazine*, New York, July 1960, p. 55.

122 Prince interview.

125 Peter Gennaro, in discussion with the author, October 12, 1999.

Walter Kerr, "Theatre: New George Abbott Musical, Fiorello La Guardia Wins Again," *Sunday Herald Tribune*, New York, December 6, 1959, Sec. 4, p. 1

126 Patton Campbell (assistant designer), in discussion with the author, October 6, 1999.

130 Kerr, December 6, 1959.

Harold Clurman, "The Theatre," *The Nation*, New York, December 19, 1959. It was

Clurman who wrote, "Eckarts' settings communicate the feeling of *amiable crudity* which is the distinctive mark of the show. Their work has real style, in contrast to the usual sets for musicals, which are efficient and pretty and that is not enough." The italics are mine.

Hal Prince, *Contradictions: Notes on Twenty-six Years in the Theatre*, New York, Dodd, Mead and Company, 1974, p. 59.

John Chapman, "It Was a Good Town Once," *Sunday News*, New York, December 6, 1959, Sec. 2, p.1.

131 Mary Rodgers interview.

Feast or Famine

133 Aaron Frankel, in discussion with the author, October 12, 1999. Burry Fredrik (stage manager), in discussion with the author, October 14, 1999.

136 Art Carney was a major talent with many credits. Broadway audiences had recently seen him as James Hyland in a serious play, *The Rope Dancers* (1957).

138 Howard Taubman, "Tyranny of the One-Set Play," *Sunday New York Times*, December 31, 1961, Sec. 2, p. 1.

Prince interview.

Jean Eckart interviewed by Farley, Jane Mary, "Couple Sets Stage for Make-Believe World," *Milwaukee Journal*, February 2, 1964, Pt. 6, p. 6.

139 Edith Oliver, "Off Broadway (Laughter)," *The New Yorker,* March 10, 1962, p. 84.

140 Jerome Weeks, in discussion with the author, January 17, 2005.

141 Elliot Martin (producer) interview.

She Loves Me

143 " Romantic Atmosphere" copyright 1963 by Sheldon Harnick, courtesy of Mr. Harnick.

William Eckart as interviewed by Hale, Alice M., "*She Loves Me*, A Romantic Atmosphere," *Theatre Crafts*, New York, May 1986, p. 26. Prince interview.

145 Ethan Morddan, *Open a New Window, the Broadway Musical in the 1960s*, New York: Palgrave, 2001, p. 65.

150 Prince interview.

Bone, *Variety*, New York, March 20, 1963.

Curiously, Walter Kerr, the *Herald Tribune* was the lone dissenter among the New York critics. Kerr thought the show "a little shopworn around the corner."

Mikos Laszlo to Mr. and Mrs. William J. Eckart, April 30, 1963, (EC).

151 Prince, *Contradictions*, p. 99.

Walton interview.

Express Yourself

153 Stuart Ostrow, the producer and a protégé of Frank Loesser's (*Guys and Dolls*), took over directing when Norman Jewison was fired out-of-town. Jewison, who later made his mark as a film director (*Fiddler on the Roof*), asked the Eckarts, "Why do we have dark masking? Why don't we have all the masking white?" They were shocked by the question, but explained how much more it would cost to light the show if they had attempted masking in white.

154 Ostrow interview also in Ostrow, Stuart. *A Producer's Broadway Journey*, Westport, CT.: Praeger, 1999, p. 73.

155 caption Ostrow interview.

caption Musser interview.

156 Herbert Ross, in discussion with the author, August 2, 1999. Ming Cho Lee's set broke the stage into different levels, a major problem for Ross as choreographer.

158 Henry T. Murdock, "*Anyone Can Whistle* Opens," *Philadelphia Inquirer*, March 3, 1964, p. 12

Anne Sloper, "Blow hard for the absurd," *Christian Science Monitor*, Boston, MA., April 8, 1964

"Elsie the Cow Show," the Eckarts worked with Miles White, who designed the costumes for the puppets.

161 Hobe. *Variety*, June 3, 1964, p. 80.

William Torbert Leonard, *Broadway Bound, A Guide* to *Shows that Died Aborning*, Metuchen, NJ: Scarecrow Press, 1983, p. 431.

162 Prince, *Contradictions*, p. 118

163 Al Kasha and Joel Hirschhorn, *Notes on Broadway*, New York: Simon and Schuster, 1987, p. 101.

164 Prince interview.

165 Prince, *Contradictions*, pp. 118-9.

166 Elinor Hughes, "Theater, *Flora the Red Menace* Travels Erratic Course," *Boston Globe*, April 13, 1965.

Mame

175 Grayson interview.

178 Angela Lansbury, in discussion with the author, November 4, 1999.

Terry Little interview.

180 caption Robert Fryer (producer), in discussion with the author, March 5, 1999.

Jerry Gaghan, "Mame Cakewalks on the Shubert Stage," *Philadelphia Daily News*, April 5, 1966, p. 34.

181 Jay Hamann, "Caesars Palace," *The Hollywood Reporter*, Los Angeles, January 27, 12969, p. 26.

Disenchantment: Age of Aquarius

183 Other Eckarts' activities included staging and producing "*Seventeen's* Fall Trends Show," Grand Ballroom, Waldorf-Astoria, June 3, 1966. Decorating Gracie Mansion for Mayor John V. Lindsay, Mary Lindsay to Bill and Jean Eckart, June 12, 1967, The Eckarts designed a stage on a flat-bed trailer which also toured New York beaches with such stars as Liza Minnelli to boost Lindsay's mayoral campaign (Perry, James M. "But We Got So Much Talent You Never Saw," *New York Observer*, July 4, 1965, Vol. 4, #26, p. 1.

186 Betty Comden as quoted by Mandelbaum, Ken, *Hallelujah Baby!*, Original Broadway Cast, compact disc, Sony Broadway, SK 48218, © 1992, p.9.

190 Ken Mandelbaum, *Not Since Carrie, Forty Years of Broadway Musical Flops*, New York: St. Martin's Press, 1991, p. 290.

caption Martin Aronstein (lighting designer), in discussion with the author, April 20, 1999.

Ken Billington (assistant lighting designer), in discussion with the author, May 20, 1999.

192 Bea Arthur, in discussion with the author, May 25, 1999.

193 Billington interview. Also, Mandelbaum, *Carrie*, p. 187.

Adler, *You Gottta Have Heart*, p. 253

195 In the 1960s, there were three *My Son…*albums. "Hello Muddah, Hello Fadduh" was a single from *My Son, the Nut* (1963), the third album. Sherman wrote over hundred parody songs in the five years he spent at the top of the charts.

Grayson interview.

John Bowab (producer), in discussion with the author, March 21, 1999.

196 Billington interview

198 Bowab interview.

Epilogue

201 Stanley Marcus to Mr. and Mrs. William Eckart, May 10, 1971, (EC). Their arrival in Dallas was marked by a flurry of celebratory newspaper articles and interviews.

203 Martin interview

A list of shows that might have been New York bound includes, *The President's Gang* (1974), *Scream* (1978), *Triptych* (1979), *Walls* (1982), *Lucky Guy* (1987), and *Better Half Dead* (1995).

Bibliography

Abbott, George. *Mister Abbott*. New York: Random House, 1963.

Adams, Edie and Robert Windeler. *Sing A Pretty Song, The "Offbeat" Life of Edie Adams, Including the Ernie Kovacs Years*. New York: William Morrow and Co., 1990.

Adler, Richard with Lee Davis. *You Gotta Have Heart*. New York: Donald I Fine, 1990.

Anderson, Walt. *The Little Screwball*. New York: Unpublished MS, 1951. (Typescript).

Appia, Adolphe. *Richard C. Beacham Essays, Scenarios and Designs*. Trans. Walter R. Volbach. Ann Arbor: U of Michigan Press, 1989.

Aronson, Arnold. *American Set Design*. New York: TCG, 1985.

Atkinson, Brooks and Albert Hirschfeld. *The Lively Years 1920-1973, A Half-Century of the Most Significant Plays on Broadway*. New York: Associated Press, 1973.

Atkinson, Brooks. "Six Vital Stage Sets," *The New York Times Magazine*. New York: *The New York Times*, April, 11, 1954, pp. 24-5.

Atkinson, Brooks. *Broadway*. Revised. New York: Macmillan, 1974.

Bablet, Denis and Marie-Louise Bablet. *Adolphe Appia*. New York: Riverrun Press, 1982.

Bagnold, Enid. *Gertie*. New York: Unpublished MS, 1952. (Typescript).

Banham, Martin (Ed). *The Cambridge Guide to Theatre*. Cambridge: Cambridge University Press, 1995.

Bay, Howard. *Stage Design*. New York: Drama Book Specialists, 1974.

Beckerman, Bernard and Howard Siegman (Eds.) *On Stage, Selected Theater Reviews from The New York Times 1920-1970*. New York: Arno Press, Quadrangle, 1973.

Bernard, Rosemary Eckart. "'Oh, Dad,' One of the Most Elaborately Propped Shows in the History of Off-Broadway Theatre Done by Louisianan and His Wife." New Iberia, LA: Unpublished MS, 1962, (EC).

Bissell, Richard. *Say, Darling*. Boston: Little, Brown and Co., 1957.

Blitzstein, Marc. *Reuben Reuben*. New York: Unpublished MS, 1955, (EC).

Blitzstein, Marc. *The Cradle Will Rock*. New York: Random House, 1938.

Blumenthal, Eileen with Julie Taymor. *Julie Taymor Playing With Fire*. New York: Harry N. Abrams, 1995.

Bordman, Gerald. *American Musical Theatre, A Chronicle*. 2nd Edition. New York: Oxford University Press, 1992.

Bordman, Gerald. *The Oxford Companion to American Theatre*. New York: Oxford University, 1987.

Burnett, Carol. *One More Time*. New York: Random House, 1986.

Burris-Meyer, Harold and Edward C. Cole. *Scenery for the Theatre, The Organization, Processes, Materials and Techniques Used to Set the Stage*. Revised Ed. Boston: Little Brown and Co., 1971.

Burrows, Abe. *Honest, Abe Is There Really No Business Like Show Business*. Boston: Little, Brown and Co., 1980.

Capp, Al. *Li'l Abner* "Comes Love," "The Law of Sadie Hawkins Day!," "Marryin' Sam Rides Again" New York: King Features Syn., 1939.

Challender, James Winston. "The Function of the Choreographer in the Development of The Conceptual Musical, An Examination of the Work of Jerome Robbins, Bob Fosse, and Michael Bennett on Broadway Between 1944 and 1981." Ann Arbor UMI (Diss. U of Florida), 1986.

Chodorov, Edward. *Oh, Men! Oh, Women!* New York: Samuel French, 1955.

Clark, Ron and Sam Bobrick. *Norman, Is That You?* New York: Unpublished MS, Nov. 28, 1969. (Typescript).

Comden, Betty. *Off Stage*. New York: Simon Schuster, 1995.

Condee, William F. *The Theatrical Space, A Guide for Directors and Designers*. Lanham, MD: The Scarecrow Press, 1995.

Conrad, Glenn R. (Ed.) *New Iberia, Essays on the Town and Its People*. 2nd Edition. Lafayette, LA: University of Southwestern Louisiana, 1986.

Contino, Rosalie H. "Costume Designer Patricia Zipprodt, Her Contribution to the American Theatre." New York: NYU Unpublished Diss, 1997. (Typescript)

Crawford, Cheryl. *One Naked Individual, My Fifty Years in the Theatre*. Indianapolis: Bobbs-Merrill Co., 1977.

Davies, Valentine. *Mircle on 34th Street*. New York: Harcourt, Brace and Co., 1947.

Davis, Ronald L. (Int. by) "Interview of Jean Eckart." Number 352. Dallas, TX: Southern Methodist University, 14 May 1986, Oral History Program. (Typescript).

Davis, Ronald L. (Int. by) "Interview of William Eckart." Number 351. Dallas, TX: Southern Methodist University, 12 May 1986, Oral History Program. (Typescript).

Dietz, Steve (Ed). *National Museum of American Art Smithosian Institution*. Boston: Bullfinch Press, Little, Brown and Company, 1995.

Drutt, Matthew (Ed). *Thannhauser, The Thannhauser Collection of the Guggenheim Museum*. New York: Guggenheim Museum Publications, 2001.

Edelman, Rob and Audrey E. Kupferberg. *Angela Lansbury, A Life on Stage and Screen*. New York: Birch Lane Press, 1996.

Engel, Lehman. *The Critics*. New York: Macmillan, 1976.

Feinsod, Arthur. *This Simple Stage*. New York: Greenwood Press, 1992.

Fraser, Barbara Means. "A Structural Analyses of the American Musical Theatre Between 1955 and 1965, A Cultural Perspective." Eugene, OR: U of Oregon Unpublished Diss., 1982. (Typescript).

Friedman, Bruce and Jay Richard Adler. *A Mother's Kisses*. New York: Unpublished MS., 1968. (Typescript).

Frommer, Myrna Katz and Harvey Frommer. *It Happened on Broadway An Oral History of the Great White Way*. New York: Harcourt Brace and Co, 1998.

Galacki, Julius. "Alumni Profile, William Eckart ('49)," *Yale Drama Alumni Magazine*. Summer. New Haven, CT: 1998.

Garfield, David. *A Player's Place, The Story of the Actors Studio*. New York: Macmillan, 1980.

Gillette, A. S. *Stage Scenery, Its Construction and Rigging*. 2nd Edition. New York: Harper and Row, 1972.

Goldman, William. *The Season, A Candid Look at Broadway*. New York: Harcourt, Brace and World, 1969.

Gordon, Eric A. *Marc the Music, The Life and Work of Marc Blitzstein*. New York: St. Martin's Press, 1989.

Gordon, Joanne. *Art Isn't Easy, The Theatre of Stephen Sondheim*. New York: Da Capo Press, 1992.

Gorelik, Mordecai. *New Theatres for Old*. New York: E. P. Dutton, Co., 1962.

Gottfried, Martin. *Broadway Musicals*. New York: Harry N. Abrams, 1984.

Gottfried, Martin. *More Broadway Musicals, Since 1980*. New York: Harry N. Abrams, 1991.

Gottfried, Martin. *All His Jazz, The Life and Death of Bob Fosse*. New York: Bantam, 1990.

Gottfried, Martin. *Balancing Act, the Authorized Biography of Angela Lansbury.* Boston: Little, Brown and Company, 1999.

Grad, Bonnie Lee. *Milton Avery.* Royal Oak, MI: Strathcona, 1981.

Green, Richard William. "William and Jean Eckart, An Examination of the Settings and Scene Changes for *The Golden Apple, Fiorello,* and *Mame*." Ann Arbor, MI: UMI (U of Miami, MA Thesis (69) 1970.

Green, Stanley. *The World of Musical Comedy.* 4th Edition, Enlarged. New York: Da Capo Press 1984.

Guernsey Jr., Otis L. (Ed) *Broadway Song and Story, Playwrights, Lyricists, Composers Discuss Their Hits.* New York: Dodd, Mead and Co., 1985.

Haagensen, Erik. "Getting to the Core of *The Golden Apple*." Fall 1995, *Show Music,* pp. 33-7, 66.

Halberstam, David. *The Fifties.* New York: Random House, 1993.

Henderson, Amy and Dwight Blocker Bowers. *Red Hot and Blue, A Smithsonian Salute to the American Musical.* Washington: Smithsonian Institution Press, 1997.

Herman, Jerry and Marilyn Stasio. *Showtune, A Memoir.* New York: Penguin Group, 1996.

Hirsch, Foster. *Harold Prince and the American Musical Theatre.* New York: Cambridge University Press, 1989.

Hollander, Anne. *Seeing Through Clothes.* New York: Viking Press, 1978.

Hughes, Robert. *American Visions, The Epic History of Art in America.* New York: Alfred A. Knopf, 1997.

Ilson, Carol. *Harold Prince, from Pajama Game to Phantom of the Opera.* Ann Arbor, MI: UMI 1989.

Inman, David. *The TV Encyclopedia.* New York: Putnam Publishing Group, 1991.

Jackson, Arthur. *Best Musicals from Show Boat to A Chorus Line.* New York: Crown, 1977.

Jarvis, Everett G. *Final Curtain, Death of Noted Movie and TV Personalities.* New York: Citadel Press, 1993.

Jones, James Earl and Penelope Niven. *James Earl Jones, Voices and Silences.* New York: Charles Scribner's Sons, 1993.

Jones, Robert Edmund. *The Dramatic Imagination.* New York: Theatre Arts Books, 1969.

Jordan, Richard Tyler. *But Darling, I'm Your Auntie Mame!* Santa Barbara: Capra Press,1998.

Kasha, Al and Joel Hirschhorn. *Notes on Broadway, Intimate Conversations with Broadway's Greatest Songwriters.* New York: Simon and Schuster, 1987.

Kaufmann, Stanley. *Theatre Criticisms.* New York: Performing Arts Journal Publications, 1983.

Kerr, Walter. *Pieces at Eight.* New York: Simon and Schuster, 1957.

Komisarjevsky, Theodore and Lee Simonson and C. G. Holme. *Settings and Costumes of the Modern Stage.* New York: The Studio, 1933.

Kranzfelder, Ivo. *Edward Hopper 1882-1967 Vision of Reality.* Koln: Benedikt Taschen 1995.

Larson, Orville K. *Scene Design In the American Theatre From 1915 to 1960.* Fayetteville, AK: U of Arkansas Press, 1989.

Latouche, John and Jerome Moross. *The Golden Apple* Revised 1977. New York: Unpublished MS 1977. (Typescript).

Laufe, Abe. *Broadway's Greatest Musicals.* 1977 Revised. New York: Funk and Wagnalls, 1977.

Laurents, Arthur Betty Comden, Adolph Green, Jule Styne *Hallelujah, Baby!* New York Unpublished MS 1967, (EC). BE 4

Laurents, Arthur. *Original Story By A Memoir of Broadway and Hollywood.* New York: Alfred A. Knopf, 2000.

Law, John John Wright and Mark Salad. *Brewer's Theater, A Phrase and Fable Dictionary.* New York: Harper Collins, 1994.

Lee, Ming Cho and Elizabeth Lee. "In Memoriam," *Yale Drama Alumni Newsletter.* New Haven, Winter, 1993.

Leigh, Wendy. *Liza Born A Star* New York: Dutton, 1993.

Leiter, Samuel L. *Ten Seasons New York Theatre in the Seventies.* New York: Greenwood Press, 1986.

Leonard, William Torbert. *Broadway Bound, A Guide to Shows That Died Aborning.* Metuchen, NJ: The Scarecrow Press 1983.

Levin, Phyllis Lee. "No Campaign Is Won Without Support." New York: Unpublished MS February 2 and 14 (revised), 1960. (EC).

Lewis, Robert. *Slings and Arrows, Theater in My Life.* New York: Stein and Day, 1984.

Lippman, Monroe. "The Current Production." Vol. I, #1 New Orleans, LA: *Tulane University Theatre Magazine Program, (EC).*

Little, Stuart W. *Off-Broadway, The Prophetic Theatre.* New York: Coward, McCann and Geoghegan, 1972.

Lloyd, Norman. *Stages, Of Life in Theatre, Film and Television.* New York: Limelight Edition, 1993.

Lynes, Russell. *The Lively Audience, A Social History of the Visual and Performing Arts in America 1890-1950.* New York: Harper and Row, 1985.

MacDougal, Roger. *To Dorothy, A Son.* New York: Unpublished MS, 1952, (EC).

MacGowan, Kenneth and Robert Edmund Jones. *Continental Stagecraft.* New York: Harcourt Brace and Co., 1922.

MacGowan, Kenneth. *The Theatre of Tomorrow.* New York: Boni and Liverwright, 1921.

Mandelbaum, Ken. *Not Since Carrie, 40 Years of Broadway Flops.* New York: St. Martin's Press, 1991.

Mantle, Burns (Ed) *The Best Plays of 1946-47 and the Yearbook of the Drama in America.* New York: Dodd, Mead and Company, 1947-98. (Series 1946-1998).

Meilziner, Jo. *Designing for the Theatre, A Memoir and A Portfolio.* New York: Bramhall House, 1965.

Middleton, Herman David. "The Use of the Design Elements in the Stage Designs of Robert Edmund Jones and Lee Simonson." Gainesville, FL: U of Florida Diss, 1964.

Mikotowicz, Thomas J. "Oliver Smith, An American Scenographer (Broadway, Ballet, New York)." New York: New York University Diss, 1985.

Mikotowicz, Thomas J. (Ed.). *Theatrical Designers, An International Biographical Dictionary.* New York: Greenwood Press, 1992.

Miller, D. A. *Place for Us, Essay on the Broadway Musical.* Cambridge, MA.: Harvard University Press, 1998.

Mordden, Ethan. *Better Foot Forward, The History of American Musical Theatre.* New York: Viking, 1976.

Mordden, Ethan. *Coming Up Roses, The Broadway Musical in the 1950's.* New York: Oxford University Press, 1998.

Mordden, Ethan. *The American Theatre.* New York: Oxford University, 1981.

Moussinac, Leon. *The New Movement in the Theatre, A Survey of Recent Development in Europe and America.* New York: Benjamin Blom, 1967.

Murphy, Brenda. *American Realism and American Drama, 1880-1940.* Cambridge: Cambridge University Press, 1987.

Nicoll, Allardyce. *The Development of the Theatre, A Study of Theatrical Art from the Beginnings to the Present Day*. 5th Revised. New York: Harcourt, Brace Jovanovich, 1966.

Novick, Julius. *Beyond Broadway, The Quest for Permanent Theatres*. New York: Hill and Wang, 1968.

Oenslager, Donald. *Scenery Then and Now*. New York: W. W. Norton, 1936.

Oenslager, Donald. *Stage Design, Four Centuries of Scenic Invention*. New York: Viking Press, 1975.

Oenslager, Donald. *The Theatre of Donald Oenslager*. Middleton, CT: Wesleyan University Press, 1978.

Oram, Robert E. "The Popular Theatre and Broadway: Recommendations for Survival by Walter Kerr." Detroit: Wayne State University Diss, 1973.

Ostrow, Stuart. *A Producer's Broadway Journey*. Westport, CT: Praeger, 1999.

Parker, W. Oren and Harvey K. Smith. *Scene Design and Stage Lighting*. 4th Edition. New York: Holt, Rinehart and Winston, 1979.

Pecktal, Lynn. *Costume Design, Techniques of Modern Masters*. New York: Watson-Guptill, 1993.

Pecktal, Lynn. *Designing and Painting for the Theatre*. New York: Holt, Rinehart and Winston, 1975.

Penn, Irving. *Moments Preserved, Eight Essays in Photographs and Words*. New York: Simon and Schuster, 1960.

Penn, Irving. *Worlds in a Small Room*. New York: Viking Press, 1974.

Philips, Jerold Allan. *The New Stagecraft in America, A History of Scenic Design, 1915-1949*. New York: New York University Diss, 1975.

Polley, Robert L. (Ed). *The Beauty of America in Great American Art*. Waukesha, WI: Country Beautiful Foundation, 1965.

Prince, Hal. *Contradictions, Notes on Twenty-six Years in the Theatre*. New York: Dodd, Mead and Co., 1974.

Raphaelson, Samson. *Three Screen Comedies*. Madison, WI: University of Wisconsin Press, 1983.

Rich, Frank with Lisa Aronson. *The Theatre of Boris Aronson*. New York: Alfred A. Knopf, 1987.

Rico, Diana. *Kovacsland, A Biography of Ernie Kovacs*. New York: Harcourt Brace Jovanovich, 1990.

Rosenberg, Bernard and Ernest Harburg. *The Broadway Musical Collaboration in Commerce and Art*. New York: New York University Press, 1993.

Rosten, Leo. *The Return of H*Y*M*A*N K*A*P*L*A*N*. New York: Harper and Brothers, 1959.

Rothenstein, John (Ed). *New International Illustrated Encyclopedia of Art*. New York: Greystone 1967.

Rugoff, Milton (Ed). *The Britannica Encyclopedia of American Art*. Chicago: Encyclopedia Britannica, 1974.

Russell, Douglas A. *Period Style for the Theatre*. 2nd Edition. Boston: Allyn and Bacon, 1987.

Sandler, Irving. *The Triumph of American Painting, A History of Abstract Expressionism*. New York: Praeger Publishers, 1970.

Schisgal, Murray. *A Way of Life*. New York: Unpublished MS, 1968, (EC).

Secrest, Meryl. *Stephen Sondheim, A Life*. New York: Alfred A. Knopf, 1998.

Seitz, William C. *Art in the Age of Aquarius, 1955-1970*. Washington, DC: Smithsonian Institution, 1992.

Selden, Samuel and Hunton D. Sellman. *Stage Design*. 3rd Edition. New York: Appleton-Century-Croft, 1959.

Shahn, Ben. *The Shape of Content*. Cambridge, MA: Harvard U Press, 1957.

Sherman, Allan and Albert Hague. *The Fig Leaves Are Falling*. New York: Unpublished MS October 15, 1968, (EC).

Shevelove, Burt and Larry Gelbart, Stephen Sondheim. *A Funny Thing Happened on the Way to the Forum, The Frogs*. New York: Dodd, Mead and Co., 1983.

Silverman, Stephen M. *Dancing on the Ceiling, Stanley Donen and His Movies*. New York: Alfred A. Knopf, 1996.

Simonson, Lee (Ed). *Theatre Art*. New York: Cooper Square Publisher, 1969.

Simonson, Lee. *The Stage Is Set*. New York: Harcourt, Brace and Co., 1932.

Smith, Cecil and Glenn Litton. *Musical Comedy in America*. New York: Theatre Arts Books, 1981.

Smith, Ronn. *American Set Design #2*. New York: TCG, 1991.

Smith, Wendy. *Real Life Drama, The Group Theatre and America, 1931-1940*. New York: Alfred A. Knopf, 1990.

Soby, James Thrall. *Ben Shahn Paintings*. New York: Georges Braziller, 1963.

Southern, Richard. *The Seven Ages of the Theatre*. New York: Hill and Wang, 1963.

Spencer, Charles. *Cecil Beaton Stage and Film Design*. New York: St. Martin's Press. 1975.

Steinbeck, John. *Of Mice and Men*. New York: Dramatists Play Service, 1964.

Steyn, Mark. *Broadway Babies Say Goodnight*. New York: Routledge 1999.

Stott, William and Jane Stott. *On Broadway, Performance Photographs by Fred Fehl*. Austin, TX: University of Texas Press, 1978.

Suskin, Steven. *Opening Night on Broadway, A Critical Quotebook of the Golden Era of the Musical Theatre, Oklahoma! (1943) to Fiddler on the Roof (1964)*. New York: Schirmer, Macmillan, 1990.

Thompson, James Robert. "Twentieth Century Scene Design, Its History and Stylistic Origins" Ann Arbor UMI (U of Minnesota Diss) 1957.

Wallock, Leonard (Ed). *New York, Culture Capital of the World 1940-1965*. New York: Rizzoli, 1988.

Wetzsteon, Ross (Ed). *The Obie Winners, the Best of Off-Broadway*. Garden City: Doubleday and Co., 1980.

Willis, John (Ed). *Theatre World*. New York: Crown, 1950-71. (Series 1950-1971).

Windeler, Robert. *Julie Andrews, A Life of Stage and Screen*. New York: Birch Lane Press, 1997.

Wingler, Hans M. and Joseph Stein. *The Bauhaus: Weimar, Dessau, Berlin, Chicago*. Trans. Wolfgang Jabs. Cambridge, MA: MIT Press, 1969.

Zadan, Craig. *Sondheim and Co., The authorized, behind-the-scenes story of the making of Stephen Sondheim's musicals*. 2nd Edition. New York: Harper and Row, 1986.

Zakrewski, Paul and Wally Harper. *Sensations*. New York: Unpublished MS, 1971, (EC).

Zavin, Benjamin Bernard and Paul Nassau, Oscar Brand. *The Education of H*Y*M*A*N K*A*P*L*A*N*. New York: Unpublished MS, Jan. 23, 1968, (EC).

Zeigler, Joseph Wesley. *Regional Theatre, The Revolutionary Stage*. New York: Da Capo Press, 1977.

Index

FLAGPOLE FROM *THE GOLDEN APPLE* (EC)
FOLLOWING PAGE:
MAME FLYING
WINDOW DROP (EC)